Launching the Imagination

A Guide to Three-Dimensional Design

Launching the Imagination

A Guide to Three-Dimensional Design

fourth edition

Mary Stewart

Mc Graw Hill

Connect
Learn
Succeed™

Published by McGraw-Hill, an imprint of The McGraw-Hill Companies, Inc., 1221 Avenue of the Americas, New York, NY 10020. Copyright © 2012, 2008, 2006, 2002. All rights reserved. No part of this publication may be reproduced or distributed in any form or by any means, or stored in a database or retrieval system, without the prior written consent of The McGraw-Hill Companies, Inc., including, but not limited to, in any network or other electronic storage or transmission, or broadcast for distance learning.

This book is printed on acid-free paper.

1 2 3 4 5 6 7 8 9 0 DOW/DOW 9 8 7 6 5 4 3 2 1

ISBN: 978-0-07737981-0
MHID: 0-07-737981-0

Vice President Editorial: *Michael Ryan*
Publisher: *Christopher Freitag*
Associate Sponsoring Editor: *Betty Chen*
Director of Development: *Rhona Robbin*
Developmental Editor: *Cynthia Ward*
Editorial Coordinator: *Sarah Remington*
Executive Marketing Manager: *Pamela S. Cooper*
Senior Production Editor: *Carey Eisner*
Design Manager: *Preston Thomas*
Interior Designer: *Linda Robertson*
Cover Designer: *Bill Stanton*
Lead Photo Research Coordinator: *Alexandra Ambrose*
Photo Researcher: *Deborah Anderson*
Buyer II: *Tandra Jorgensen*
Media Project Manager: *Bethuel Jabez*
Composition: *10.5/14 Palatino Roman by Lachina Publishing Services*
Printing: *70# Sterling Ultra Web Dull, R.R. Donnelley & Sons*

Cover: Top right: Marilyn da Silva, *Reap What You Sow; A Prescription for Life*, 2004. © Marilyn da Silva. Photo by M. Lee Fatherree; Center: Daniel E. Kelm and Timothy C. Ely, *Rubeus*, 1990. Courtesy of Daniel E. Kelm and Timothy C. Ely; Far left: Devorah Sperber, *After van Eyck*, 2006. © Devorah Sperber. Photo: Aaron Deetz; Middle left: Zac Freeman, *Steve*, 2006. Photo courtesy of J. Johnson Gallery; Bottom: Maya Lin, *Blue Lake Pass* (detail), 2006. Photograph by G.R. Christmas, courtesy The Pace Gallery. © Maya Lin Studio, Inc. Courtesy The Pace Gallery.

Library of Congress Cataloging-in-Publication Data

Stewart, Mary, 1952-
  Launching the imagination : a comprehensive guide to basic design / Mary Stewart. — 4th ed.
    p. cm.
  Also issued in parts titled: Launching the imagination : a comprehensive guide to two-dimensional design, and Launching the imagination : a comprehensive guide to three-dimensional design.
  Includes bibliographical references and index.
  ISBN-13: 978-0-07-337924-1 (softcover : alk. paper)
  ISBN-10: 0-07-337924-7 (softcover : alk. paper)
  ISBN-13: 978-0-07-737980-3 (softcover : alk. paper)
  ISBN-10: 0-07-737980-2 (softcover : alk. paper)
  ISBN-13: 978-0-07-737981-0 (softcover : alk. paper)
  ISBN-10: 0-07-737981-0 (softcover : alk. paper)
  1. Design. I. Title. II. Title: Comprehensive guide to basic design.
  NK1510.S74 2011
  745.4—dc22
                                    2010045154

The Internet addresses listed in the text were accurate at the time of publication. The inclusion of a Web site does not indicate an endorsement by the authors or McGraw-Hill, and McGraw-Hill does not guarantee the accuracy of the information presented at these sites.

www.mhhe.com

Launching the Imagination:
A Guide to Three-Dimensional Design
is dedicated to Jeff Boshart

Launching the Imagination treats *design* as both a verb and a noun—as both a process and a product. By covering the process of creative and critical thinking as well as presenting the elements and principles used in creating a product, this book offers a unique resource for foundations courses.

The title *Launching the Imagination* suggests the goals of this book and of the foundations year as a whole. Through an immersion in 3-D concepts and problems, students are encouraged to develop ways of thinking visually that will serve them throughout their studies and careers. They learn that design is deliberate—a process of exploring a wide range of solutions and choosing the most promising option for further development. And they find inspiration in the work of others, analyzing the art of the past and the present for insights into how composition informs communication. This book supports these goals in the following ways:

UNIQUE COVERAGE OF "PROCESS" AS WELL AS "PRODUCT"

Every artist/designer faces challenges in getting started, generating and evaluating visual ideas, managing long-term projects, working with others, and handling critiques. **Part Two: Concepts and Critical Thinking** offers practical advice and examples that students can consult at any point in the course. Chapter Eight in Part Two also explores the question of meaning in art from the artist's perspective.

APPLICATIONS TO STUDIO PRACTICE

For the practicing artist/designer, it is not enough to recognize the elemtns and principles in the work of others. **Key Questions** throughout the book challenge students to apply concepts to their own works in progress. **Studio project ideas** on the book's Web site invite a hands-on exploration of chapter topics. A list of some of these studio projects can be found at the end of each chapter.

CONVERSATIONS WITH PRACTICING ARTISTS AND DESIGNERS

Just as guest lecturers enrich the classroom by contributing different perspectives on how and why we make art and create designs, so the **artist and designer profiles** at the end of each chapter add other voices and experiences to the text. In these interviews, students learn about working processes and career choices from a remarkable group of professionals, including photographer Samuel Yates, metalsmith Marilyn da Silva, sculptor Kendall Buster, and ceramicist David MacDonald.

Profile:
Kendall Buster, Sculptor
Biological Architecture

Kendall Buster's large-scale "biological architecture" projects have been exhibited at Artist's Space and the American Academy of Arts and Letters in New York City; the Hirshhorn Museum and the Kreeger Museum in Washington, DC; the Kemper Museum in Kansas City; Suyama Space in Seattle; the Nevada Museum of Art in Reno; and the KZNSA Gallery in South Africa. Buster has created commissioned sculptures for the Washington, DC, Convention Center; Massey Cancer Center in Richmond, VA; and the Agave Library in Phoenix. Current projects include commissions for the new chemistry building at Princeton University, Johns Hopkins University, and the Indianapolis Museum of Art.

MS: Microbiology was your initial academic passion, and you worked in this field for twelve years. What attracted you to microbiology, and what did you learn from it?

KB: Peering into a microscope gave me access to an intricate and beautiful world that was beyond ordinary perception. As I learned more, I became increasingly interested in the architecture of natural forms—the way cells are constructed to maximize efficiency or the permeability of a particular cell wall. The sculptures I now create begin with an internal skeleton that I wrap in a fabric or plastic skin. And, I am still fascinated by shifts in perception, from very small scale to very large scale. For me, art and science are simply aspects of the same impulse.

MS: How do you translate your ideas into large-scale objects? Most of your recent projects could fill an entire gymnasium!

KB: Ideas often occur just as I am waking up. At this point, they are more intuitive than intentional. I begin to record possibilities through pencil drawings. Drawing is crucial—it is the first step in getting the idea out of my head and into the world. I then move to what I see as three-dimensional sketching, using carved Styrofoam, wire, or various types of board.

Further work is done with an entire team of collaborators. Computer-aided design helps us explore variations further and analyze the structural requirements and possibilities of the forms. With my studio team, I create physical models of the building in which the artwork will be placed in order to study

the ways in which the sculpture converses with the site. I have a project coordinator who communicates with the client on the architectural particulars of the site and a rigger who is an installation specialist.

MS: How are the pieces actually constructed?

KB: My large-scale sculptures are made with many interlocked parts, and so creating patterns for the parts is critical. These patterns, both computer generated and hand drawn on the studio floor, are used for shaping and welding the steel frames or cutting planar material. The frames are professionally powder-coated, and when the frames are covered in cloth I might work with as many as ten to twenty helpers in a marathon "screening party."

MS: Please talk us through *New Growth*, installed in the Boise Art Museum.

KB: *New Growth* is an inventory of architectural models that function like biological systems. In this imagined city, old forms generate new forms through processes that suggest germination, budding, merging, hybridization, or absorption. The model city is conceived as a single organism constructed from many interdependent parts. Some structures are connected by passageways that suggest either umbilical cords or parasitic invasions. Contiguous membranes create distinct regions in the city, and the transparency of these membranes allows inner layers to be visible through the outer shell.

Architectural structures form and re-form the fabric of cities over time. To evoke this process, I wanted

to build a structure that seems to be based on a precise blueprint, while at the same time contradict this idea by creating a structure that seems dynamic, continually changing. I am also interested in exploring the tension between what is revealed and what is concealed; how windows link interior space with exterior place to create shifting sight lines; how narrow entryways or low passages act in direct confrontation with the body; how space is compressed and movement directed; how one is at times hidden, and at times exposed.

New Growth is also a response to the particulars of the Boise Art Museum site. On my first visit I visualized a kind of floating cityscape made up of forms that behaved both as individual structures and as a continuous membrane. The sculpture that I finally built connected to the exhibition site in unexpected ways. Curved rooftops in my architectural models seemed to echo the arched beams in the ceiling, and the ever-changing light penetrating through the floor-to-ceiling windows created subtle shades of white and gray on the transparent layers of fabric.

Scale shifts between the viewer's initial "panoramic" overview and the more closely observed details were also important. At one moment, the viewer is dwarfed by the artwork; at another, the artwork reads as a model that the viewer can command. As a result, the viewer is enveloped, embraced, and engaged—all at the same time.

MS: What advice do you have for beginning students?

KB: I have three bits of advice. First, realize that each of us has our own work process and embrace the process that is right for you. Second, find the right balance between conceptual breadth (lateral thinking) and conceptual depth (vertical thinking). Too much lateral thinking can result in superficiality, while too much vertical thinking can narrow your possibilities. Finally, embrace the idea of an ongoing and preferably daily studio practice. Complex ideas and structures don't happen overnight!

Kendall Buster, *New Growth*, 2007. Dimensions variable, as installed in Boise Art Museum.

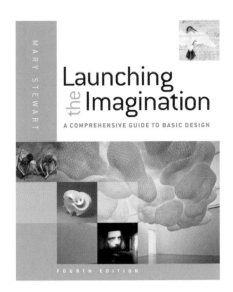

AN UNMATCHED VISUAL RESOURCE

By looking closely at as many outstanding illustrations as possible, students can build a mental library of images that can then serve as a launching pad for their own work. The **300-plus color reproductions** in this book encompass contemporary and traditional art, craft, media arts, and design, from both Western and world cultures. In addition, instructors who adopt the book can tap into **Connect Image Bank,** a way to easily browse and search for images and to download them for use in class presentations.

THOROUGH COVERAGE OF DESIGN VOCABULARY

A carpenter stocks his shop with a variety of tools, including a table saw, band saw, jig saw, and radial saw. Each has distinct capabilities and uses. Similarly, when students master the visual and verbal vocabulary of basic design, they can more eloquently express their ideas using a variety of tools. *Launching the Imagination* covers all of the topics common to most foundations courses, thus offering a coherent approach to a full-year curriculum.

Key terms are clearly explained and illustrated within the text, with at least one visual example provided for each concept. Students can review these terms in a Key Terms list at the end of each chapter and can test their understanding in an online flashcard and quiz program. A glossary of terms starting on page 294 serves as a comprehensive resource.

FLEXIBLE FORMATS

As in the past, *Launching the Imagination* is available in three formats so that professors can choose the coverage that best fits their curriculum:

1. A **comprehensive volume** for full-year courses. This volume covers 2-D, 3-D, and 4-D time design, plus creativity and problem solving (Parts One to Four).
2. A **2-D volume** that also includes chapters on creativity and problem solving (Parts One and Two).
3. A **3-D volume** that also includes chapters on creativity and problem solving (Parts Two and Three). This volume has been substantially expanded to better serve the 3-D classroom.

CourseSmart, a new way for faculty to find and review eTextbooks, is also a great option for students who are interested in accessing their course materials digitally and saving money. CourseSmart offers thousands of the most commonly adopted textbooks across hundreds of courses from a wide variety of higher-education publishers. It is the only place faculty can review and compare the full text of textbooks online, providing immediate access without the environmental impact of requesting print examination copies. At CourseSmart, students can save up to 50 percent off the cost of a print book, reduce their impact on the environment, and gain access to powerful Web tools for learning, including full text search, notes and highlighting, and e-mail tools for sharing notes among classmates.

Craft your teaching resources to match the way you teach. With **McGraw-Hill Create, www.mcgrawhill create.com,** you can easily rearrange chapters, combine material from other content sources, and quickly upload content you have written such as your course syllabus or teaching notes. Find the content you need in Create by searching through thousands of leading McGraw-Hill textbooks. Arrange your book to fit your teaching style. Create even allows you to personalize your book's appearance by selecting the cover and adding your name, school, and course information. Order a Create book and you'll receive a complimentary print review copy in 3–5 business days or a complimentary electronic review copy (eComp) via email in about one hour. Go to www.mcgrawhillcreate.com today and register. Experience how McGraw-Hill Create empowers you to teach your students your way.

NEW TO THE FOURTH EDITION

Working with invaluable feedback from other foundations teachers and my students, I have made the following improvements to the text:

- **Expanded and improved coverage of 3-D design.** The coverage in Part Three, Three-Dimensional Design, has been improved in several ways. Topics such as "form," in Chapter Nine, have been reorganized to work better as a unit of study. Coverage of 3-D elements and principles has been expanded, and Part Three has 12 additional examples of concepts, for a total of 200 full-color images. Every image has been carefully evaluated to ensure that it clearly illustrates the concept, and more than 30 examples have been replaced. Many more examples of contemporary sculpture have been included, representing works by artists such as Ann Hamilton, Kiki Smith, Ned Kahn, Nick Cave, Liza Lou, Olafur Eliasson, Jaume Plensa, Xu Bing, and Tara Donovan.

- **Reorganized and streamlined Part Two, Concepts and Critical Thinking.** The chapters in Part Two have been resequenced to align more closely with the steps in the design process. The first chapter in this part, Chapter Five, focuses on strategies for initiating a project. Tips for cultivating creativity as a daily practice and suggestions for managing creative projects from start to finish are now covered in Chapter Six. As in past editions, Chapters Seven and Eight cover critical thinking and constructing meaning in art. New image

choices create a stronger balance between 2-D and 3-D examples representing both art and design.

- **Increased focus on contemporary art.** The focus on contemporary art and artists has been increased throughout, with a particularly strong emphasis on sculptural works. There are 34 new examples by artists and designers, including works by John Paul Miller, Petah Coyne, William Kentridge, and Dan Sutherland.

- **New artist profiles.** Painter Suzanne Stryk discusses the value of the close observation of nature and connections between her sketchbooks and more developed artworks (Chapter Six), while sculptor Kendall Buster discusses her large-scale public art projects and the collaborative process through which they are made (Chapter Seven).

SUPPLEMENTS

Led by Mathew Kelly from Central College, a remarkable team of collaborators has developed an extensive online Instructor's Manual and an accompanying Web site. Advice on course construction, critique skills, and technical resources are included, along with more than 70 assignments. Divided into sections on Two-Dimensional Design, Three-Dimensional Design, Four-Dimensional Design, Color, Creativity, and Digital Design, this manual provides the basic information on which the teacher can build a rich and informative course.

Online Learning Center at www.mhhe.com/stewart4e

The Online Learning Center offers resources for each chapter of the text, including chapter objectives, vocabulary flashcards, activities, and studio projects. For instructors, lecture PowerPoints and an Instructor's Manual filled with advice on course construction, critique skills, and technical resources are available, along with assignment ideas.

MyArtStudio at www.mhhe.com/ArtStudio

Students have access to MyArtStudio, a rich and comprehensive Web site with interactions that allow students to study and experiment with various elements and principles of art and to view videos of art techniques and artists at work. Exercises on the Online Learning Center guide students to MyArtStudio at appropriate points in the text.

ACKNOWLEDGMENTS

Images are at the heart of this book. I would like to thank all the artists and designers who granted permission for use of their artworks and the galleries, museums, archives, and private donors who provided the high-resolution images. Photo researcher Deborah Anderson was remarkably tenacious in pursuing each permission and inventive in suggesting alternatives when necessary. Recommendations by developmental editor Cynthia Ward greatly improved the structure in Part Three and improved overall clarity; fine-tuning by copyeditor Mary Roybal improved consistency. At McGraw-Hill, I would like to thank production editor Carey Eisner, marketing manager Pamela Cooper, and, especially, sponsoring editor Betty Chen—truly the model of grace under pressure. Eric Zeiter did an exemplary job with the layout of this challenging book and William Stanton again created the beautiful covers. Thank you to Denise Wright and her team at Southern Editorial Publication Management, LLC, for all of their hard work with the supplements.

The artists I interviewed have been remarkably generous and supportive. In this edition, I would particularly like to thank Kendall Buster and Suzanne Stryk. At Florida State University, I would like to thank Dean Sally McRorie for all of her support and her relentless work in the service of the arts.

This book is dedicated to three of my colleagues. The comprehensive version is dedicated to Dr. Richard Siegesmund, from the University of Georgia, in recognition of his exemplary work with Integrative Teaching International, a nonprofit college teaching organization. The 2-D split edition is dedicated to Adam Kallish, who has served as both the catalyst for action and the designer for the same organization. The 3-D split edition is dedicated to Jeff Boshart, in recognition of over 25 years of service to F.A.T.E. (Foundations in Art: Theory and Education) and his repeated contributions as a reviewer for various editions of this book.

For the Fourth Edition:

The following reviewers provided valuable insights and suggestions:

Donald Barrie, *Seattle Central Community College*
Nicholas Bonner, *Northern Kentucky University*
Jeff Boshart, *Eastern Illinois University*
Keith Bryant, *University of North Carolina at Charlotte*
Marie Bukowski, *Louisiana Tech University*
Jessica Calderwood, *University of Wisconsin, Oshkosh*
Ben Cunningham, *Millersville University*
Eileen Doktorski, *Utah State University*
Scott Dooley, *Wittenberg University*
Frankie Flood, *University of Wisconsin, Milwaukee*
Paul Gebhardt, *University of Maine at Fort Kent*
David Griffin, *Eastern Illinois University*
Dan L. Henderson, *Art Institute of Atlanta*
Kevin W. Hughes, *Missouri State University*
Dawn Hunter, *University of South Carolina*
Imi Hwangbo, *University of Georgia*
Rosalie Rosso King, *Western Washington University*
Casey McGuire, *Metropolitan State College*
Erik Miller, *The Community College of Baltimore County*
Alan Moss, *Kent State University*
Gary Nemcosky, *Appalachian State University*
Jane Nodine, *University of South Carolina Upstate*
Laura Prange, *University of Southern Mississippi*
Ann Coddington Rast, *Eastern Illinois University*
Laura Ruby, *University of Hawaii*

For the Third Edition:

Scott Betz, *Winston-Salem State University*
Denise Burge, *University of Cincinnati*
Holly Earhart, *Full Sail Real World Education*
Sarah Gjertson, *University of Denver*
Marth McLeish, *Indiana State University*
Julia Morrisroe, *University of Florida—Gainesville*
John Nettleton, *Ontario College of Art & Design*
Gayle Pendergrass, *Arkansas State University*
Renee Sandell, *George Mason University*
Kyle Trowbridge, *University of Miami*
Jeremy Waltman, *Florida State University*
Peter Winant, *George Mason University*

For the Second Edition:

Kathleen Arkles, *College for Creative Studies*
Donald Barrie, *Seattle Central Community College*
Julie Baugnet, *St. Cloud State University*
Donna Beckis, *Fitchburg State College*
Nancy Blum-Cumming, *University of Wisconsin—Stout*

Debra K. D. Bonnello, *Lansing Community College*

Jeff Boshart, *Eastern Illinois University*

Jacquelin Boulanger, *New College of Florida*

Stephanie Bowman, *Pittsburgh State University*

Peter Brown, *Ringling School of Art*

John Carlander, *Westmont College*

Steven Cost, *Amarillo College*

Michael Croft, *University of Arizona*

Cat Crotchett, *Western Michigan University*

Claire Darley, *Art Academy of Cincinnati*

Anita M. DeAngelis, *East Tennessee State University*

Beverly Dennis, *Jones County Junior College*

Tracy Doreen Dietzel, *Edgewood College*

Jim Doud, *American University*

Clyde L. Edwards, *Valdosta State University*

James Elniski, *School of Art Institute at Chicago*

Jane Fasse, *Edgewood College*

John Ford, *Labette Community College*

Corky Goss, *Cazenovia College*

Arlene Grossman, *Art Institute of Boston at Lesley University*

Danielle Harmon, *West Texas A&M University*

Christopher Hocking, *University of Georgia*

Carol Hodson, *Webster University*

Sara M. Hong, *University of Arizona*

Lorie Jesperson, *Lake Michigan College*

C. Ann Kittredge, *University of Maine—Presque Isle*

Deborah Krupenia, *Endicott College*

Michelle La Perriere, *Maryland Institute College of Art*

In Shile Lee, *Tompkins Cortland Community College*

Richard F. Martin, *New York Institute of Technology*

Christine McCullough, *Youngstown State University*

Julie McWilliams, *Sussex County College*

Nancy Morrow, *Kansas State University*

Byron Myrich, *Jones Junior College*

Kelly Nelson, *Longwood University*

Soon Ee Ngoh, *Mississippi State University*

Lara Nguyen, *California State University, Long Beach*

Grace O'Brien, *Purdue University*

Mark O'Grady, *Pratt Institute*

Sally Packard, *University of North Texas*

William Potter, *Herron School of Art–IUPUI*

Patsy C. Rainey, *University of Mississippi*

Gerson M. Rapaport, *New York Institute of Technology*

Cherri Rittenhouse, *Rock Valley College*

Gil Rocha, *Richland Community College*

William B. Rowe, *Ohio Northern University*

Kim Schrag, *Tompkins Courtland Community College*

Jean Sharer, *Front Range Community College*

Todd Slaughter, *Ohio State University*

Robert Smart, *Lawrence University*

Karen Spears, *Eastern Kentucky University*

Mindy Spritz, *The Art Institute of Atlanta*

Teresa Stoll, *Lake City Community College*

Katherine Stranse, *University of Arkansas—Little Rock*

Rob Tarbell, *Limestone College*

William Travis, *Rowan University*

Linda Vanderkolk, *Purdue University*

Carolynne Whitefeather, *Utica College*

Reid Wood, *Lorain County Community College*

Marilyn H. Wounded Head, *Mesa State College*

Alice Zinnes, *NYC College of Technology, CUNY*

For the First Edition:

Scott Betz, *Weber State University*

Jeff Boshart, *Eastern Illinois University*

Peter Brown, *Ringling School of Art and Design*

Brian Cantley, *California State University, Fullerton*

Laurie Beth Clark, *University of Wisconsin, Madison*

Michael Croft, *University of Arizona*

John Fillwalk, *Ball State University*

David Fobes, *San Diego State University*

Albert Grivetti, *Clarke College*

Imi Hwangbo, *University of Louisville*

Michelle Illuminato, *Bowling Green State University*

Ann Baddeley Keister, *Grand Valley State University*

Margaret Keller, *St. Louis Community College*

Dan Lowery, *Southwestern Illinois College*

Karen Mahaffy, *University of Texas at San Antonio*

Richard Moses, *University of Illinois*

Gary Nemcosky, *Appalachian State University*

Helen Maria Nugent, *Art Institute of Chicago*

Rick Paul, *Purdue University*

Ron Saito, *California State University, Northridge*

Karen Schory, *Johnson County Community College*

Susan Slavick, *Carnegie Mellon University*

Paul Wittenbraker, *Grand Valley State University*

William Zack, *Ball State University*

Three-Dimensional Design 179

part three

Author Mary Stewart with *Labyrinth* book.

Mary Stewart is currently Director of Art Foundations at Florida State University. She has received two grants from the Pennsylvania Council on the Arts and has participated in over 95 exhibitions, nationally and internationally.

From 1994 to 2004, Stewart worked with Greek philosophy as a primary source for her images. In Plato's famous dialogues, Socrates led his students through a series of conversations on the nature of beauty and the role of memory in developing knowledge. For Socrates, life was a process of self-discovery, a search for essential truths remembered from a pre-birth state. Unlike Aristotle, who argued that knowledge was derived from experience, Socrates suggested that knowledge was inherent and universal. *Labyrinth,* shown in the top photo, is composed of 11 etchings based on cave paintings, fragments of early writing, and Greek sculpture. When collapsed, the book presents a cohesive composition; when opened, the images become fragmented, creating a sense of mystery.

In her current work, Stewart constructs invented landscapes from her digital photographs. Based on multiple north Florida sites, *Stormfury #4* presents a world that is both treacherous and awe-inspiring. Line, shapes, textures, and colors expand, compress, and collide within an apocalyptic panorama.

Mary Stewart, *Stormfury #4,* 2008. Digital photocopy with prismacolor and acrylics, 90 × 44 in. (228.6 × 111.76 cm).

i.1 **Bill Viola,** *Slowly Turning Narrative,* **1992.** Bill Viola's *Slowly Turning Narrative* consists of a large, rotating screen onto which moving images are projected. One side of the screen is a mirror, which reflects distorted images back into the room.

BEGINNER'S MIND, OPEN MIND

You are ready to embark on a marvelous journey. New technologies and exhibition venues offer dazzling new ways to produce, perform, and publicize visual ideas. Contemporary art has expanded to include performances, earthworks, and installations (i.1). Metalsmiths now use everything from plastics to precious metals to create inventive small-scale sculptures (i.2). Graphic designers develop many forms of visual communication, from shopping bags and exhibitions (i.3) to Web sites, logos, and brochures. Film and video are becoming increasingly integrated with the Internet, which promises to extend visual communication even further (i.4). The opportunities for exploration are endless (i.5). It is a great time to be studying art and design!

i.2 **Keith E. LoBue,** *Where Music Dwells,* **1993.** A broken pocket watch can become an evocative artwork when images and words are added.

i.3 Bill Cannan & Co., NASA's Participating Exhibit at the 1989 Paris Air Show. To suggest the mystery of space travel and highlight individual displays, this NASA exhibition used dramatic pools of light within a mysterious dark setting.

i.4 Hans-Jürgen Syberberg, *Parsifal,* 1982. Syberberg combined live actors with oversized projections of dreamlike landscapes in his filmic interpretation of Richard Wagner's opera.

i.5 Xu Bing, *A Book from the Sky*, 1987–91. Hong Kong Museum of Art. Mixed mediums.

A journey of a thousand miles begins with one step. As a beginner, your first steps are especially important. Free of the preconceptions or habitual patterns that can paralyze more advanced students, beginners enter the learning experience with an open mind and an intense desire to explore new ideas. With no reputation to defend, they can more easily make the mistakes that are so essential to learning. Having taught students at all levels, I have found that beginners of any age are the most courageous by far. The open, unencumbered "beginner's mind" is wonderfully receptive and resilient. As a result, remarkable changes can occur during your first year.

DEFINING DESIGN

As a verb, *design* can be defined four ways:

- To plan, delineate, or define, as in designing a building
- To create a deliberate sequence of images or events, as in developing a film storyboard (i.6)
- To create a functional object, as in product design (i.7)
- To organize disparate parts into a coherent whole, as in composing a brochure

439 Melanie — Run — Run.

440 Children (foreground against Sodium Screen) Background Bodega school with michelle and 2 or 3 children

440A continuation of 440. - Melanie runs past camera

i.6 Harold Michelson, Storyboard for Alfred Hitchcock's *The Birds*. Storyboards are used to plan the sequence of events and compose the specific shots in a film. Alfred Hitchcock, who began his career as an artist, preplanned his films with exacting care.

i.7 Designworks/USA, Home Pro Garden Tool Line. These five gardening tools are all based on the same basic combination of handle, blades, and simple pivot. Variations in proportion determine their use.

As a noun, *design* can be defined as

- A plan or pattern, such as the layout for a garden (i.8)

- An arrangement of lines, shapes, colors, and textures into an artistic whole, as in the composition of a painting or sculpture (i.9)

Design is deliberate. Rather than hope for the best and accept the result, artists and designers explore a wide range of solutions to every problem, then choose the most promising option for further development. Even when chance is used to generate ideas, choices are often made before the results are shown. Design creates a bridge between artistic intention and compositional conclusion. As painter Joseph Albers noted, "To design is to plan and to organize, to order, to relate and to control."

Two-dimensional compositions are constructed from lines, shapes, textures, values, and colors that have been arranged to create a unified whole (i.10). Lines, planes, volumes, masses, and space are the basic components of a three-dimensional composition (i.11). Time design (including video, photography, performance, kinetic sculpture, and the book arts) is based on the juxtaposition of images and events (i.12). A great idea never saved a bad painting. Art and design are visual forms of communication: without careful composition, a great idea may be lost.

Developing a wide range of solutions to every problem is the quickest way to master composition. Small, quick studies are often used to explore the possibilities. By translating a mental image into a rough sketch, you can immediately see whether the idea has potential. Furthermore, the best way to have a good idea is to have a lot of ideas. By selecting the best rough composition from 20 sketches, you will have a better beginning point for your final design.

In the pages that follow, the basic elements, principles, and implications of design are explored in depth. Over 650 images supply visual examples from many cultures and in all areas of art and design. Fifteen interviews with living artists provide insight into the creative process.

i.8 Garden Design. An extensive layout is generally used for planning a garden. Matching the plants to the soil conditions, setting, climate, and overall intent saves money and improves results. In this case, the design is not an artwork in itself but, rather, a plan of action.

i.9 Claude Monet, *Waterlily Pond (Le Bassin des Nymphéas),* 1904. Impressionist Claude Monet moved to the village of Giverny in 1883 and built an extensive water garden. The waterlilies he grew there inspired his last major series of paintings. Monet combined lines, shapes, textures, and colors to create a compelling illusion of a shimmering space.

i.10 Sam Francis, *Flash Point,* 1975. Surrounded by explosive energy, the white square in the center of this painting provides a unifying focal point.

Reading this book, however, is just the first step. True understanding comes through your own efforts, combined with the direction your teachers can provide. Remember that basic drawing and design courses provide the foundation on which all subsequent courses are built. You are a college beginner only once in your entire life: this is not a rehearsal. By using your time well, you really *can* get the rocket off the launching pad.

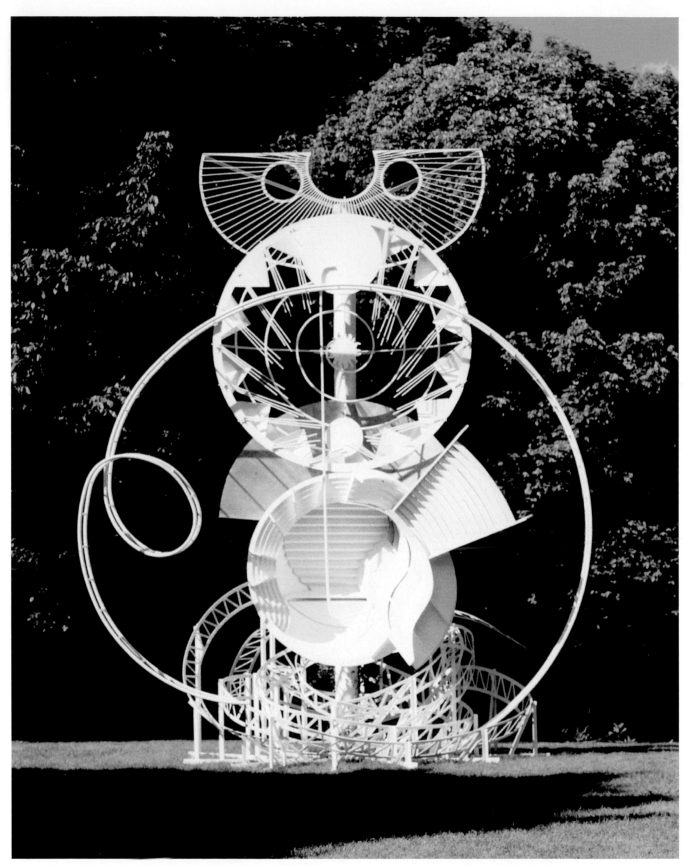

i.11 Alice Aycock, *Tree of Life Fantasy: Synopsis of the Book of Questions Concerning the World Order and/or the Order of Worlds*, 1990–92. Inspired by the double-helix structure of DNA and by medieval illustrations representing the entrance to paradise as a spinning hole in the sky, Aycock has combined a linear structure with a series of circular planes and a lot of open space. The resulting sculpture is as open and playful as a roller coaster.

i.12 Paul Jenkins and Jae Lee, from *Inhumans*: "First Contact," March 1999. Comic books, like films, rely on the development of characters, the use of "camera" angles, and the organization of multiple images.

Launching the Imagination

A Guide to Three-Dimensional Design

Georgiana Nehl and David Browne, *Solstice Greetings,* **1998.** Color photograph of constructed assemblage, 5 × 5 in. (12.7 × 12.7 cm).

Concepts and Critical Thinking

In *A Kick in the Seat of the Pants,* Roger Von Oech identifies four distinct roles in the creative process.

First, the *explorer* learns as much as possible about the problem. Research is crucial. Ignorance may result in a compositional or conceptual cliché.

Second, the *artist* experiments with a wide variety of solutions, using all sorts of combinations, proportions, and materials. By creating 10 answers to each question, the artist can select the best solution rather than accepting the only solution.

Third, the *judge* assesses the work in progress and determines what revisions are required. Innovative ideas are never fully developed when first presented; most need extensive revision and expansion. Rather than discard an underdeveloped idea, the judge identifies its potential and determines ways to increase its strength.

Finally, the *warrior* implements the idea. When obstacles appear, the warrior assesses the situation, determines the best course of action, and then moves ahead decisively.

We will explore each of these roles in the next four chapters. Chapter Five deals with concept development and visual problem solving. Strategies for cultivating creativity and improving time management are discussed in Chapter Six. Chapter Seven is devoted to critical thinking and provides specific ways to improve any design. In Chapter Eight, we expand our discussion of visual communication and consider ways to create more meaningful artworks.

Part Two

A
IS FOR APOLLO, WHOSE
ARROWS NEVER MISS

U
IS FOR URANIA THE MUSE OF
CELESTIAL FORCES IS SHE

chapter five

Problem Seeking and Problem Solving

By mastering the basic elements and principles of design, you can increase the visual power of your work. Composition, however, is only part of the puzzle. With the increasing emphasis on visual communication, the ideas being expressed by artists and designers have become more varied and complex. Conceptual invention is just as important as compositional strength.

New ideas invite development of new types of artwork. When the concept is fresh and the composition is compelling, expression and communication expand. In this chapter, we consider ways in which artists and designers define problems and explore various problem-solving strategies.

PROBLEM SEEKING

The Design Process

In its most basic form, the design process can be distilled down to four basic steps. When beginning a project, the designer asks

1. What do we need?
2. What existing designs are similar to the design we need?
3. What is the difference between the existing designs and the new design?
4. How can we transform, combine, or expand these existing designs?

By studying the classic Eames chair, we can see this process clearly. Charles and Ray Eames were two of the most innovative and influential designers of the postwar era. Charles, trained as an architect, was a master of engineering and had a gift for design integration. Ray, trained as a painter, contributed a love of visual structure, a sense of adventure, and an understanding of marketing. Combining their strengths, this husband-and-wife team designed furniture, toys, exhibitions, and architecture and directed over 80 experimental films.

Their first breakthrough in furniture design came in 1940, when they entered a chair competition sponsored by the Museum of Modern Art in New York City. Many architects had designed furniture, and the Eameses were eager to explore this field.

Many similar products existed. The most common was the overstuffed chair, which continues to dominate American living rooms. Extensive padding on a boxy framework supported the sitter. Another popular design was the

5.1 Marcel Breuer, *Armchair*, 1925. Tubular steel, canvas, 28¹¹⁄₁₆ × 30⁵⁄₁₆ × 26¾ in. (72.8 × 77 × 68 cm).

5.2 Alvar Aalto, *Paimio Lounge Chair*, 1931–33. Laminated birch, molded plywood, lacquered, 26 × 23¾ × 34⅞ in. (66 × 60.5 × 88.5 cm).

Adirondack chair, made from a series of flat wooden planes. Of greatest interest, however, were designs by architects such as Marcel Breuer (5.1) and Alvar Aalto (5.2). These designs used modern materials and clearly displayed their structure.

By comparing existing chairs with the chair they wanted, Charles and Ray could identify qualities they needed to retain and qualities that needed to be changed. The familiar overstuffed chair (5.3) was bulky and awkward, but it was comfortable. The Adirondack chair (5.4) was easy to mass-produce but too large for interior use. The modern chairs were elegant and inventive but were expensive to produce and often uncomfortable. The Eameses wanted to create a modern chair that was comfortable, elegant, and inexpensive.

During World War II, the Eames team had designed and manufactured molded plywood splints, which were used by doctors in the U.S. Navy. After extensive research and experimentation, they had mastered the process of steaming and reshaping the sheets of plywood into complex curves. In developing their competition entry, they combined their knowledge of splints, love of modern chairs, understanding of anatomy, and mastery of architecture. Their plywood chair, designed in collaboration with architect Eero Saarinen, won the first prize.

5.3 Overstuffed chair.

5.4 Adirondack chair.

5.5 Charles and Ray Eames, *Side Chair, Model DCM*, 1946.
Molded ash plywood, steel rod, and rubber shockmounts,
28¾ × 19½ × 20 in. (73 × 49.5 × 50.8 cm).

5.6 Frank Gehry, *Cross Check Armchair*, 1992. Maple,
33⅝ × 28½ × 28½ in. (85.3 × 72.4 × 72.4 cm).

A series of Eames designs followed, including a metal and plywood version in 1946 (5.5) and numerous cast plastic versions. To create the plastic chairs, the Eames team invented a new manufacturing process. This led to a breakthrough in the field of furniture design.

By addressing a need, researching existing designs, making comparisons, and combining the best characteristics of existing chairs, the Eames team produced a new kind of chair and thus firmly established themselves as leaders in the design field.

The Fine Art Process

For a designer, the problem-solving process begins when a client requests help or the designer identifies a societal need. With the Eames chair, the museum competition provided the impetus for an experiment that reshaped an industry.

By contrast, contemporary sculptors, filmmakers, painters, and other fine artists generally invent their own aesthetic problems. Ideas often arise from personal experience and from the cultural context. Combining self-awareness with empathy for others,

many artists have transformed a specific event into a universal statement. For example, Picasso's *Guernica* (see figure 8.24, page 168), painted in response to the 1937 bombing of a specific Spanish village, is now seen as a universal statement about the horrors of war. Working more independently and with fewer deadlines, artists can explore ideas and issues of personal interest. Adam Kallish's interview at the end of this chapter emphasizes the design process, while interviews with Suzanne Stryk, Kendall Buster, and Roger Shimomura emphasize the fine art process.

Sources of Ideas

Regardless of the initial motivation for their work, both artists and designers constantly scan their surroundings in an omnivorous search for images and ideas. As demonstrated by the profiles that appear throughout this book, the most improbable object or idea may provide inspiration. Memories of growing up in small-town America provide the stimulus for *Storefront Stories,* by Nancy Callahan and Diane Gallo. Biological systems and architecture inspire sculptor Kendall Buster. Ordinary vegetables and African vessels influence ceramicist David MacDonald. If you are at a loss for an idea, take a fresh look at your surroundings. Here are three strategies.

Transform a Common Object

Architect Frank Gehry based the exuberant armchair in figure 5.6 on the wood-strip bushel basket used by farmers (5.7). If you consider all the ideas that can be generated by a set of car keys, a pair of scissors, or a compass, you will have more than enough to get a project started.

5.7 Wood-strip bushel basket.

Study Nature

Ceramicist Ray Rogers is inspired by many natural forms, including mushrooms, stones, and aquatic life. His spherical pots (5.8) often suggest the colors, textures, and economy of nature. In figure 5.9, Vera Lisková used the fluidity and transparency of glass to create a humorous version of a prosaic porcupine. Through an inventive use of materials, both artists have reinterpreted nature.

Visit a Museum

Artists and designers frequently visit all kinds of museums. Carefully observed, the history and physical objects produced by any culture can be both instructive and inspirational. Looking at non-Western artwork is especially valuable. Unfamiliar concepts and compositions can stimulate creativity. Beau Dick's *Mugamtl Mask* (5.10) is one example. First developed by a man who had revived from a

5.8 Ray Rogers, *Vessel*, New Zealand, 1984. Large, pit-fired (porous and nonfunctional) with "fungoid" decorative treatment in relief. Diameter approximately 21⅝ in. (55 cm).

5.9 Vera Lisková, *Porcupine*, 1972–80. Flame-worked glass, 4¼ × 11 in. (10.8 × 28.2 cm).

deadly illness, it depicts the supernatural abilities (including flight) that he gained during his experience. His descendants now have the right to construct and wear this special mask. By understanding the story and studying this mask, you can more readily design a mask based on your own experiences.

Historical examples such as Albrecht Dürer's *The Knight, Death and the Devil* (5.11) can be equally inspiring. Two hundred years before this print was made, the Black Plague killed nearly half the population of Europe. This horrific disease remained a threat in Dürer's time. As a result, Renaissance conceptions of life and death were very different from our contemporary viewpoint. This difference can spark a new way of thinking and lead you to a fresh idea.

Characteristics of a Good Problem

Regardless of its source, the problem at hand must fully engage either the artist or the designer. Whether it is assigned or invented, a good problem generally includes the following characteristics.

Significant

When substantial amounts of time, effort, and money are being spent, it is wise to prioritize problems and focus on those of greatest consequence. Identifying your major goals can help you determine the significance of a job.

5.10 Beau Dick, *Mugamtl Mask (Crooked Beak)*, 1993. Red cedar, cedar bark, paint, 24 × 26 × 16 in. (61 × 66 × 40.6 cm).

5.11 Albrecht Dürer, Detail of *The Knight, Death and the Devil*, 1513. Engraving, 11 × 14 in. (28 × 36 cm).

Socially Responsible

With the human population approaching 7 billion, it is unwise to pursue a project that squanders natural resources. What resources will be required for a major project, and how will you dispose of resulting waste? Increasingly, artists and designers consider the environmental as well as the economic implications of each project.

Comprehensible

It is impossible to solve a problem you don't fully understand. Ask questions if the assignment specifications and objectives are unclear to you.

Open to Experimentation

It is important to distinguish between clear definition and restrictive limitations. Consider the following two assignment descriptions:

1. Organize at least 20 photocopies in such a way that they convey an idea or emotion.

2. Organize 20 photographs by American Civil War photographer Mathew Brady in order to tell a story about the life of Abraham Lincoln.

In the first case, the requirements of the project are clearly stated, but the solution remains open. In the second case, the *solution* as well as the *problem* is described. For the professional artist or designer, there are no "bad" problems, only bad solutions. However, when limited to a narrow range of possible solutions, even the most inventive person will become frustrated. If you find yourself in a straitjacket, rethink the problem and try a new approach.

Authentic

Regardless of the source, every person approaches each problem on his or her own terms. Each of us has a unique perspective, and the connections we make will vary. As a student, you will learn more when you really embrace each assignment and make it your own. Ask questions, so that you can understand the conceptual implications of each project. When you reframe the *question* in your own terms, the creative possibilities will expand and your imagination will soar.

CONVERGENT AND DIVERGENT THINKING

To see how it all works, let's work our way through an actual assignment, using two different problem-solving strategies.

> *Problem:* Organize up to 20 photocopies from library sources so that they tell a story. Use any size and type of format. Any image can be enlarged, reduced, cropped, or repeated.

Using Convergent Thinking

Convergent thinking involves the pursuit of a predetermined goal, usually in a linear progression and through a highly focused problem-solving technique. The word *prose* can help you remember the basic steps:

1. Define the *problem*.
2. Do *research*.
3. Determine your *objective*.
4. Devise a *strategy*.
5. *Execute* the strategy.
6. *Evaluate* the results.

In convergent thinking, the end determines the means. You know what you are seeking before you begin. For this reason, clear definition of the problem is essential: the most brilliant idea is useless if it doesn't solve the problem.

Convergent thinking is familiar to most of us in the scientific method, which follows the same basic procedure. It is orderly, logical, and empirical; there are clear boundaries and specific guidelines. Clearly focused on the final result, convergent thinking is a good way to achieve a goal and meet a deadline. Let's analyze each step.

Define the Problem

Determine all of the physical and technical requirements of the assignment and ask whether there are any stylistic limitations. Be sure that you understand the preliminary steps as well as the final due date.

Next, assess your strengths and weaknesses relative to the problem assigned, and determine your best work strategy. Let's consider the approaches taken by two hypothetical students, Jeremy (as a convergent thinker) and Angela (as a divergent thinker).

Using a dictionary, Jeremy begins by analyzing the words *story* and *images*. He finds that a *story* is shorter than a novel, that it may be true or fictitious, that a series of connected events is needed, and that it may take many forms, including a memoir, a play, or a newspaper article. Next, he determines that an *image* is a representation of a person or thing, a visual impression produced by reflection in a mirror, or a mental picture of something—an idea or impression. This means that photographs from books or magazines and reproductions of paintings are fair game. Jeremy realizes that he can even include a mirror in the project, to reflect the viewer's own image.

He spends the first hour of class on brainstorming, then decides to develop a story about Irish immigration to America in the 1890s.

Do Research

Creativity is highly dependent on seeking connections and making new combinations. The more information you have, the more connections you can make. Through research, you can collect and assess technical, visual, and conceptual possibilities.

For this assignment, Jeremy reads extensively, then develops a plausible story based on immigrant diaries. He begins to collect images of ships, cities, and people.

Determine Your Objective

Jeremy now has the raw material needed to solve the problem. However, many questions remain unanswered, including

- What happens in this story? Is it fiction or nonfiction?

- Who is the storyteller? A 12-year-old boy will tell a very different story than a 20-year-old woman.

- What is the best format to use? A dozen letters sent between fictitious brothers in Dublin and Boston? A Web site describing actual families? A photo album?

At this point, Jeremy pauses to rethink his strategy. What does he really want to communicate? He considers:

- *Does it solve the problem?* He reviews the assignment parameters.

- *Is the solution conceptually inventive?* Is it really intriguing, or is it something we've all seen before, a cliché?

- *Is the planned solution visually compelling?*

- *Can this solution be completed by the due date?* To meet the due date, it may be necessary to distill a complex problem down to an essential statement. In this case, Jeremy decides to simplify his project by focusing on one main character.

Devise a Strategy

While some assignments can be done in an afternoon, three-dimensional projects and multiple-image works tend to take longer. Jeremy determines the supplies he needs and considers the best time and place to work on the project.

Execute the Strategy

Now, Jeremy just digs in and works. He has found it best to work with great concentration and determination at this point, rather than second-guessing himself.

Evaluate the Results

At the end of each work session, Jeremy considers the strengths and weaknesses of the work in progress. What areas in each composition seem cluttered or confusing? How can those areas be strengthened? He finally presents the project for a class critique.

Convergent Thinking Applications

Convergent thinking is most effective when

- The problem can be defined clearly.
- The problem can be solved rationally.
- The problem must be solved sequentially.
- Firm deadlines must be met.

Because many problems in science and industry fit these criteria, convergent thinking is favored by scientists, businesspeople, and graphic designers.

Using Divergent Thinking

The advantages of convergent thinking are clarity, control, focus, and a strong sense of direction. For many tasks, convergent thinking is ideal. In some cases, however, convergent thinking can offer *too* much clarity and not enough chaos. Inspiration is elusive. Over-the-edge creativity is often messy and rarely occurs in an orderly progression. If you want to find something completely new, you will have to leave the beaten path.

In **divergent thinking,** the means determines the end. The process is more open-ended; specific results are hard to predict. Divergent thinking is a great way to generate completely new ideas.

There are two major differences between convergent and divergent thinking. First, in divergent thinking, the problem is defined much more broadly, with less attention to "what the client wants." Research is more expansive and less tightly focused. Second, because the convergent thinker discards weak ideas in the thumbnail stage, the final image is more pre-planned and predictable. The divergent thinker, on the other hand, generates many variables, is less methodical, and may have to produce multiple drafts of a composition in order to get a polished result.

While convergent thinking is usually more efficient, divergent thinking is often more inventive. It opens up unfamiliar lines of inquiry and can lead to a creative breakthrough. Divergent thinking is a high-risk/high-gain approach. By breaking traditional rules, the artist can explore unexpected connections and create new possibilities.

Let's try the same assignment again, now using Angela's divergent thinking.

Problem: Organize up to 20 photocopies from library sources so that they tell a story. Use any size and type of format. Any image can be enlarged, reduced, cropped, or repeated.

Realizing that the strength of the source images is critical, Angela immediately heads for the section of the library devoted to photography. By leafing through a dozen books, she finds 40 great photographs, ranging from images of train stations to trapeze artists. She photocopies the photographs, enlarging and reducing pictures to provide more options. Laying them out on a table, she begins to move the images around, considering various stories that might be generated. Twenty of the images are soon discarded; they are unrelated to the circus story she decides to develop. She then finds five more images to flesh out her idea.

At this point, her process becomes similar to the final steps described in the preceding section. Like Jeremy, she must clarify her objective, develop characters, decide on a format, and construct the final piece. However, because she started with such a disparate collection of images, her final story is more likely to be nonlinear. Like a dream, her images may *evoke* feelings rather than *describe* specific events.

Divergent Thinking Applications

Divergent thinking is most effective when

- The problem definition is elusive or evolving.
- A rational solution is not required.
- A methodical approach is unnecessary.
- Deadlines are flexible.

Many creative people have used divergent thinking to explore the subconscious and reveal unexpected new patterns of thought. Surrealism, an art movement that flourished in Europe between the world wars, provides many notable examples of divergent thinking in art and literature. More interested in the essential substance of ideas and objects than in surface appearances, painter Yves

5.12 Yves Tanguy, *Multiplication of the Arcs,* **1954.** Oil on canvas, 40 × 60 in. (101.6 × 152.4 cm).

5.13 Giorgio de Chirico, *The Mystery and Melancholy of a Street,* **1914.** Oil on canvas, 24¼ × 28½ in. (62 × 72 cm).

Tanguy constructed *Multiplication of the Arcs* (5.12) from evocative abstract shapes. In *The Mystery and Melancholy of a Street* (5.13), Giorgio de Chirico used distorted perspective and threatening cast shadows to create a feeling of anxiety. More interested in stimulating the viewer's own response than in imposing a specific vision, the surrealists rejected rational thought.

Which is better—convergent or divergent thinking? A good problem-solving strategy is one that works. If five people are working on a Website design, a clear sense of direction, agreement on style, an understanding of individual responsibilities, and adherence to deadlines are essential. On the other hand, when an artist is working independently, the open-ended divergent approach can lead to a major breakthrough. As noted in the Adam Kallish interview at the end of this chapter, combining convergent and divergent thinking is ideal. When you need to expand an idea through open-ended exploration, use divergent thinking. When focus or distillation is needed, shift to convergent thinking.

BRAINSTORMING

Brainstorming plays an important role in both convergent and divergent thinking. It is a great way to expand ideas, see connections, and explore implications. Following are four common strategies.

Make a List

Let's say that the assignment involves visualizing an emotion. Start by listing every emotion you can, regardless of your interest in any specific area. Getting into the practice of opening up and actively exploring possibilities is crucial—just pour out ideas!

> **joy   sorrow   anger   passion   jealousy   sympathy   horror   exaltation**

From the list of emotions, circle one that looks promising. To move from the intangible name of the emotion to a visual solution, develop a list of the *kinds, causes,* and *effects* of the emotion. Following is one example, using *anger* as a starting point.

KINDS	CAUSES	EFFECTS
annoyance	wrong number phone call at 5 A.M.	slammed down phone
smoldering rage	friend gets award you want	argument with friend
desperate anger	fired from job	shouted at your child
anger at self	poor performance on test	major studying

By investigating specific kinds of anger and determining the causes and the effects, you now have some specific images to develop, rather than struggling with a vague, intangible emotion.

Use a Thesaurus

Another way to explore the potential of an idea is to use a thesaurus. Be sure to get a thesaurus that lists words conceptually rather than alphabetically. Use the index in the back to look up the specific word you need. For example, *The Concise Roget's International Thesaurus* has a section titled "Feelings," including everything from *acrimony* to *zeal*. Here is a listing of synonyms from the section on resentment and anger: *anger, wrath, ire, indignation, heat, more heat than light, dudgeon, fit of anger, tantrum, outburst, explosion, storm, scene, passion, fury, burn, vehemence, violence, vent one's anger, seethe, simmer,* and *sizzle!* Thinking about a wide range of implications and connections to other emotions can give you a new approach to a familiar word.

Explore Connections

By drawing a conceptual diagram, you can create your own thesaurus. Start with a central word. Then, branch out in all directions, pursuing connections and word associations as widely as possible. In a sense, this approach lets you visualize your thinking, as the branches show the patterns and connections that occurred as you explored the idea (5.14).

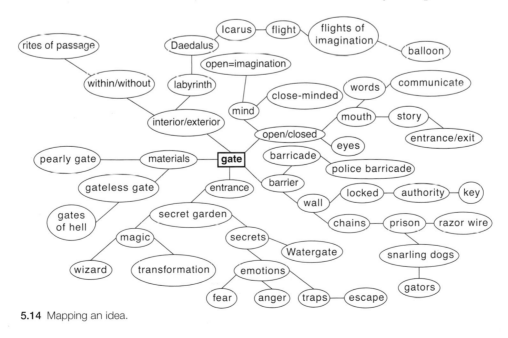

5.14 Mapping an idea.

If I am going to make drawings or photographs which include a bicycle, I might go for a bike ride, but more importantly I would fantasize about a bike. I would picture a bike in my mind. The most obvious depiction is the side view because this is the significant profile. I would then imagine a standing bicycle with no rider, looking from above, directly down on the bike, or from behind or in front of the standing bike with my eye-level midway between the ground and the handlebars. In these three positions the bicycle is seen from the least significant profile. It is a thin vertical line with horizontal protrusions of the pedals, seat and handlebars. The area viewed is so minimal that the bicycle almost disappears.

Before long in examining a bike I would become involved with circles. Looking at the tires, I think about the suspension of the rim and the tire, indeed, the entire vehicle and rider, by the thin spokes. It amazes me that everything is floating in space, connected only by thin lines. I imagine riding the bike through puddles and the trace of the linear journey from the congruent and diverging water marks left by the tread on the pavement. I might think about two friends together and separated. Symbolism.

I think about cycles of being with friends and apart. And again I would think literally of cycles, circles and tires.

I would think of the full moon as a circle and how in its cycle it turns into a line. I would see the tires from the significant profile and in my mind I would turn it in space and it would become an ellipse.

If I turned it further, until it was on an axis 90 degrees from the significant profile, it would no longer be a circle or an ellipse, but it would be a line. So again, line comes into my thoughts.

A circle is a line.

A circle is a straight line.[1]

5.15 Keith Smith. Brainstorming.

In *Structure of the Visual Book,* Keith Smith demonstrates the value of verbal connections. Smith seeks immersion in his subject. He wants to know it so well that he can pursue his images intuitively, with all the power and grace of a skilled cyclist. Try to follow the steps in figure 5.15, as he explores the word *bicycle.* Using a single object, he explores movement, friendship, and geometry.

Keep a Journal

Keeping a journal or a sketchbook is an ideal way to record your ideas and create connections. In it, you can

- Classify, arrange, and record information
- Develop new ideas
- Examine your current beliefs and analyze the beliefs of others
- Record your responses to critiques
- Make connections among your various classes

Recording your ideas at the end of each class and reviewing them at the beginning of the next can help you construct your own learning process. Anything that expands your thinking is fair game, including

- Plans for projects, such as thumbnail sketches and rough drafts
- Comments on how your work can be improved
- Notes from textbook readings and clippings from magazines
- Notes on visiting artists or gallery visits
- Technical notes or information on materials used in class
- Questions you want to pose in the next class meeting

Your record keeping can take many forms, including

- Drawings and diagrams
- Written ideas, descriptions, and lists
- Poetry and song lyrics

Periodically ask yourself the following questions:

- What was the most compelling image I saw today? What made it compelling?
- What similarities and differences were there among my studio classes this week?
- What connections were there between my lecture classes and my studio classes?
- What do I need to know in order to push my ideas further?

Viewing the journal as a record of your creative process is liberating. A random idea today can help you solve a visual problem tomorrow. Indeed, it is wise to review the journal as you move into upper level classes. Many ideas that were too ambitious for a first-year class are perfectly suited to further development later on.

Collaborative Creativity

Designers generally use group brainstorming. This helps them explore a wider range of possibilities and better meet client needs. In *The Art of Innovation*, IDEO general manager Tom Kelley lists seven characteristics of effective group brainstorming. The following list is based on a chapter titled "The Perfect Brainstorm."

1. Sharpen your focus. A good brainstormer will generate a lot of ideas. When these ideas all address the same problem, many viable solutions result. On the other hand, when participants don't understand the problem, chaos can result.

2. Use playful rules, such as "write it down" and "think bigger." A visual and verbal record of your ideas is helpful. Premature criticism is not.

3. Number your ideas. Numbers ("Let's aim for 50 ideas in the next hour") can create quantitative targets and provide a record of the order in which ideas occurred.

4. Build and jump. As the momentum builds, more and more ideas burst forth. A thoughtful question can then help the group leap to the next level, rather than getting stuck on a plateau.

5. The space remembers. Fill your brainstorming space with 22 × 30 in. Post-it notes covered with ideas the group has developed. By seeing the information, you can more easily spot bridges and build connections.

6. Warm up. If you are working with a completely new group, it may be necessary to provide an icebreaker to build trust. This is especially true if the participants are unfamiliar with brainstorming. I often ask each participant to present one succinct question or to draw a quick cartoon of the problem as they see it. It may be an enraged elephant, a tangle of thorns, or a whirling chain saw. Both the questions and the cartoons can reveal participant insights without demanding too much too soon.

7. Get physical. A wide range of simple materials opens up possibilities, especially if you are brainstorming a three-dimensional design problem. Cardboard, plasticine, and canvas all behave very differently. Playing with various materials can lead to a wider range of possibilities.

VISUAL RESEARCH

Thumbnail Sketches

Now let's practice turning ideas into images.

Return to your original list of emotions you developed in the brainstorming exercise. Circle the most promising words or phrases you have generated and look for connections between them. Start working on thumbnail sketches, about 1.5 × 2 in. in size (5.16). Be sure to draw a clear boundary for the sketches. The

5.16 Examples of thumbnail sketches.

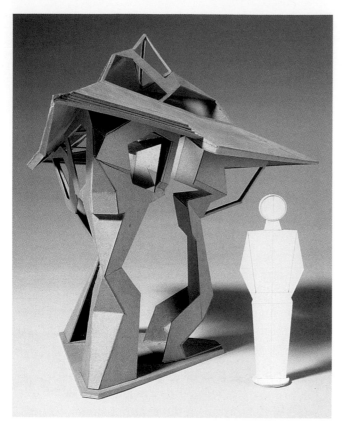

5.17A Peter Forbes, Models for *Shelter/Surveillance Sculpture*, 1994. Mixed mediums, 10½ × 9½ × 9 in. (27 × 24 × 23 cm).

size of the sculpture relative to the viewer and developed a construction strategy. As a result, when he constructed the final, 11-foot-tall sculpture (5.17B), Forbes was able to proceed with confidence. A **model** is a technical experiment. A **prototype** can be quite refined, such as the fully functional test cars developed by automobile companies. In addition to the aesthetic benefit of these preliminary studies, they often are needed to help solve technical problems at this stage. Is the cardboard you are using heavy enough to stand vertically, or does it bow? Is your adhesive strong enough? If there are moving parts, is the action fluid and easy, or does the mechanism constantly get stuck?

By completing these preliminary studies, you can refine the idea, strengthen the composition, and improve the craft of the final piece. As with a well-rehearsed performance, the work you bring to the critique now is really ready for discussion.

5.17B Peter Forbes, *Shelter/Surveillance Sculpture*, 1994. Mixed mediums, 11 ft 2 in. × 10 ft 4 in. × 10 ft (3.4 × 3.2 × 3 m).

edge of the frame is like an electric fence; by using the edge wisely, you can generate a lot of power!

As with the verbal brainstorming, move fast and stay loose at this point. It is better to generate 10 to 20 possibilities than to refine any single idea. You may find yourself producing very different solutions, or you may make a series of multiple solutions to the same idea. Either approach is fine—just keep moving!

Model Making

When working two-dimensionally, it is often necessary to make one or more full-sized rough drafts to see how the design looks when enlarged. Refinements made at this stage can mean the difference between an adequate solution and an inspired solution.

Prototypes, models, and maquettes serve a similar purpose when you are working three-dimensionally. A **maquette** is a well-developed three-dimensional sketch. Figure 5.17A shows Peter Forbes's maquette for *Shelter/Surveillance Sculpture*. In this chipboard "sketch," Forbes determined the

AN OPEN MIND

The very best artists and designers are often accomplished in more than one field. For example, Michelangelo was acclaimed as a painter, sculptor, and poet, while Leonardo da Vinci was a master of art, biology, and engineering. The study of philosophy has had a major impact on videographer Bill Viola and on installation artist Robert Irwin. Performer Laurie Anderson is equally an artist and a musician and derives many of her ideas from literature. Whenever the base of knowledge expands, the range of potential connections increases. When the islands of knowledge are widely scattered, as with interdisciplinary work, the imaginative leap is especially great.

The message is clear: the more you know, the more you can say. Read a book. Attend a lecture. Take a course in astronomy, archaeology, psychology, or poetry. Use ideas from academic courses to expand your studio work. Art and design require conceptual development as well as perceptual and technical skill. By engaging your heart, your eye, your hand, and your mind, you can fully use your emotional, perceptual, technical, and conceptual resources to create your very best work.

SUMMARY

- Concept and composition are equally important aspects of art and design.
- Designers usually solve problems presented by clients. Artists usually invent aesthetic problems for themselves.
- Ideas come from many sources, including common objects, nature, mythology, and history.
- Good problems are significant, socially responsible, comprehensible, and authentic. They provide basic parameters without inhibiting exploration.
- Convergent thinking is highly linear. The word *prose* can help you remember the steps.

- Divergent thinking is nonlinear and more open-ended than convergent thinking. It is less predictable and may lead to a creative breakthrough.
- Any idea can be expanded or enriched using brainstorming. Making lists, using a thesaurus, making a conceptual diagram, and creating connections are all common strategies.
- Visual and verbal research can provide the background information needed to create a truly inventive solution.
- The best artists and designers have a wide range of interests and approach new challenges with an open mind.

KEY TERMS

brainstorming	**divergent thinking**	**model**	**prototype**
convergent thinking	**maquette**		

STUDIO PROJECTS

To apply the concepts from this chapter in the studio, check out the Projects page in the Online Learning Center at www.mhhe.com/stewart4e. The following is a sample of the chapter-related assignments that are described in step-by-step detail.

Poster Design. Discovering the importance of research to creating an effective ad.
Limited/Unlimited. Using the limitations of a design problem as a springboard to solutions.
Superhero Mask/Headgear Design. Exploring a variety of strategies for developing a three-dimensional design.

Profile:
Adam Kallish, Designer/Consultant

Creativity by Design

Adam Kallish has dedicated his career to brand design with underpinnings in business consulting and collaborative deployment of innovation teams for large corporations. His interests range from traditional graphic design and brand strategy to organizational design. These areas are integrated through multidisciplinary teams and program management, linking vision (desire) to requirements (specifications) to results (benefits).

MS: You are an advocate of "Design Methods," which is a particular approach to solving problems. Why?

AK: Designers are often invited into a project after many crucial decisions have been made. They are then urged to "be creative." While developing a great composition is important, the outcome may miss the mark because the designer is entering too late in the game. Design Methods presents a disciplined approach to creativity from the very start.

MS: Please give me some historical background.

AK: Design Methods was developed by John Chris Jones and others in reaction to the scientific reductivism of the post–World War II world. It recognized a new way to solve the world's problems by striking a balance between intuition (imagination, experience, and beliefs) and logic (objectivity, phenomenology, and repeatability).

The convergent and divergent strategies described in Chapter Five are a part of Design Methods. In fact, they are interdependent. Rather than simply solve a problem as presented, through Design Methods, we redefine the problem itself, which often leads to a creative breakthrough. From the outset Design Methods combines rationality, proof, and definitions with experience, feelings, and precedent.

MS: Why seek a balance between intuition and logic?

AK: Intuition is based on established patterns derived from our personal experiences. We use it every day, especially when making quick decisions. Yet, a purely intuitive response can only illuminate what has been experienced, not what *can* be experienced.

Thus, intuition provides a narrow doorway into the future. Rationality is based upon logical patterns that many people can understand. But a purely rational approach tends to oversimplify problems and the results are often mediocre.

Innovation acts as a bridge between the two by exploring three key areas: what is desirable, what is possible, and what is viable. Innovation is difficult to achieve because it requires us to move from desirability to viability.

MS: It sounds pretty daunting!

AK: In the beginning, it can feel counterintuitive. But with practice, Design Methods leads to a deeper understanding of both problem seeking and problem solving.

MS: You are really talking about ways to invent the future. What are the essential questions that apply to *all* change processes?

AK: The act of designing is difficult because we tend to seek future solutions using past and current information. For example, the solutions to global warming we develop today will work only if our predictions of the future are correct.

For simple problems involving incremental change, the future is pretty easy to understand. The redesign of an existing object like a poster or a coffee cup has many constraints that are fairly obvious, and a single designer can solve these problems. However, for highly complex problems involving many designers, many interdependencies, and many unknowns, the act of designing can easily fall apart. These four key questions can guide us when discussing the future. What should we stop doing; what should we start doing; what should we continue doing; and how can we become more effective in what we do?

MS: What is the typical Design Methods sequence?

AK: Step one is Divergence (sometimes called Analysis or Discovery). This stage is about generating doubts, posing insightful questions, exploring what is critical to the stakeholders, including the client and the users.

Step two is Transformation (sometimes called Genesis or Development). This stage is about creating appropriate boundaries and prioritizing information. The criteria and specifications that begin to emerge help the design team agree on a specific course of action.

Step three is Convergence. This stage is about focusing on an emerging solution and narrowing as many variables as possible in implementing a designed result.

With complex problems (such as systems or technological change), this sequence may need to be repeated several times before reaching a final result.

MS: It seems that Design Methods is best used in collaborative situations.

AK: It actually *requires* collaboration among various stakeholders, including clients, marketing personnel, manufacturing, users, and the designers themselves. While individualism seems easier, each of us has too many blind spots and prejudices to create a balanced future. Collaboration provides us with multiple lenses. Through these lenses, we can see our problem more fully. Even though they are harder to manage, teams bring the critical mass of skills and ideas we need when creating the best future for the greatest number of people.

MS: Let's see Design Methods in action.

AK: We can use a project from one of my classes as an example. The Nehring Center, a nonprofit art center in DeKalb, Illinois, needed to expand membership and increase attendance. Working with center director Jessica Witte, we began with an overview of the organization, discussing its goals and objectives, and noting areas for possible improvement. We interviewed a wide range of stakeholders, reviewed activities offered at the Center, analyzed its program content, and considered its affiliations to other institutions. Students began to delve deeply into its operational, marketing, and philanthropic activities and created a prioritized list of challenges.

Students then divided into two teams, one of which focused on issues of identity and the other on fundraising, which were seen as interdependent. Using convergent thinking, the teams redefined their topics and recommended specific actions. Finally, the students presented their findings to Ms. Witte, to a board member, and to School of Art faculty members. After the final presentation, she wrote:

"Design Methods sketches out a plan for the gallery's future and its current needs. I am really thankful that the presentation did not just put a Band-Aid of a logo together for me. Addressing the issue of the gallery in a greater scope . . . is really valuable."

MS: Essentially, it sounds like you took the long way around, and arrived at a more interesting end point.

AK: Yes. Despite its initial difficulty, the full process provoked the students to intensify their investigation. Their conceptual tool kit then allowed them to dig deeper and wrestle with a much more expansive problem space.

Increasing complexity   Increasing certainty

Initial understanding of problem

Divergence "seeking"

What is desirable?
Precedent
Social dimension
Political dimension
Economic dimension
Technological dimension

Exploring the problem space (solving) or opportunity space (seeking) and searching for ideas

What is possible?
Boundary shifting
Classifications
Emerging criteria

Transformation "redefinition"

Exploring and defining the problem structure

What is viable?
Selecting criteria
Ranking & weighting
Value analysis
Systematic search
Boundary search
Prototyping

Prototyping and producing a design response

Convergence "solving"

Release and measure effectiveness

Cultivating Creativity

"The heart of all new ideas lies in the borrowing, adding, combining or modifying of old ones. Do it by accident and people call you lucky. Do it by design and they'll call you creative."

Michael LeBoeuf, in *Imagineering*

The problem-seeking and problem-solving processes described in Chapter Five seem methodical and deliberate. The creative challenges we actually confront in the studio are often much messier. This chapter is designed to help you bridge the gap between the ideal situation and your actual experience. In it we consider characteristics of creative people, discuss goal setting, list time-management strategies, and explore habits of mind and habits of work that can increase success.

SEVEN CHARACTERISTICS OF CREATIVE THINKING

"Conditions for creativity are to be puzzled, to concentrate, to accept conflict and tension, to be born every day, to feel a sense of self."

Erich Fromm, in *Creativity and Its Cultivation*

Creativity is inherently unpredictable. Through creative thinking, old habits are broken and familiar patterns of thought are transformed. Anything can happen. Predicting the future based on past experience becomes inadequate when a creative breakthrough occurs. Like a shimmering drop of mercury, creativity eludes capture.

We can actively encourage creative thinking, however. Rather than waiting for inspiration, we can set up the conditions favorable to creativity. Based on observation and on interviews, various researchers have noted the following characteristics in many creative people.

Receptivity

Creative people are open to new ideas and welcome new experiences. Never complacent, they question the status quo and embrace alternative solutions to existing problems. Listening more and talking less is helpful. As journalist Larry King says, "I never learn anything new when I'm the one talking!"

Curiosity

A good designer brings an insatiable curiosity to each project. Researching unfamiliar topics and analyzing unusual systems is a source of delight for most creative people. "How does it work?" and "How can it work better?" are frequently asked questions.

Wide Range of Interests

With a broad knowledge base, a creative person can make a wider range of connections. Consider the number of words you can create from the letters in the word *image:*

age, game, gem, am, aim, a, I, me

Try the same game with the word *imagination:*

gin, nation, gnat, ton, tan, not, man, again, gain, oat, got, tag, am, aim, ant, no, on, tin, gamin, inn, ingot, main, a, I

With more components, the number of combinations increases. Likewise, an artist who has a background in literature, geology, archery, music, and history can make more connections than can a narrow-minded specialist.

Attentiveness

Realizing that every experience is valuable, creative people pay attention to seemingly minor details. Scientists often develop major theories by observing small events, which they then organize into complex patterns. Artists can often see past superficial visual chaos to discern an underlying order. Playwrights develop dramatic works by looking past the surface of human behavior to explore the substance of the human condition. By looking carefully, creative people see possibilities that others miss.

Connection Seeking

Seeing the similarity among seemingly disparate parts has often sparked a creative breakthrough. For example, Egyptian hieroglyphs became readable when a young French scholar realized that they carried the same message as an adjacent Greek inscription on a slab of stone. By comparing the two and cracking the Rosetta Stone code, Jean-François

Champollion opened the door for all subsequent students of ancient Egyptian culture.

Conviction

Creative people value existing knowledge. Since new ideas are often derived from old ideas, it is foolish to ignore or dismiss the past. However, creative people also love change. Never satisfied with routine answers to familiar questions, they constantly consider new possibilities and often challenge the status quo.

Complexity

In lecture classes, we must take notes, memorize facts, and collect and analyze data. We are encouraged to think rationally, write clearly, and present our ideas in a linear progression. In studio classes, exploration, experimentation, and intuition are encouraged, especially during brainstorming sessions. Synthesis, intuition, visualization, spatial perception, and non-linear thinking are highly valued.

To be fully effective, a creative person needs to combine the rational with the intuitive. While intuition may be used to generate a new idea, logic and analysis are often needed for its realization. As a result, the actions of creative people are often complex or even contradictory. As noted by psychologist Mihaly Csikszentmihalyi,[1] creative people often combine

- Physical energy with a respect for rest. They work long hours with great concentration, then rest and relax, fully recharging their batteries. They view balance between work and play as essential.

- Savvy with innocence. Creative people tend to view the world and themselves with a sense of wonder, rather than cling to preconceptions or stereotypes. They use common sense as well as intellect in completing their work.

- Responsibility with playfulness. When the situation requires serious attention, creative people are remarkably diligent and determined. They realize that there is no substitute for hard work and drive themselves relentlessly when nearing completion of a major project. On the other hand, when the situation permits, a playful, devil-may-care attitude may prevail, providing a release from the previous period of work.

- Risk-taking with safe-keeping. Creativity expert George Prince has noted two behavioral extremes in people.[2] Safe-keepers look before they leap, avoid surprises, punish mistakes, follow the rules, and watch the clock. A safe-keeper is most comfortable when there is only one right answer to memorize or one solution to produce. Risk-takers are just the opposite. They break the rules, leap before they look, like surprises, are impetuous, and may lose track of time. A risk-taker enjoys inventing multiple answers to every question.

  An imbalance in either direction limits creativity. Fear inhibits the safe-keeper, while irresponsibility may inhibit the risk-taker. Creative thinking requires a mix of risk-taking and safe-keeping. When brainstorming new ideas, open-ended exploration is used. But, when implementing new ideas, deadlines, budgets, and feasibility become major concerns. The risk-taker gets the job started; the safe-keeper gets the job done.

- Extroversion with introversion. When starting a new project, creative people are often talkative and gregarious, eager to share insights and explore ideas. When a clear sense of direction develops, however, they often withdraw, seeking solitude and quiet work time. This capacity for solitude is crucial. Several studies have shown that talented teenagers who cannot stand solitude rarely develop their creative skills.

- Passion with objectivity. Mature artists tend to plunge into new projects, convinced of the significance of the work and confident of their skills. Any attempt to distract or dissuade them at this point is futile. However, when the model or rough study is done, many will pause to assess their progress. This analysis and judgment may occur in a group setting or may be done by the artist alone. In either case, the emotional attachment required while creating is now replaced by a dispassionate objectivity. Work that does not pass this review is redone or discarded, regardless of the hours spent in its development. In major projects, this alternating process of creation and analysis may be repeated many times.

- Disregard for time with attention to deadlines. Time often dissolves when studio work begins. An artist or a designer can become engrossed in a project: when the work is going well, 6 hours can feel like 20 minutes. On the other hand, an acute attention to deadlines is necessary when preparing an exhibition or working for a client.

- Modesty with pride. As they mature, creative people often become increasingly aware of the contributions to their success made by teachers, family, and colleagues. Rather than brag about past accomplishments, they tend to focus on current projects. On the other hand, as creative people become aware of their significance within a field, they gain a powerful sense of purpose. Distractions are deleted from the schedule, and increasingly ambitious goals are set.

When the balance is right, all of these complex characteristics fuel even greater achievement.

GOAL SETTING

Human behavior is strongly goal-directed. Every action occurs for a reason. When we focus our attention on a specific task, we can channel our energy and better manage our time. When we reach our goals, our self-esteem increases, which then helps us overcome obstacles. And, with each goal met, our knowledge increases. Michael LeBoeuf has diagrammed this effect clearly (6.1).

A Goal-Setting Strategy

Self-knowledge is essential. No matter how hard we try, we can never really fulfill our potential when pursuing goals set by others. The following exercise can help you clarify your personal interests.

1. Get a package of Post-it notes. Working spontaneously, write one of your characteristics on each note, such as "I am creative," "I love music," "I write well." Identify as many attributes as possible.

2. When you finish, lay out the notes on a table and look at them for a while. Consider the type of person they describe. What are this person's strengths? What additional interests might this person need to develop?

3. On a fresh stack of notes, write a new set of responses, this time dealing with the question

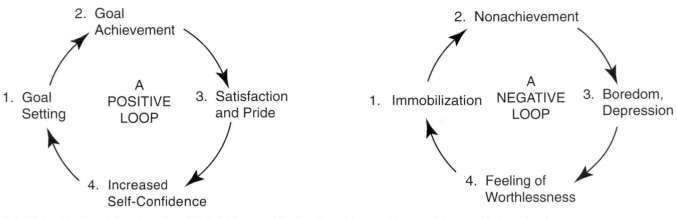

6.1 Michael LeBoeuf, *Imagineering*, 1980. Achievement feeds self-confidence, while nonachievement induces inertia.

"Why not?" as an expansion of your interests. Why not travel to Tibet? Why not learn Spanish? Why not master canoeing? Add these to the grid.

4. Then take a break. Let your subconscious mind play with the possibilities suggested by your notes.

5. Next, organize the notes into four general categories: intellectual goals, personal-relationship goals, spiritual or emotional goals, physical fitness goals. If you are an extreme safe-keeper, add a category called "Adventure." If you are an extreme risk-taker, consider adding a category called "Organization." Since a mix of activities helps feed the psyche, working with each of these categories is helpful.

6. Choose one goal from each category and develop an implementation strategy. Be specific! "I want to become a better artist" is too vague. Consider specific actions you can take to improve your artwork. "I need to improve my drawing" is better. "I want to learn anatomy" is better still. To learn anatomy, you can take a class, study an anatomy book, or draw from a skeleton. These are tangible actions—you now know what to do.

7. Prioritize your goals and develop a rough timetable, listing weekly goals, semester goals, and one-year goals. It is not necessary to list career goals just yet. Most of us explore many ideas during our first year of college, and formalizing career goals prematurely is counterproductive.

8. At least once a month, review your chart and add or delete information as necessary. If you

realize that you are overextended this term, shift one of your minor goals to next semester. This system is intended to provide clear targets, not to create a straitjacket.

9. If you achieve all your goals, congratulate yourself — then set more ambitious goals next term. If you achieve half of your goals, congratulate yourself — then prioritize more carefully next term. You may have taken on too many tasks. Because there is always a gap between intention and outcome, a 70 to 80 percent completion rate is fine.

Characteristics of Good Goals

Ambitious yet Achievable

Too modest a goal will provide no sense of accomplishment. Too ambitious a goal will reduce, rather than increase, motivation. No one wants to fight a losing battle! Knowing your strengths and weaknesses will help you set realistic goals.

Compatible

Training for the Boston Marathon while simultaneously trying to gain 20 pounds is unwise, since you will burn off every calorie you consume. Trying to save a thousand dollars while touring Europe is unrealistic, since travel always costs more than you expect. On the other hand, by taking a dance class or joining a hiking club, you may be able to combine a fitness goal with a social goal.

Self-Directed

Avoid goals that are primarily dependent on someone else's actions or opinions. "I want to earn an A in drawing" is a common example. Since the grade is determined by a teacher, your control in this area is limited. Instead, focus on improving your drawing as much as possible. This will increase your receptivity to learning and focus your attention on actions you can control. When you do your best work, good grades generally follow.

Temporary

Set clear target dates, get the job done, and move on to the next project. Each completed task increases your self-confidence and adds momentum. By contrast, unfinished work can drain energy and decrease momentum. If you are overloaded, delete secondary goals so that you can complete primary goals.

TIME MANAGEMENT

Time management can help you achieve your goals. Working smarter is usually more effective than simply working harder. In a world bursting with opportunity, using your work time well can increase the time available for travel, volunteer work, or socializing. The following time-management strategies have been used by many artists and designers.

Set the Stage

Choosing when and where to work can significantly increase your output. If you are a lark, bursting with energy and enthusiasm early in the morning, tackle major projects before noon. If you are an owl, equipped with night vision and able to hunt after dark, work on major projects after dinner. If you are distracted by clutter, clean your desk before beginning your workday, and tidy up your desk before you leave. These seemingly minor actions can substantially increase your productivity.

Prioritize

Note which tasks are most *urgent* and which tasks are most *important*. Timing can be crucial. When you pay your phone bill on time, you easily complete an urgent but unimportant task. When your phone bill is overdue and the service is cut off, this unimportant task becomes a major headache. Dispense with urgent tasks quickly so that you can focus on more important issues.

See the Big Picture

Use monthly calendar pages to record your major projects and obligations. A calendar that is organized by months can help you see which weeks will be packed with deadlines and which weeks will be relatively quiet. To avoid all-nighters, distribute large, important tasks over several weeks. To avoid missing a pivotal lecture or critique, schedule out-of-town trips during "slow" weeks.

Work Sequentially

Many activities are best done in a specific sequence. If you are writing a 20-page paper, it is best to start with research, make an outline, complete a rough draft, make corrections, then write the final draft. If you are designing a poster, it is best to start with research, make thumbnail sketches, assess the results, make a full-size rough layout, consult the client, and *then* complete the poster. Trying to cut out the intermediate steps and move directly to the final draft is rarely effective. With most large projects, you learn more, save time, and do better work by following the right sequence of tasks.

Use Parts to Create the Whole

Seen as a whole, a major project can become overwhelming. In an extreme case, creative paralysis sets in, resulting in a condition similar to writer's block. Breaking down big jobs into smaller parts helps enormously. In *Bird by Bird,* Anne Lamott gives a wonderful description of this process:

> Thirty years ago my other brother, who was ten years old at the time, was trying to get a report on birds written that he'd had three months to write. [It] was due the next day. . . . He was at the kitchen table close to tears, surrounded by binder paper and pencils and unopened books on birds, immobilized by the hugeness of the task ahead. Then my father sat down beside him, put his arm around my brother's shoulder, and said, "Bird by bird, buddy. Just take it bird by bird."[3]

By doing the job incrementally, you are likely to learn more and procrastinate less.

Make the Most of Class Time

Psychologists tell us that beginnings and endings of events are especially memorable. An experienced teacher knows that the first 10 minutes of class set the tone for the rest of the session and that a summary at the end can help students remember the lesson. Similarly, the wise student arrives 5 minutes early for class and maintains attention to the end of class.

Be an active learner. You can use that 5 minutes before class to review your notes from the previous session and organize your supplies. This helps create a bridge between what you know and the new information to be presented. Try to end the class on a high note, either by completing a project or by clearly determining the strengths and weaknesses of the work in progress. By analyzing your progress, you can organize your thinking and provide a solid beginning point for the next work session.

When in Doubt, Crank It Out

Fear is one of the greatest obstacles to creative thinking. When we are afraid, we tend to avoid action and consequently miss opportunities.

Both habit and perfectionism feed fear. If you consistently repeat the same activities and limit yourself to familiar friendships, you will become more and more fearful of new experiences. Perfectionism is especially destructive during brainstorming, which requires a loose, open approach.

Creativity takes courage. As IBM founder Thomas Watson noted, "If you are not satisfied with your rate of success, try failing more." Baseball player Reggie Jackson is renowned for his 563 home runs—but he also struck out 2,597 times. Thomas Edison's research team tried over 6,000 materials before finding the carbon-fiber filament used in lightbulbs.

"When in doubt, don't!" is the safe-keeper's motto. "When in doubt, do!" is the risk-taker's motto. By starting each project with a sense of adventure, you increase your level of both learning and creativity.

Work Together

Many areas of art and design, including filmmaking, industrial design, and advertising design, are often done collaboratively. Working together, artists and designers can complete projects that are too complex or time-consuming to be done solo. Collaborative thinking helps us break familiar patterns and teaches us to listen to alternative or opposing ideas.

Here is one example. Gather 20 people. Start with a copied fragment from an existing image, such as *Metamophosis II,* an 8 × 160 in. banner by M. C. Escher (6.2). In this case, design students were provided with a 1-inch strip of the banner to create a beginning point and another 1-inch strip of the banner to create the ending point (6.3A). Each person invented an 8½ × 11 in. connection between the two strips. Buildings, plants, chess pieces, and other images were used to bridge the gap between the strips at the beginning and the end. The images were then connected end to end, like cars in a train. When combined, they created a collaborative banner 20 feet long. One piece of the banner is shown in figure 6.3B. Students had to negotiate with the person ahead of them in the line and with the person behind them in order to make a continuous image with graceful transitions. In effect, all 20 participants became members of a creative team. Finally, each 8½ × 11 in. section was photocopied and traded, providing each person with the completed artwork. In a collaboration of this kind, everyone gains, both in the learning process and in the sharing of the final product.

6.2 M. C. Escher, Part of *Metamorphosis II*, 1939–40. Woodcut in black, green, and brown, printed from 20 blocks on three combined sheets, 7½ × 153⅜ in. (19 × 390 cm).

6.3A Examples of Escher Starter Images.

6.3B Mary Stewart and Jesse Wummer, **Expanded Escher Collaboration.** Student work.

VARIATIONS ON A THEME

When we work creatively, the idea develops right along with the image. As the project evolves, we see other implications that go beyond our initial intention. By courageously pursuing these implications, we can exceed our original expectations. Just as the landscape appears to expand when we climb a mountain, so an image can expand when our conceptual understanding increases.

One way to get a lot of mileage out of an idea is through variations on a theme. Professional artists rarely do just one painting or sculpture of a given idea—most do many variations before

6.4A Katsushika Hokusai, *Thirty-Six Views of Mount Fuji: Under the Mannen Bridge at Fukagawa,* Edo Period, c. 1830. Color woodblock print, 10¹⁄₁₆ × 14¹¹⁄₁₆ in. (25.7 × 37.5 cm).

moving to a new subject. *Thirty-Six Views of Mount Fuji* is one example. Printmaker Katsushika

6.4B Katsushika Hokusai, *Thirty-Six Views of Mount Fuji: The Great Wave off Kanagawa*, **Edo Period, c. 1830.** Color woodblock print, 10⅜ × 14¹⁵⁄₁₆ in. (25.9 × 37.5 cm).

6.4C Katsushika Hokusai, *Thirty-Six Views of Mount Fuji: Near Umezawa in Sagami Province*, **Edo Period, c. 1830.** Color woodblock print, 10¹⁄₁₆ × 14⅞ in. (25.6 × 37.8 cm).

Hokusai was 70 years old when he began this series. The revered and beautiful Mount Fuji appeared in each of the designs in some way. Variations in the time of year and size of the mountain helped Hokusai produce very different images while retaining the same basic theme (6.4A–C).

Variations on the standard chess set are shown in the next three figures. Completed by industrial design students in response to a design competition, each set offers a unique approach to an ancient game. Eddie Chui's *Let's Dance* (6.5) retains the familiar forms of the various pieces but adds a curved bottom. Rather than sitting stoically in place, the knights, pawns, and other pieces tend to dance back and forth, while magnets connect them to the board. Deborah Tan used a very different approach. Her set (6.6) is designed for blind players. To help them distinguish each piece, Tan created a collection of very distinctive forms. Depressions in the board help secure each piece in place. Finally, Sergio Silva provided a carrying case along with his set of geometric forms (6.7). Created from square and rectangular forms, the set is crisp and highly unified.

Many variations on a cube are shown in figure 6.8. Submitted by beginning architecture students at Auburn University, they demonstrate one advantage of studying art and design in a classroom setting: you get to see variations on a theme every time an assignment is due.

6.5 Eddie Chui, *Let's Dance*, **2005.** Maple, magnets, and silicon.

6.6 Deborah Tan, *Chess Set*, **2005.** Plaster and plastic.

6.7 Sergio Silva, *Chess Set*, 2005. Anodized aluminum and wood.

6.8 Cubes from above, study models from Auburn University School of Architecture.

HABITS OF MIND AND WORK

Habits of Mind

Dr. Arthur L. Costa and Dr. Bena Kallick have identified 16 "habits of mind" essential to success. Here their list has been distilled down to four attributes that characterize the most effective art and design students, with commentary added.

Flexibility

Convergent, divergent, and collaborative problem-solving strategies present distinct advantages and disadvantages. Limiting yourself to just one approach reduces your ability to solve a wide range of problems. Flexibility, on the other hand, gives you the ability to question existing assumptions, adopt new ideas, and shift strategies as needed.

Analytical Thinking

In general, designers are hired to solve a client's problem. Limitations imposed by time, materials, and budget complicate matters. An analytical mindset helps the designer solve the real problem rather than wasting time on an imagined problem.

Capacity for Synthesis

Synthesis may be defined as the capacity to combine separate parts to create a coherent whole. Two aspects of synthesis are particularly important for artists and designers. First, they must be able to combine lines, shapes, textures, and so on to create

a compositional whole. Second, they must be able to apply past knowledge to new situations. By retaining your understanding of each problem solved, you accumulate a vast storehouse of knowledge and experience.

Responsible Risk Taking

Risk-takers are willing to risk failure in order to achieve success. They view setbacks as opportunities for growth rather than occasions for despair. Irresponsible risk-takers leap before they look. Responsible risk-takers weigh benefits and hazards, gather their energy, and then leap.

Habits of Work

To provide beginning designers with a realistic checklist, Professor Rusty Smith and his colleagues in the School of Architecture at Auburn University have developed the following list of "habits of work" for architects.

Self-Reliance

Essentially, self-reliance creates an active approach to work. Rather than waiting for directions or blaming others for delays, each architecture student actively generates possibilities, weighs benefits, and makes choices. To a substantial degree, self-reliant students drive their own learning process.

Organized Persistence

Beating your head against a brick wall is an example of mindless persistence. It is impressive but ineffective. Chiseling away at the mortar between the bricks until the wall falls apart is an example of organized persistence. It may take weeks, but eventually organized persistence results in a solution. It gives us the ability to prevail, even when we are faced with the most daunting task.

Daily Practice

Momentum is extremely powerful when you are working on a difficult problem. Daily practice helps maintain momentum. For example, when learning a new computer program, practicing for a couple of hours each night is better than working on it one full day a month.

Appropriate Speed

Some tasks are best completed quickly, with brisk decision making and decisive action. Slowing down to reframe a question and weigh alternative solutions is necessary in other cases. Knowing when to speed up and when to slow down is one mark of a "master learner."

Valuing Alternative Viewpoints

Listening to others, understanding diverse points of view, and considering alternatives expand our capacity to solve a wide variety of problems. Even when the advice is off-base, we can often use the idea as a springboard to a fresh approach.

Incremental Excellence

Most art and design problems are best developed in a series of stages. Ideas evolve, skills improve, compositions are distilled. Rather than trying for the "perfect solution" on the first day of work, it is better to start with a "funky junky" draft.

Direct Engagement

Talk is cheap. Work is hard. The only way to solve most art and design problems is to get involved. You will never win a race when you are standing on the sidelines!

SUMMARY

- Creativity and design both require new combinations of old ideas.

- Creative people are receptive to new ideas, are curious, have a wide range of interests, are attentive, seek connections, and work with great conviction.

- A combination of rational and intuitive thinking feeds creativity. While intuition may be used to generate a new idea, logic and analysis are often needed for its completion. As a result, the actions of creative people are often complex or even contradictory.

- Goals you set are goals you get. Establishing priorities and setting appropriate goals will help you achieve your potential. Good goals are ambitious but achievable, compatible, self-directed, and temporary. Deadlines encourage completion of complex projects.

- Completing tasks in an appropriate sequence, making the most of each work period, maintaining momentum, and reducing stress are major aspects of time management.

- Collaborative work can help you expand your ideas, explore new fields, and pursue projects that are too complex or time-consuming to do alone.

- Ideas can be explored more fully using variations on a theme.

- Flexibility, analytical ability, the capacity for synthesis, and responsible risk taking are effective habits of mind.

- Self-reliance, organized persistence, daily practice, appropriate speed, valuing alternative viewpoints, incremental excellence, and direct engagement are effective habits of work.

STUDIO PROJECTS

To apply the concepts from this chapter in the studio, check out the Projects page in the Online Learning Center at www.mhhe.com/stewart4e. The following is a sample of the chapter-related assignments that are described in step-by-step detail.

Collaborative Compositions. Digitally creating a collaborative collage.
Expanding Escher. Working within the boundaries of a partner's design.
Audio Assemblage. Building a musical instrument from found objects as a team.

Profile:
Suzanne Stryk, Painter

An Art of Observation

Suzanne Stryk's artwork has appeared in over 60 group shows, and in solo exhibitions at the National Academy of Sciences, the Morris Museum of Art, the Eleanor B. Wilson Museum, and the William King Museum (an affiliate of the Virginia Museum of Fine Arts). Among the collections that own her work are the Tennessee State Museum, Bank of America's Southeastern Collection, the Taubman Museum of Art, and the Smithsonian Institution.

MS: You initially studied fine art and biology and then shifted to major in art history. Why?

SS: When I began my studies, I didn't really fit into the abstract expressionist and pop art approaches that were prevalent at the time. I was fascinated—and still am—with the depiction of nature in the art of different cultures. My papers explored topics such as animals in Egyptian tomb painting and nature marginalia drawn into medieval manuscripts. This "detour" into art history turned out to be invaluable to me as an artist.

MS: You then developed a career as a scientific illustrator. What kinds of jobs did you do, and what did you learn from these jobs?

SS: Seeking to merge my interest in nature and art, I studied scientific illustration in the early eighties. I then worked in a university biology department, drawing graphs and charts, along with the fun stuff—plant specimens and animals. The job required discipline and patience, which remains with me to this day, along with the arrows, labels, measurements, and grids that fill my images.

MS: When and why did you shift toward more self-directed studio work?

SS: Scientific illustration stimulated more and more questions. I wondered, "What does my precise drawing really say about an animal? Doesn't it say more about us as a species of observers?" In the mid-eighties, I discovered Russian icons, which often use a grid format to depict events in a saint's life. I decided to put a cicada's life cycle in a similar grid. This inspired a whole series called *Life Cycles*. Then, a couple of these paintings were selected for my first major exhibition in Chicago. You know, if

you're doing work that makes you think, "Either this is the stupidest thing in the world or really profound," then you might be onto something! It was the turning point in my discovery of personal voice.

MS: What are the greatest challenges in your work?

SS: Well, it's always a great challenge to make the concept and the visual idea seamless. Right now, I'm constructing life-sized birds from printouts of their genomic sequences. The finished birds will perch or hang around my paintings. I've done very little three-dimensional work and must therefore become fluent in a new "language."

MS: Your sketchbooks are numbered and lined up on a shelf in your studio, thirty in a row. Why are they so well organized, and what do they contribute to your studio practice?

SS: My sketchbooks are the primary source for my finished images. They include drawings of creatures surrounded by my notes, dates, measurements, and names, like a field naturalist's journal. But you'll also find interpretive notes about my personal response to the animal. As an illustrator, I focus on observation. As an artist, I must turn my observations into meaning.

MS: You look up the specific species of beetle or other subject. Why is specificity important?

SS: Knowing the species leads me to learn more about the animal, about its special features or behaviors. For example, I may discover a plump green caterpillar with tiny bristles and reddish dots. When I identify it as a Luna moth larva, I learn to feed it walnut leaves. I can then witness it pupate and, if lucky, watch it emerge as a huge milky-green adult. This is no small thing for me, for my whole worldview—as reflected in my art—centers on the awareness of other lives.

MS: You emphasize the importance of intuition. Please describe intuition and give us an example.

SS: It may sound like a contradiction, but a lot of intuition is learned. For instance, in my *Genomes and Daily Observations* series, I invent microorganisms or insect parts from the accidental stains and drips on the paper. I recognize that it just "feels right." These examples of intuition may take years of painting and familiarity with biological forms to do convincingly. Louis Pasteur got it right when he said, "Chance favors the prepared mind."

I can also be very analytical. While working on a drawing, I may use a high-powered magnifier to help me meticulously paint tiny bristles on a beetle's leg. But isn't the analytical—knowing where and when to use it—informed by the intuitive? For me, the analytical and the intuitive are partners.

MS: Do you purposely seek subjects for your work?

SS: Not with the *Daily Observations* series. When my path crosses with, say, a salamander, then it's a salamander painting that day. This series is simultaneous with the other art projects I do—it keeps me grounded with actual living things.

MS: You show your work in a wide variety of settings, from galleries and museums to science centers. What do you most want to communicate?

SS: Art humanizes science. It suggests nature is not just something "out there" or in the realm of laboratories, but part of our own story. I'm humbled when my work hangs next to the armature of a dinosaur or a display of beetles in a natural history museum. Evolution is, in the end, the greatest artist of all.

Recently I painted a blue finch on what looks like a torn piece of paper floating in a suggestive landscape. I'd like viewers to ask questions, such as, "Is this image about our partial understanding of the natural world? About the fragmentation of nature? Our own fragmentation? Is it a memory? A personal dream?" But a viewer said, "Oh, I love the blue of that bird against the white!" So you see, the first communication begins as a purely visual experience. The conceptual sneaks in there after the eye is seduced.

MS: Do you have any advice for my students?

SS: Find your own voice. Ask yourself, "What sight makes me want to make an image? Soldiers on a battlefield? Graffiti? The patterned wing of a moth?" The answer should help point you in a personal direction. Probe what it is that attracts you, visually and conceptually. As artists, we must embrace a life that is fully engaged, connected to the experience of being alive. I think of a life in art as analogous to evolution: it winds around, mutates, some creations live, others fail, and along the way surprising and even marvelous things are made.

Suzanne Stryk, *Genomes and Daily Observations Series*, 2005. Mixed media on paper, 10 × 14 in. (25.4 × 35.6 cm).

Developing Critical Thinking

chapter seven

Critical thinking combines

- Evaluation of all available information
- Analysis of visual relationships
- Exploration of alternative solutions

Never complacent, the best artists and designers continually seek to improve each image and expand each idea. Critical thinking is used to determine compositional strengths, develop concepts, and improve visual communication. Knowing what to keep and what to change is crucial. By enhancing the best aspects of a design and deleting the weak areas, we can dramatically strengthen both communication and expression.

ESTABLISHING CRITERIA

Establishing the criteria on which judgments will be made is the first step. For example, if technical skills are being emphasized in an assignment, craftsmanship will be highly valued. Likewise, if the assignment must be done in analogous colors, a black-and-white painting will not meet the criteria, no matter how well it is composed. By determining the major questions being raised in each problem, we can understand the basis on which judgments will be reached. Consider the following questions:

- What is the purpose of the assignment? Does your teacher want you to learn any specific skills? What compositional and conceptual variables will you need to explore?
- What are the basic assignment parameters? Are there limitations in the size, style, or materials?
- When is the assignment due and in what form must it be presented?

It is important to distinguish between understanding assignment criteria and seeking the "right answer." In the first case, by determining the boundaries, you can fully focus your energy when you begin to work. Just as a magnifying glass can be used to focus sunlight into a powerful beam, so assignment parameters can help you focus creative energy. On the other hand, students who try to determine the right answer to a problem often simply want to know the teacher's solution. Such knowledge is rarely helpful. The assignment simply sets a learning process in motion: you learn through your work!

FORM, SUBJECT, CONTENT

Form may be defined as the physical manifestation of an idea or emotion. Two-dimensional forms are created using line, shape, texture, value, and color. The building blocks of three-dimensional forms are line, plane, volume, mass, space, texture, and color. Duration, tempo, intensity, scope, setting, and chronology are combined to create time-based art forms. For example, film is the form in which *Star Wars* was first presented.

The **subject,** or topic, of an artwork is most apparent when a person, an object, an event, or a setting is clearly represented. For example, the conflict between the rebels and the Empire provides the subject for *Star Wars.*

The emotional or intellectual message of an artwork provides its **content,** or underlying theme. The theme of *Star Wars* is the journey into the self. Luke Skywalker's gradual understanding of himself and acceptance of Darth Vader as his father provide an essential emotional undercurrent to the entire series.

STOP, LOOK, LISTEN, LEARN

Any of these three aspects of design can be discussed critically. A **critique** is the most common structure used. During the critique, your peers or professors analyze your work. Many solutions are presented, demonstrating a wide range of possibilities. The strengths and weaknesses in each design are identified, and areas needing revision are revealed. These insights can be used to improve the current design or to generate possibilities for the next assignment.

Critiques can be extremely helpful, extremely destructive, or just plain boring, depending largely on the amount and type of student involvement. Specific recommendations are most helpful. Be sure to substantiate each judgment so that your rationale is clear.

Whether you are giving or receiving advice, come with your mind open, rather than with your fists closed. A critique is not a combat zone! Listen carefully to any explanations offered and generously offer your insights to others. Likewise, receive suggestions gracefully rather than defensively. You will make the final decision on any further actions needed to strengthen your design; if someone gives you bad advice, quietly discard it. A substantial and supportive critique is the best way to determine the effect your design has on an audience, so speak thoughtfully and weigh seriously every suggestion you receive.

When beginning a critique, it is useful to distinguish between objective and subjective criticism. **Objective criticism** is used to assess how well a work of art or design utilizes the elements and principles of design. Discussion generally focuses on basic compositional concerns, such as

- The type of balance used in the composition and how it was created

- The spatial depth of a design and its compositional effect

- The degree of unity in a design and how it was achieved

Objective criticism is based on direct observation and a shared understanding of assignment parameters. Discussion is usually clear and straightforward. Alternative compositional solutions may be discussed in depth.

Subjective criticism is used to describe the personal impact of an image, the narrative implications of an idea, or the cultural ramifications of an action. Discussion generally focuses on the subject and content of the design, including

- The meaning of the artwork

- The feelings it evokes

- Its relationship to other cultural events

- The artist's intent

Because subjective criticism is not based on simple observation, it is more difficult for most groups to remain focused on the artwork itself or to reach any clear conclusions regarding possible improvements. The discussion may become more general and wide-ranging as political or social questions raised by the works of art and design are analyzed. Because of the potential lack of clarity, subjective criticism may be used sparingly during the foundation year.

TYPES OF CRITIQUES

Description

The first step is to look carefully and report clearly. Without evaluating, telling stories, drawing conclusions, or making recommendations, simply describe the visual organization of the work presented. A **descriptive critique** can help you see details and heighten your understanding of the design. The student whose work you describe learns which aspects of the design are most eye-catching and which areas are muddled and need work.

This is a particularly useful exercise when analyzing a complex piece, such as figure 7.1A. In an art history class, you might write:

> *Place de l'Europe on a Rainy Day* is a rectangular painting depicting a street in Paris. A vertical lamppost and its shadow extend from the top edge to the bottom edge, neatly dividing the painting in half. A horizon line, extending from the left side and three-quarters of the way to the right, further divides the painting, creating four major quadrants. Because this horizon line is positioned just above center, the bottom half of the composition is slightly larger than the top half. A dozen pedestrians with umbrellas occupy the bottom half of the painting. At the right edge, a man strides into the painting, while next to him a couple moves out of the painting, toward the viewer. To the left of the lamppost, most of the movement is horizontal, as people cross the cobblestone streets.

When using description in a spoken critique in a studio class, it is useful to note essential compositional characteristics:

- What is the shape of the overall composition? A circle or sphere presents a very different compositional playing field than does a square or a cube.

- What range of colors has been used? A black-and-white design is very different from a full-color design.

- What is the size of the project? Extremes are especially notable. A sculpture that is 10 feet tall or a painting that is 1 inch square will immediately attract attention.

- Is the visual information tightly packed, creating a very dense design, or is the design

7.1A Gustave Caillebotte, *Place de l'Europe on a Rainy Day,* **1877.** Oil on canvas, 83½ × 108¾ in. (212.2 × 276.2 cm).

more spacious, with a lot of space between shapes or volumes?

The Key Questions that appear throughout this book can provide a springboard into a critique.

Cause and Effect

A descriptive critique helps us analyze the compositional choices made by the artist. A **cause-and-effect critique** (also known as a **formal analysis**) builds on this description. In a simple description, you might say that the design is primarily composed of diagonals. Using cause and effect, you might conclude that, *because* of the many diagonals, the design is very dynamic. In a cause-and-effect critique, you discuss consequences as well as choices. Analyzing the same painting, you might write:

> *Place de l'Europe on a Rainy Day* depicts a city street in Paris near the end of the nineteenth century. A lamppost, positioned near the center, vertically dissects the painting in half. The horizon line creates a second major division, with 45 percent of the space above and 55 percent below this line.

A dozen pedestrians in dark clothing cross the cobblestone streets from left to right, creating a flowing movement. To the right of the post, the pedestrians move in and out of the painting, from background to foreground. Both types of movement add compositional energy. Two men and one woman are the most prominent figures. The man at the far right edge pulls us into the painting, while the couple to his immediate left moves toward us, pushing out of their world and into our world. The movement that dominates each side of the painting is arrested by the lamppost. It is almost as if we are getting two paintings on one canvas.

As shown in figure 7.1B, a visual diagram can be used to support your written comments.

While a written formal analysis is used more often in art history classes than in studio classes, artists often mentally assess their own work using the same strategy. Sculptor Rodger Mack described *The Oracle's Tears* (7.2) as follows:

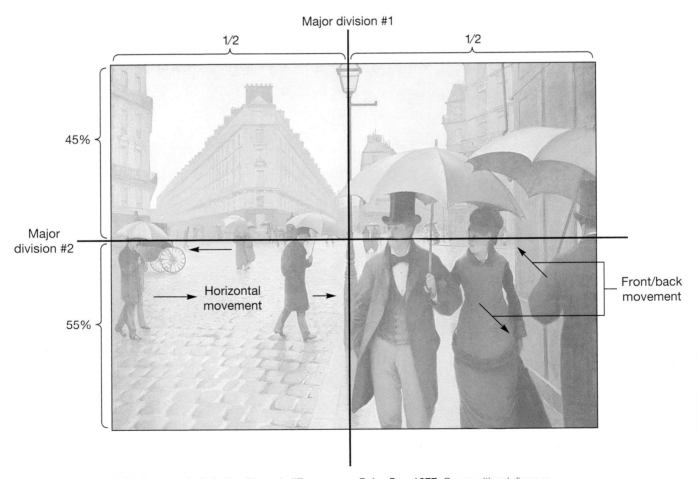

7.1B Gustave Caillebotte, *Place de l'Europe on a Rainy Day*, 1877. Compositional diagram.

This sculpture is made from five major parts. The column dominates, structurally and conceptually. Just above it, I have placed a form that has reappeared in my work for 30 years, the Oracle. It is like an image on a tarot card, the hanging man, perhaps. A smaller piece, based on a shape I found in a market in Athens, connects the oracle and the column. The tears are created using three descending lines. The base is the final element. It provides a stable support and adds a sense of completion.

A description of technical aspects of the project can enhance the viewers' understanding of the artwork. Professor Mack wrote:

I used a combination of fabrication and casting. The oracle form was made by cutting shapes from a sheet of ⅛-inch bronze and welding them together. The tears and the column were cast in sections, then welded. A potassium dichloride patina, applied using a blowtorch, gives the piece its golden color.

Professor Mack then concluded his commentary with a subjective discussion of his intentions:

I've always been drawn to ancient cities and architectural forms and have been working with mythological themes for the past six years. I've completed a series of maidens, a minotaur, a Trojan horse, and several oracles so far. When I visit these ancient civilizations, it saddens me that they are gone, destroyed to make way for new civilizations.

Because written descriptions of this kind are often required in fellowship applications and grant proposals, developing your analytical skills and your writing ability can really pay off professionally.

7.2 Rodger Mack, *The Oracle's Tears*, 1999. Cast and welded bronze, 17 × 6 × 4 ft (5.18 × 1.83 × 1.22 m).

Compare and Contrast

In a **compare/contrast critique,** similarities and differences between two images are noted. Let's return to the Caillebotte painting one more time, now comparing the perspective used with the perspective in Raphael's *The School of Athens* (7.3).

The city streets depicted in *The School of Athens* and *Place de l'Europe* demonstrate many differences between Renaissance and Impressionist perspective.

The one-point perspective used in Raphael's painting leads our eyes to Plato and Aristotle, positioned just below the center of the composition. The other figures in the painting are massed in a horizontal band from the far right to the far left side and in two lower groups, to the right and left of the central figures. Our eyes are led back to the philosophers by a man sprawled on the steps to the right and by the scribes' tables on the left. Like a proscenium arch in a theater, a broad arch in the foreground frames the scene. Overlapping arches add to the depth of the painting. This composition combines the stability of one-point perspective with a powerful illusion of space.

In the Caillebotte painting, a lamppost occupies center stage, rather than a philosopher. The perspective in the cobblestone street and in the buildings on the right is complicated by the perspective used for a large background building on the left. This unusual illusion of space, combined with the movement of the pedestrians, creates a feeling of instability.

Compare and contrast essays are often used in art history classes. This form of analysis helps demonstrate differences in historical periods or artistic styles. The same approach, however, may be used in the studio, for either spoken or written critiques. The following, written by two students in a basic design class, is an example. The assignment was to complete an 18 × 24 in. design, transforming the music building (Crouse College) into a labyrinth.

7.3 Raphael, *The School of Athens*, 1509–11. Fresco, 26 × 18 ft (7.92 × 5.49 m). Stanza della Segnatura, Vatican, Rome.

7.4 Cally Iden, *Transforming Crouse College into a Labyrinth.* Student work, 18 × 24 in. (45.7 × 61 cm).

7.5 Tricia Tripp, *Transforming Crouse College into a Labyrinth.* Student work, 24 × 18 in. (61 × 45.7 cm).

Looking at Cally's design (7.4), Trish wrote:

Cally's piece uses strong black-and-white contrast, with both negative and positive space clearly defined. In contrast, my design is brightly colored, representing a kaleidoscope based on the stained glass windows in the building.

We both use the staircase as a major element. Cally's stair leads you in and around the building, creating a way to explore the space. My stair becomes part of the overall pattern.

I thought of the labyrinth as an abstract puzzle, a design you could draw your pencil through to find the ending. I wanted my design to be playful. Cally's design focuses on the psychological, creating an entry into the human mind. Cally's design is mysterious. Her staircases lead nowhere.

We both use lines very deliberately. Where one line ends, another begins. Without lines in a labyrinth, it wouldn't be as puzzling or mysterious. It would just be another design, rather than a puzzle to solve or a fun house to explore.

Looking at Trish's design (7.5), Cally wrote:

My labyrinth uses black and white to form a high-contrast composition, whereas Trish uses color to transform the building into a complex pattern. My vertical format helps suggest the height of the building, which is dominated by two amazing staircases. Trish's horizontal format contains a design that is as abstract as a computer circuit board.

Next, I notice conceptual differences between our solutions. My drawing is representational, depicting a psychological labyrinth, whereas Trish's turns the labyrinth into a puzzle. The space is generally flat in her design: color is used to create a balanced composition rather than being used to create any illusion of space. On the other hand, because my design is representational, I used size variation to create a convincing interior space.

One similarity between our drawings is in the inclusion of the staircase. Trish used the stairs as a background shape that adds dynamism to the composition. I used the stair as a primary motif, a means by which people using the building can explore their own minds.

For me, Trish's design creates a sense of alienation. There is no evidence of human experience here—it is a purely visual world, made up of complex shapes. It is as beautiful as an image in a kaleidoscope.

On the other hand, there are hints of "the human" in my composition, but it is lost within the maze of repetitive stairs: only traces remain. I want to convey the feeling of being caught in a labyrinth, solving mysteries, and finding one's self.

Both critiques are honest without being abusive and offer a discussion of both concept and composition. While the critiques are very different, each student clearly respects the approach taken by the other.

Greatest Strength/ Unrealized Potential

Many projects have one notable strength and one glaring weakness. To create a positive atmosphere, start by pointing out the strength in the work. Begin by looking for

- The level of unity in the design and how it was achieved

- The amount of variety in the design and how much energy it generates

- The type of balance used and its emotional effect

- The attention to detail. This could include craftsmanship, conceptual nuance, or compositional economy.

- A conceptual spark. We all love to see an unexpected solution that redefines the imaginative potential of a project.

Using figure 7.6A as an example, you could say:

> The primary strength of this project is unity. The use of black marker throughout gives the design a simple, clean, and consistent look. The repetition of the arches helps tie it all together. Vertical and horizontal lines dominate, creating a type of grid.

Next, consider ways to improve the project. Mentally arm yourself with a magic wand. If you could instantly transform the design, what single aspect would you change? How can the potential of the project be more fully realized? Here are some basic questions:

- Is it big enough? Is it small enough?

- Is it bold enough? Is it subtle enough?

- How rich is the concept? Can it be expanded?

- How can the concept be communicated more clearly? How can the concept be communicated more fully?

The assignment was to create a labyrinth. Figure 7.6A is spatially shallow. To strengthen the composition, you might suggest:

> When I think about a labyrinth, I think of it as a mysterious place that I can enter and explore. As it

7.6A Initial design.　　　**7.6B** Design variation.

now stands, this design is spatially flat: it gives me no place to go. You might try increasing the illusion of space. Greater size variation in the arches, with larger ones in the front and smaller ones in the back, could help. Overlapping some of the arches could increase the space and add rhythm to the work. And have you considered using gray marker for the background shapes? This would reduce the contrast and push those shapes back in space.

The resulting design (7.6B) is more spatially complex.

DEVELOPING A LONG-TERM PROJECT

Critical thinking is useful at many points in a project, not just at the end. When working on a project for 10 hours or more, it is useful to assess progress at the beginning or the end of each work period. This may be done in a large-group critique, in small teams, in discussion with your teacher, or on your own. Several effective strategies follow.

Week One Assessment

Determine Essential Concept

As a project begins to evolve from brainstorming to thumbnails to rough drafts, the concept may also evolve. Your initial idea may expand or shift during the translation from the mind to the hand to the page. Stopping to reconsider your central concept and refine your image can bring great clarity and purpose to the work. What is the design *really* about? You can speak more forcefully when you know what you want to say.

Explore Polarities

Sometimes, the best way to strengthen an idea is to present the exact opposite. For example, if you want to show the *joy* a political prisoner feels on being released from jail, you may need to show the *despair* she felt before her release. To increase the *dynamism* in a design, add some emphatically *static* elements. The contrast created by polarities can heighten communication.

Move from General to Specific

"Be specific!" demands your writing teacher. Just as vague generalities weaken your writing, so vague generalities can weaken your designs. Details are important. "A bird watched people walk down the street" is far less compelling than "Two vultures hovered over University Avenue, hungrily watching the two hapless students stagger from bar to bar." Specifying the kind of bird, type of people, and exact location makes the image come alive.

Move from Personal to Universal

Autobiography is an especially rich source of images and ideas. The authenticity of personal experience is extremely powerful. However, if you focus too tightly on your own family, friends, and experiences, the viewer must know you personally in order to appreciate your design. Try expanding your field of vision. Use a story about your high school graduation to say something about *all* rites of passage from childhood to adulthood.

Week Two Assessment

A well-developed rough draft or a full-scale model may be presented at this stage. The purpose of this critique is to help the artist or designer determine ways to increase the visual and conceptual impact of an existing idea. Following are three major strategies.

Develop Alternatives

By helping someone else solve a problem, we can often solve our own problem. Organize a team of four or five classmates. Working individually, design 5 to 10 possible solutions to a visual problem using 2 × 3 in. thumbnail sketches. Then have one person present his or her ideas verbally and visually. Each team member must then propose an alternative way to solve the problem. This can be done verbally; however, once you get going, it is more effective and stimulating if everyone (including the artist) draws alternative solutions. This process helps the artist see the unrealized potential in his or her idea. And, because of the number of alternatives presented, the artist rarely adopts any single suggestion. Instead, the exercise simply becomes a means of demonstrating ways to clarify, expand, and strengthen intentions already formed.

Edit Out Nonessentials

Have you ever found it difficult to determine the real point of a lengthy lecture and thus lost interest? In our zeal to communicate, teachers sometimes provide so many examples and side issues that students get lost. Likewise, if your design is overloaded with peripheral detail or if a secondary visual element is given the starring role, the result will be cluttered and impact will be lost. Look carefully at your design, focusing on visual relationships. Are there any shapes or volumes that can be deleted?

Amplify Essentials

Just as it is necessary to delete extraneous information, it is equally important to strengthen the essential information. Review the section on emphasis in Chapter Three and consider ways to increase your compositional power. Try "going too far," wildly exaggerating the size, color, or texture of an important visual element. The only way to get an extraordinary image is to make extraordinary compositional choices.

Developing a Self-Assignment

On pages 149 and 150, Jason Chin describes the development of a month-long self-assignment he completed near the end of his freshman year. The original project proposal is given at the top of the first page. The rest of the text is devoted to Jason's analysis of his actual work process. This type of personal assessment can bring an extended project to a memorable conclusion.

Self-Assignment:
Jason Chin
The Mythological Alphabet

Original Proposal

Description: I plan to make an illustrated alphabet book with 32 pages and a cover. The theme of the book will be myths and heroes. I am interested in illustrating the essence of each hero's story. Specifically, how can I visually communicate the story of a tragic hero versus a triumphant one? Further concerns with the book will be making it work as a whole. That means keeping it balanced and making it flow: I don't want the images to become disjointed.

Primary Concerns

1. How do I communicate the individual nature of the characters?
2. How do I connect each hero to all the others?
3. How will the book affect the reader? I want to get the reader fully involved in the book.
4. How can I best use the unique characteristics of the book format?

Time Management

Week 1: Research myths and heroes. Identify possible characters for the book.

Week 2: Bring at least 20 thumbnail sketches to the first team meeting.

Week 3: Bring finalized design/layout for book. Each page must have a final design in the form of thumbnails.

Week 4: Complete half of the pages.

Week 5: Finish remaining pages and present at the critique.

Commentary

The independent project was both a blessing and a curse. Given the freedom to do what I chose was liberating, but the burden of what to do with that freedom was great. Ultimately, it became one of the best learning experiences of my freshman year.

I had decided to pursue illustration as my major, because of my interest in storytelling. This interest in stories led me to choose to make a book for my project. The next step was to find a story to tell. To limit my workload, I looked for a story that had already been told, one that I could reinterpret, as opposed to writing my own story. At this point, I came across two books, one of Greek myths, and an alphabet book illustrated by Norman Rockwell, and my initial concept was born.

Once the idea was initiated, I set to work researching Greek myths. The idea was to find one character for each letter of the alphabet. It proved more difficult than I had first thought. I found about 20 names with no problem, but I soon realized that several letters in our alphabet did not exist in the Greek alphabet. To overcome this hurdle, I took some liberties on the original problem and did not limit myself strictly to characters from myths (for example, I included the White Island for the letter W). Once the subject of each illustration was chosen, I set about the task of doing the images and designing the format of the book.

Doing the illustrations and designing the format of the book all came together at about the same time.

As I was working out the drawings I made several key decisions that heavily influenced the outcome of the project. First, I decided that each picture would have to be black and white if I was going to pull this whole thing off. Second, I knew that they would have to be relatively small. Through my art history class, I gained a strong interest in Japanese woodblock prints and was especially attracted to their strong compositional sensibility. This became the focus of my attention while working out the illustrations. Finally, the decision to make the illustrations small helped determine the way I used text in the book, because it all but eliminated the possibility of overlaying text on image.

I designed each image in my sketchbook, doing thumbnails and comp sketches of all sizes and shapes, until I found the image that I felt best represented the character. For example, Zeus has the biggest and busiest frame in the book because he is the king of the gods, while the image of the White Island is quite serene because it is a burial ground.

When I had each individual image worked out, I redrew them in order in the pages of my sketch book as if they were in the real book. I could now see how each image would work as a double-page spread, as well as how well the book could flow visually. With this mockup of the book in front of me it was very easy to see obvious mistakes and correct them before going to final art.

I did the final illustrations in pen and ink, on illustration board, and when they were finished, it was time to drop in the text. My first concept for the text was to be very minimal; each page would read, "A is for," "B is for," and so on. However,

I soon realized that making each page rhyme would drastically increase the reader's interest in the book. So I wrote a more extensive text and put the rhyming parts on opposite pages in order to give the reader one more incentive to turn the page.

The final touch for the book was putting the colored paper down. The decision to do this came when I went to place the type. The only means I had to get good type was to print it out on the computer, but I had no way to print it on the illustration board. So I had to put it on printer paper and cut and paste it. No matter how carefully I cut the paper and pasted it on, it just didn't look right. I came up with two solutions: one, print the words on colored paper and paste it on, or two, cut frames of colored paper to cover over the entire page except for the image and the text. I chose the latter and was pleased to discover that the local art store had a vast selection of handmade and colored papers.

Today I look back on this project as a pivotal experience in my art education, because I had free range to pursue storytelling, something that has since become an essential aspect of my art. In the professional world, bookmaking is rarely an individual process. It is a collaborative process, involving editors, artists, and writers, so for me to be able to pursue it on my own was in fact a blessing. I got to make a book the way that I thought it should be done, and pursue my own personal vision of what a Mythological Alphabet should be. By making this book, I discovered something that I love to do, and want to make a career of doing, and to me the vision that I have gained from this experience is invaluable.

Jason Chin, *A Is for Apollo* (left) and *U Is for Urania* (right). Student work.

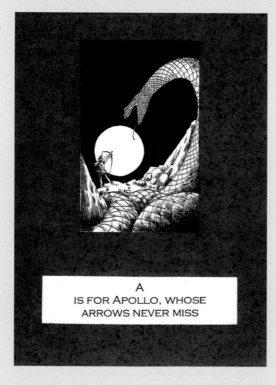

A
IS FOR APOLLO, WHOSE
ARROWS NEVER MISS

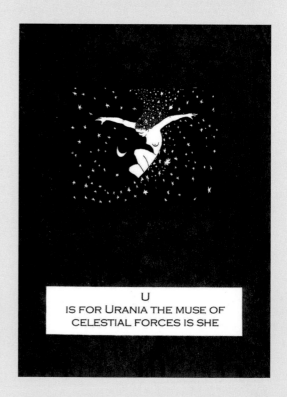

U
IS FOR URANIA THE MUSE OF
CELESTIAL FORCES IS SHE

7.7A Linear design.

7.8A Visual clutter.

7.9A Completed labyrinth design.

7.7B Adding invented texture.

7.8B Visual clarity.

7.9B Divided labyrinth design.

TURN UP THE HEAT: PUSHING YOUR PROJECT'S POTENTIAL

Some compositions are so bold that they seem to explode off the page. Other compositions have all the right ingredients but never really take off. By asking the following questions, you can more fully realize the potential of any assignment.

Basic Arithmetic

1. Should anything be *added* to the design? If your composition lacks energy, consider adding another layer of information or increasing the illusion of space. Notice how texture changes the composition in figures 7.7A and 7.7B.

2. Should anything be *subtracted*? If the composition is cluttered, try discarding 25 percent of the visual information. Then use the remaining shapes more deliberately (7.8A and B). Get as much as possible from every visual element. Economy is a virtue.

3. What happens when any component is *multiplied*? As shown in figures 7.6A and 7.6B, repetition can unify a design, add rhythm, and increase the illusion of space.

4. Can the design be *divided* into two or more separate compositions? When a design is too complicated, it may become impossible to resolve. Packing 20 ideas into a single design can diminish rather than improve communication. In figures 7.9A and 7.9B, a complicated source image has been separated into several different designs, creating a series of stronger images.

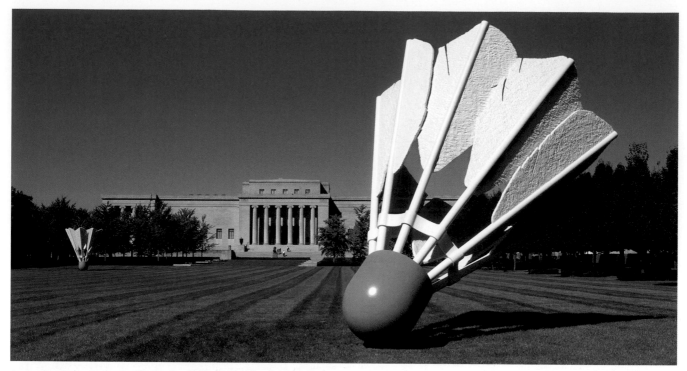

7.10 **Claes Oldenburg and Coosje van Bruggen,** *Shuttlecocks,* **1994.** South facade of the Nelson-Atkins Museum of Art and the Kansas City Sculpture Park. Aluminum, fiberglass-reinforced plastic, and paint. 230⁹⁄₁₆ × 191⁷⁄₈ in. (585.63 × 487.36 cm).

7.11A   7.11B

7.11C   7.11D

7.11E   7.11F

Transformation

Works of art and design present ideas in physical form. Each composition is strongly influenced by the materials used, the relationships created, and the viewing context chosen. Consider the following alternatives:

1. What happens when the material is changed? Even when the shapes stay the same, a silver teapot is very different from a glass, steel, or ceramic teapot. Sculptors Claes Oldenburg and Coosje van Bruggen used transformations in material extensively, often changing hard, reflective materials into soft vinyl. This form of transformation is especially effective when the new material brings structural qualities and conceptual connotations that challenge our expectations.

2. What is the relationship of the piece to the viewer? What is the relationship between the artwork and its surroundings? What happens when a chair is reduced to the size of a salt shaker? Or when a 19-foot-tall badminton shuttlecock is placed in front of a museum (7.10)? How does any image change, both visually and conceptually, when size is dramatically reduced or increased?

3. Can a change in position increase impact? Working with the same four blocks, a seemingly endless number of solutions can be created (7.11A–F).

4. Is a physical object compelling from all points of view? Does the composition of the artwork encourage the viewer to view it from other angles?

5. Will a change in viewing context increase meaning? For example, a side of beef has a very different meaning when it is hung in a gallery rather than staying in a slaughterhouse. Likewise, pop artists, such as Andy Warhol and Roy Lichtenstein, brought new meaning to soup cans and comic books by using them as subject matter in their paintings.

7.12

7.13

7.14

Reorganization

Time-based work, such as visual books, comic books, film, and video, is generally constructed from multiple images. Changing the organization of the parts of the puzzle can completely alter the meaning of the piece. For example, Angela contemplates entering the building in the sequence shown in figure 7.12. Using a different organization of the same three images, Angela now wonders what will happen when she opens the door at the top of the stairs (7.13). By repeating the image of Angela, we can present a dilemma: she is now in a labyrinth—which route should she take (7.14)?

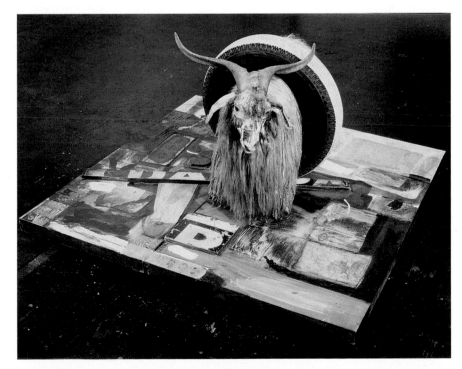

7.15 Robert Rauschenberg, *Monogram*, 1955–59. Freestanding combine, 42 × 63¼ × 64½ in. (106.7 × 160.7 × 163.8 cm).

7.16 Robert Rauschenberg, *Monogram, 1st State*, c. 1955.
Combine painting: oil, paper, fabric, wood on canvas, plus stuffed Angora goat and three electric light fixtures, approx. 75 × 46 × 12 in. (190.5 × 114.3 × 30.5 cm). No longer in existence.

7.17 Robert Rauschenberg, *Monogram, 2nd State*, c. 1956.
Combine: oil, paper, fabric, wood, plus rubber tire and stuffed Angora goat on wood, 115 × 32 × 44 in. (292 × 81.3 × 111.8 cm).

CONCEPTUAL VARIATIONS

Any compositional change affects the conceptual impact of an artwork. Henry M. Sayre provides a striking example in *A World of Art*.[1] A distilled version of his ideas follows.

Robert Rauschenberg's *Monogram* (7.15) is constructed from a stuffed goat, an automobile tire, and a painted plywood base. Seeking to combine painting and sculpture, Rauschenberg created three different versions of this piece. In the first version (7.16), he placed the goat on a shelf that extended from the center of a 6-foot-tall painting. This created a connection between the painting and the goat but diminished its sculptural impact. In the second

version (7.17), Rauschenberg placed a tire around the goat's midsection and moved the animal in front of the painting. This enhanced the artwork's three-dimensionality but created too much of a separation between the animal and the painting. He finally hit on the right combination when he placed the painting on the floor and positioned the goat in the center. The painting retained its integrity as a two-dimensional surface, the goat retained its physical presence, and a highly unified combination of the two elements was achieved. The addition of the tire enhanced the goat's sculptural form and gave the artwork a humorous twist.

ACCEPTING RESPONSIBILITY

We have explored only a few of the many approaches to critical thinking in this chapter. Every assignment presents new possibilities for critiques, and each teacher invents his or her own way to address the needs of a specific class.

Regardless of the specifics, however, two facts are inescapable. First, you will learn only what you want to learn. If you reject out-of-hand the alternatives suggested, or if you avoid responsibility for your conceptual and compositional choices, you will gain nothing from the critique, no matter what strategy is used. Second, there are no free rides. Everyone in the class is responsible for the success of the session. It is often difficult to sustain your attention or honestly assess your work or the work of others. When you get a superficial response to a project, insisting on further clarification is not easy. Every critique demands sincere and sustained attention from each participant. And, when the responses are supportive and substantial, remarkable improvements in works of art and design can be made.

SUMMARY

- Critical thinking helps us identify strengths and weaknesses in a project and determine the improvements that need to be made.

- Understanding the criteria on which a project will be judged helps focus critical thinking.

- Many artworks can be analyzed in terms of three basic aspects: form, subject, and content.

- Objective critiques focus on observable facts. Subjective critiques focus on feelings, intentions, and implications.

- Four common critique methods are description, cause and effect, compare and contrast, and greatest strength/unrealized potential.

- Many critique methods may be used when you are working on a long-term project. In all cases, there are three primary objectives: explore alternatives, delete nonessentials, and strengthen essentials.

- Basic arithmetic, transformation, and reorganization can be used to increase compositional impact.

- An open mind combined with a willingness to share ideas can strengthen any critique.

KEY TERMS

cause-and-effect critique (formal analysis)

compare/contrast critique

content

critique

descriptive critique

form

objective criticism

subject

subjective criticism

STUDIO PROJECTS

To apply the concepts from this chapter in the studio, check out the Projects page in the Online Learning Center at www.mhhe.com/stewart4e. The following is a sample of the chapter-related assignments that are described in step-by-step detail.

Capstone Project. Expanding creativity through in-depth exploration.

Profile:
Kendall Buster, Sculptor
Biological Architecture

Kendall Buster's large-scale "biological architecture" projects have been exhibited at Artist's Space and the American Academy of Arts and Letters in New York City; the Hirshhorn Museum and the Kreeger Museum in Washington, DC; the Kemper Museum in Kansas City; Suyama Space in Seattle; the Nevada Museum of Art in Reno; and the KZNSA Gallery in South Africa. Buster has created commissioned sculptures for the Washington, DC, Convention Center; Massey Cancer Center in Richmond, VA; and the Agave Library in Phoenix. Current projects include commissions for the new chemistry building at Princeton University, Johns Hopkins University, and the Indianapolis Museum of Art.

MS: Microbiology was your initial academic passion, and you worked in this field for twelve years. What attracted you to microbiology, and what did you learn from it?

KB: Peering into a microscope gave me access to an intricate and beautiful world that was beyond ordinary perception. As I learned more, I became increasingly interested in the architecture of natural forms—the way cells are constructed to maximize efficiency or the permeability of a particular cell wall. The sculptures I now create begin with an internal skeleton that I wrap in a fabric or plastic skin. And, I am still fascinated by shifts in perception, from very small scale to very large scale. For me, art and science are simply aspects of the same impulse.

MS: How do you translate your ideas into large-scale objects? Most of your recent projects could fill an entire gymnasium!

KB: Ideas often occur just as I am waking up. At this point, they are more intuitive than intentional. I begin to record possibilities through pencil drawings. Drawing is crucial—it is the first step in getting the idea out of my head and into the world. I then move to what I see as three-dimensional sketching, using carved Styrofoam, wire, or various types of board.

Further work is done with an entire team of collaborators. Computer-aided design helps us explore variations further and analyze the structural requirements and possibilities of the forms. With my studio team, I create physical models of the building in which the artwork will be placed in order to study the ways in which the sculpture converses with the site. I have a project coordinator who communicates with the client on the architectural particulars of the site and a rigger who is an installation specialist.

MS: How are the pieces actually constructed?

KB: My large-scale sculptures are made with many interlocked parts, and so creating patterns for the parts is critical. These patterns, both computer generated and hand drawn on the studio floor, are used for shaping and welding the steel frames or cutting planar material. The frames are professionally powder-coated, and when the frames are covered in cloth I might work with as many as ten to twenty helpers in a marathon "screening party."

MS: Please talk us through *New Growth*, installed in the Boise Art Museum.

KB: *New Growth* is an inventory of architectural models that function like biological systems. In this imagined city, old forms generate new forms through processes that suggest germination, budding, merging, hybridization, or absorption. The model city is conceived as a single organism constructed from many interdependent parts. Some structures are connected by passageways that suggest either umbilical cords or parasitic invasions. Contiguous membranes create distinct regions in the city, and the transparency of these membranes allows inner layers to be visible through the outer shell.

Architectural structures form and re-form the fabric of cities over time. To evoke this process, I wanted to build a structure that seems to be based on a precise blueprint, while at the same time contradict this idea by creating a structure that seems dynamic, continually changing. I am also interested in exploring the tension between what is revealed and what is concealed; how windows link interior space with exterior place to create shifting sight lines; how narrow entryways or low passages act in direct confrontation with the body; how space is compressed and movement directed; how one is at times hidden, and at times exposed.

New Growth is also a response to the particulars of the Boise Art Museum site. On my first visit I visualized a kind of floating cityscape made up of forms that behaved both as individual structures and as a continuous membrane. The sculpture that I finally built connected to the exhibition site in unexpected ways. Curved rooftops in my architectural models seemed to echo the arched beams in the ceiling, and the ever-changing light penetrating through the floor-to-ceiling windows created subtle shades of white and gray on the transparent layers of fabric.

Scale shifts between the viewer's initial "panoramic" overview and the more closely observed details were also important. At one moment, the viewer is dwarfed by the artwork; at another, the artwork reads as a model that the viewer can command. As a result, the viewer is enveloped, embraced, and engaged—all at the same time.

MS: What advice do you have for beginning students?
KB: I have three bits of advice. First, realize that each of us has our own work process and embrace the process that is right for you. Second, find the right balance between conceptual breadth (lateral thinking) and conceptual depth (vertical thinking). Too much lateral thinking can result in superficiality, while too much vertical thinking can narrow your possibilities. Finally, embrace the idea of an ongoing and preferably daily studio practice. Complex ideas and structures don't happen overnight!

Kendall Buster, *New Growth,* 2007. Dimensions variable, as installed in Boise Art Museum.

chapter eight

Constructing Meaning

Seeking and solving visual problems, cultivating creativity, and developing critical judgment all require hours of hard work. Why are these skills so highly valued by artists and designers and so strongly emphasized by college teachers?

The answer is simple. At a professional level, art and graphic design projects are done in order to communicate ideas and express emotions. Turning elusive concepts into effective communication is not easy. Clay, ink, metal, fabric, and other physical materials must somehow stimulate an audience to see, understand, and respond. In this chapter, we explore the essentials of visual communication and identify some of the strategies artists and designers use to construct meaning. The interviews at the end of each chapter provide an insider's view of this process.

BUILDING BRIDGES

Shared Language

A shared language is the basis on which all communication is built. For example, if you are fluent in English and I am effective as a writer, the ideas I want to communicate in this chapter should make sense to you. On the other hand, if English is your second language, some of the vocabulary may be unfamiliar. In that case, you may have to strengthen the bridge between us by looking up words in a dictionary.

Figure 8.1 demonstrates the importance of shared language. For a reader of Chinese, the flowing brushstrokes form characters that communicate

8.1 Huai-su, Detail of Autobiography, Tang dynasty, 7th–10th centuries. Ink on paper.

specific ideas. For those of us who know no Chinese, the calligraphy is visually enticing but conveys no specific message. We cannot understand the characters.

Historical and cultural "literacy" can create another type of bridge. As an American, I live within a framework that is driven by a capitalist economic structure, a two-party political system, and social systems based on Judeo-Christian values. South African William Kentridge brings a very different frame of reference to his artwork. Born in 1951, he experienced apartheid firsthand as the son of white civil rights lawyers and has extensive knowledge of the history of many African genocides. In *Black Box/Chambre Noir* (8.2), he uses a miniature theater to tell the story of one such genocide, which nearly wiped out the Herero people. Powered by the type of mechanism used in ink-jet printers, six automatons enter and exit the stage. Projections of historical documents, combined with fragments of music from Mozart's opera *The Magic Flute* and Namibian songs, expand the tragic story. While viewers are immediately drawn to the fascinating structure, we cannot fully understand the meaning without expanding our knowledge of African history.

Iconography

Many artworks depend on cultural and historical references to build meaning. **Iconography** (literally, "describing images") is the study of such symbolic visual systems.

Deborah Haylor-McDowell's *The Serpent Didn't Lie* (8.3) is loaded with references. An anatomical diagram copied from Leonardo da Vinci's notebooks appears in the upper-left corner, while the nude couple near the center is based on *The Kiss*, a sculpture by Auguste Rodin. Einstein's computations for the theory of relativity appear in the upper-right corner, and in the foreground a baby takes his first steps. A snakeskin border surrounds the image. What does it all mean? Haylor-McDowell says:

> Ignorance may spare us the pain of difficult decisions. However, the price we pay is high. Can humankind's greatest gifts, emotion and intellect, mature in a world that is free of suffering? In the absence of adversity, will our humanness be lost?

8.2 View of William Kentridge's *Black Box/Chambre Noire*, 2005. Miniature theater with mechanized objects, projections and sound, dimensions variable.

8.3 Deborah Haylor-McDowell, *The Serpent Didn't Lie*, 1997. Etching, 15 × 23 in. (38.1 × 58.42 cm).

8.4 Milton Glaser, *Art is . . .* , 1996. Poster.

8.5 René Magritte, *Golconde*, 1953. Oil on canvas, 31¾ × 38⅝ in. (80.65 × 98.11 cm).

The Serpent Didn't Lie is based on a biblical text dealing with good and evil in the Garden of Eden. What is the price we pay for knowledge? The images I used in the composition deal with the complexities and responsibilities of our pursuit of knowledge.

Through a sophisticated use of iconography, the artist created a puzzle that is filled with ideas for us to unravel and explore. For those who understand the cultural references, this print presents a survey of types of knowledge in a compelling visual form. For those who do not understand the references, the print is simply a beautifully crafted collection of architectural and figurative fragments.

Graphic designers are especially aware of the importance of iconography. On a purely visual level, Milton Glaser's 1996 poster for the School of Visual Arts (8.4) is intriguing and evocative in itself. The hovering hat, shadowy figure, and curious text raise all sorts of questions. When we compare the poster with surrealist René Magritte's *Golconde* (8.5), the ideas expand much further. In this and other paintings by Magritte, the man in the bowler hat represents anyone who is courageously navigating through the chaos of contemporary life. When we make the connection between Glaser and Magritte,

the School of Visual Arts poster becomes poignant as well as provocative. Like the man in the bowler hat, each art student must find a path through the complexities of contemporary life in order to develop a meaningful approach to art and design.

Audience

Just as films are targeted and rated for specific audiences, so many forms of visual communication are designed for specific viewers. George Balanchine was a master choreographer renowned for his love of classical ballet as well as his modern sensibility and commitment to endless invention. A powerful yet restrained poster was needed to publicize a performance of his work (8.6). The dancers in blue are carefully balanced by simple text on a blue background. By contrast, in *Dancing Downtown 2003* (8.7), the soloist wears a loose dress that accentuates her physicality. She dances with wild abandon. Both shows attracted diverse audiences, but the Balanchine poster was targeted at those seeking more traditional ballet, while *Dancing Downtown 2003* was targeted at those seeking a more exuberant and contemporary approach.

8.6 *Serenade* by George Balanchine, Los Angeles Ballet. Poster. Design by Catherine Kanner, photo by Reed Hutchinson.

8.7 *Dancing Downtown*, 2003. Poster. Designed by Noon.

Immediacy

When the bridge between the image and the audience is explicit, communication can occur almost instantaneously. When the iconography is elusive or complex, communication takes longer and is more varied. Each approach can be effective in the right time and place. When we are driving a car, our lives depend on the immediate message we receive when a traffic light turns red. The "Stop!" is clear and concise. When visiting a museum, we often seek greater complexity and emotional resonance.

Graphic designers generally aim for a combination of immediacy, clarity, and resonance. For them, an effective poster or billboard can be understood at a glance. Figure 8.8 is an excellent example. The bold, white hanged man immediately attracts attention, and the book title itself is simple and direct. The position of the figure's head adds another layer of meaning to this critique of capital punishment.

By contrast, *Some Words* (8.9) by Markus Schaller requires extended viewer involvement. Created

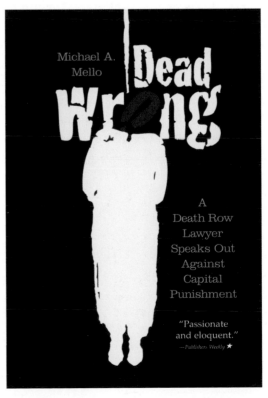

8.8 Mark Maccaulay. Book jacket.

8.9 Markus Schaller, *Some Words*, 2007. Steel, dimensions variable.

from a sequence of stream-of-consciousness texts inscribed onto 70 iron panels, this installation was designed as a meditation on the very process of thinking. Viewers entering this visual labyrinth had to be willing to puzzle over the words presented and explore their own cognitive response. The message here is neither explicit nor immediate. As with Haylor-McDowell's work (figure 8.3), the viewer must piece together a complex set of clues, then reach his or her own conclusions about the nature of knowledge and the development of literacy.

Stereotypes

A **stereotype** is a fixed generalization based on a preconception. On a benign level, when we use a stereotype, we ignore individual characteristics and emphasize group characteristics. For example, the broken wine glass in figure 8.10 is widely used on shipping crates to communicate fragility. Glass is actually a very versatile material that can be cast as bricks, spun into fiber-optic cables, and polished to create lenses. However, we are most familiar with fragile wine glasses and bottles. Relying on this *general* perception, the shipping label designer used a stereotype to communicate fragility.

Racial stereotyping, which is never benign, tends to exaggerate negative generalizations. Even when a positive assumption is made (such as "Asian Americans are brainy overachievers"), the overall effect is demeaning. Rather than learning about an individual person, we make judgments based on our preconceptions.

Stereotypes are often used to create the bridge on which communication depends. Because they are based on preconceptions, stereotypes require little thought. The viewer responds automatically. In some situations, an automatic response is ideal. Four airport pictograms are shown in figure 8.11. Can you determine the meaning of each? If the designer is successful, even an exhausted traveler from New Zealand will be able to determine at a glance where to find a baggage locker, an elevator, or a toilet. Especially notice the use of the male and female stereotypes for the toilet pictograms. Despite the wide range of clothing worn by female travelers, the designers used a dress to create a stereotypical female.

8.10 "Fragile" pictogram.

Baggage lockers   Elevator   Toilets, men Toilets, women

8.11 Roger Cook and Don Shanosky, images from a poster introducing the signage symbol system developed for the U.S. Department of Transportation, 1974.

Clichés

A **cliché** is an overused expression or a predictable treatment of an idea. Phrases such as "Let's level the playing field" and "Think outside the box" are powerful the first time we hear them. However, when we hear them repeatedly, they lose their impact and become clichés. Visual clichés are equally predictable. Skulls representing death and seagulls representing tranquility may be effective at first but tend to become worn out when used repeatedly.

Surprise

A shift in a stereotype or cliché upsets our expectations and challenges our assumptions. The resulting shock can surprise or delight an audience, making the message more memorable. Originally based on the cowboy stereotype, the Marlboro Man has been reinterpreted in figure 8.12. This ad, which begins like an ordinary cigarette commercial, quickly shifts from the heroic cowboy to a man with a hacking cough. At this point, the narrator suggests that "cowboys are a dying breed" because of the cancer caused by smoking. By breaking the stereotype, the designers attract the viewers' attention, challenge the conventional cigarette ad, and strengthen their nonsmoking message.

Na Zha Cradle (8.13) is equally surprising. Cradles are "supposed" to be soft, safe, and comforting. This cradle is metallic, threatening, and dangerous. Metaphorically commenting on the aggressive capitalism that has driven the Chinese economy in recent years, Shi Jinsong suggests that there is a price to be paid when society progresses too quickly.

Key Questions
BUILDING BRIDGES

- Are there any symbolic or cultural meanings embedded in your composition? Are these meanings consistent with the message you want to convey?
- Have you used a stereotype or a cliché? Does this strengthen or weaken your message?
- What audience do you want to reach? Are the form and content of your design appropriate for that audience?

NARRATOR: No wonder cowboys are a dying breed. If

you need help quitting, tune into project QUIT, and take

control of your life.

8.12 Agency: Ruhr/Paragon, Minneapolis. Production: Lotter, Minneapolis. Details: TV, 30 seconds, color. First appearance: February 1988. Account Supervisor: Anne Bologna. Creative Director/Art Director: Doug Lew. Associate Creative Director/Copywriter: Bill Johnson. Agency Producer: Arleen Kulis. Production Company Director: Jim Lotter.

8.13 Shi Jinsong, *Na Zha Cradle*, 2005. Stainless steel, 24 × 31.9 × 24.3 in. (61.4 × 81.7 × 62.2 cm).

PURPOSE AND INTENT

Any number of approaches to visual communication can be effective. We simply choose the style, iconography, and composition best suited to our purpose.

Let's consider four very different uses of human anatomy. *Arterial Fibrillation* (8.14) was developed for the cover of a medical journal. With equal training in art and science, medical illustrator Kim Martens combined anatomical accuracy with artistic imagination to create this design. Intent on sales, the art director for the magazine requested an image that was both physically correct and visually enticing.

Designed as an anatomical roadmap, *Understanding Healthcare* (8.15) had to present complex information in a clear and concise way. To make the text accessible to a general audience, the designers used a loose grid dominated by vertical columns at the top and a strong horizontal band at the bottom. Arrows and other visual cues help the reader navigate from page to page.

Booster (8.16) is dominated by a series of X-rays of the artist's body. In this unconventional self-portrait, Robert Rauschenberg combined a collection of personal X-rays with various examples of technological notation, including an astronomer's

8.14 Kim Martens, *Arterial Fibrillation*, 2000. Photoshop.

chart, diagrams analyzing the movement of drills and arrows, graphs, and an empty chair. The title adds further meaning, suggesting a connection to booster shots, booster rockets, and booster seats, which increase the height of an ordinary chair so that young children can sit at a table comfortably. Reduced to an X-ray image and surrounded by fragments of technological information, the artist becomes a cog in the machinery of mass culture. By contrast, the woman in Kiki Smith's *Virgin Mary* (8.17) seems both vulnerable and graceful. She displays her flayed body unapologetically, extending her open hands in a type of blessing.

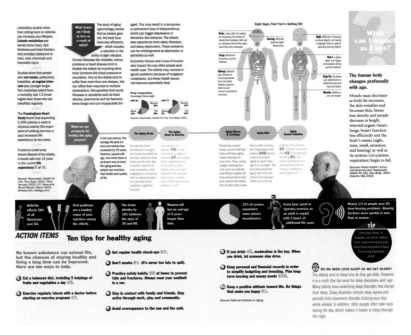

8.15 **United Healthcare Brochure.** Design Firm: Pentagram, NY. Courtesy of Richard Saul Wurman.

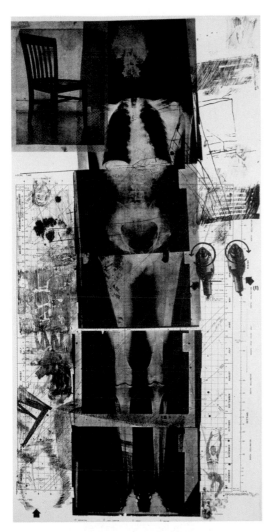

8.16 **Robert Rauschenberg,** *Booster,* **1967.** Lithograph and serigraph, printed in color, composition 71⁹⁄₁₆ × 35⅛ in. (181.7 × 89.1 cm).

8.17 **Kiki Smith,** *Virgin Mary,* **1992.** Beeswax, microcrystalline wax, cheesecloth, and wood on steel base, 67½ × 26 × 14½ in. (171.5 × 66 × 36.8 cm).

8.18 Margaret Bourke-White, *At the Time of the Louisville Flood,* 1937. Gelatin silver print.

8.19 Alfred Eisenstadt, *Winston Churchill, Liverpool,* 1957. Gelatin silver print.

CONTEXT

The compositional context in which any image appears profoundly influences meaning. In figure 8.18, the juxtaposition of a quiet line of flood survivors with a propagandistic billboard makes us rethink the phrase "There's no way like the American way."

The social context in which an image appears is equally important. In figure 8.19, Winston Churchill, the prime minister most responsible for British victory during World War II, extends two fingers to create the "V for victory" gesture he used throughout the war. If we are familiar with Churchill and know about the desperate struggle of the British people during the war, we immediately make the correct connection. In figure 8.20, the same gesture communicates a very different idea. As part of the signage for the Minnesota Children's Museum, the extended fingers now communicate the number two. Realizing that many young visitors to the museum may not be able to read, the designers used both a number and a gesture to communicate location. Finally, in Sean O'Meallie's *Out-Boxed Finger Puppets Perform the Numbers 1 Through 5 in No Particular Order* (8.21), the same gesture becomes a playful piece of sculpture as well as an indication of the number two. We now see the extended fingers in the context of a series of whimsical forms. In each of these three cases, the meaning of the two fingers depends on the context.

8.20 **Minnesota Children's Museum, Pentagram design, New York, NY.** Tracy Cameron and Michael Bierut, Designers.

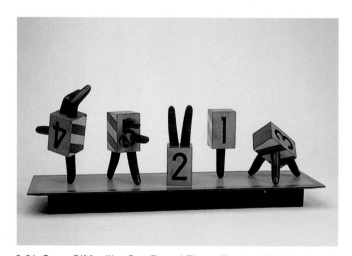

8.21 Sean O'Meallie, *Out-Boxed Finger Puppets Perform the Numbers 1 Through 5 in No Particular Order,* 1999. Polychromed wood, 17.5 × 42 × 11 in.

CONNECTIONS

Analogies, similes, and metaphors are figures of speech that link one thing to another. An **analogy** creates a general connection between unrelated objects or ideas, while a **simile** creates the connection using the word *as* or *like*, as in "She has a heart as big as Texas." A **metaphor** is more explicit: Speaking metaphorically, we would say "Her heart *is* Texas." As you can see, a substantial shift in meaning occurs when metaphor is used.

In all cases, the original word is given the qualities of the linked word. For example, when Robert Burns wrote the simile "My love is like a red red rose," he gave the abstract concept of "love" the attributes of a glorious, colorful, fragrant, thorny, and transient rose.

Metaphorical thinking can be used to connect an image and an idea. Take the phrase "I have butterflies in my stomach." This phrase is widely used to describe nervousness. Substitute other insects for butterflies, such as bees or wasps. How does this change the meaning? To push it even further, start with the phrase "My mind was full of clouds." What happens when "clouds" is replaced by mice on treadmills, rats in mazes, shadowy staircases, beating drums, screaming children—or even butterflies? When my mind is full of butterflies, I am happy, but butterflies in my stomach indicate fear. In addition to expanding ideas, metaphors can help provide specific images for elusive emotions.

Metaphorical thinking and symbolism have always been used by artists and designers to strengthen communication. Exaggerated metaphors are especially common in advertising design. The massive wave that threatens the computer user in figure 8.22 is a metaphor for the destructive power of the Y2K computer bug that once seemed likely to create massive computer failures on January 1, 2000. Editorial cartoons also rely on metaphors. In figure 8.23, a congressional hand puppet vows independence from the very lobbyist who is controlling his vote.

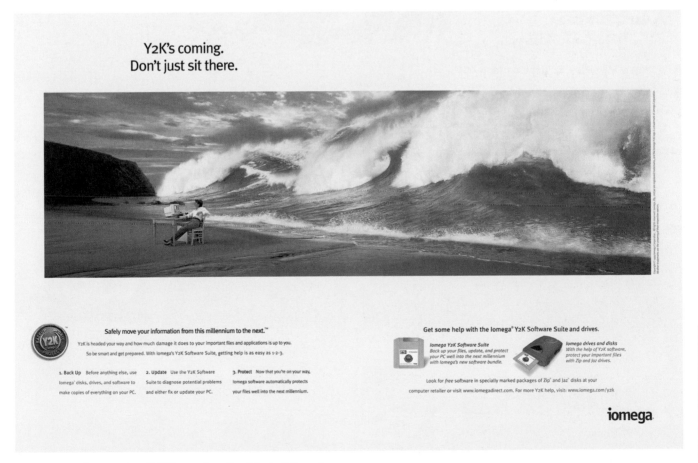

8.22 Iomega Corporation, "Y2K's coming. Don't just sit there."

8.23 Jimmy Margulies, Editorial Cartoon, 2006.

8.24 Pablo Picasso, *Guernica*, 1937. Oil on canvas, 11 ft 5½ in. × 25 ft 5¼ in. (3.5 × 7.8 m).

Picasso's *Guernica* (8.24) is also loaded with metaphors. In *A World of Art*, Henry Sayre offers the following description:

> The horse, at the center left, speared and dying in anguish, represents the fate of the dreamer's creativity. The entire scene is surveyed by a bull, which represents at once Spain itself, the simultaneous heroism and tragedy of the bullfight, and the Minotaur, the bull-man who for the Surrealists stood for the irrational forces of the human psyche. The significance of the electric light bulb at the top center of the painting, and the oil lamp, held by the woman reaching out the window, has been much debated, but they represent, at least, old and new ways of seeing.[1]

Rather than showing exploding bombs or collapsing buildings, Picasso filled his painting with abstracted animals, screaming humans, and various sources of light. In so doing, he focused on the meaning and emotion of the event, rather than its appearance.

AESTHETICS

Definitions

In *Design in the Visual Arts*, Roy Behrens noted the difference between the words *anesthetic* and *aesthetic*. An **anesthetic** is used to induce insensitivity or unconsciousness. In an anesthetic state, we are numbed and disoriented. We may not be able to determine the size or location of objects or the sequence of events. On the other hand, **aesthetics** is the study of human responses to beauty. In an aesthetic experience, our feelings are enhanced and our understanding expands. As a result, an aesthetic experience tends to heighten meaning, while an anesthetic experience tends to dull meaning. Dentists use anesthetics; artists and designers use aesthetics.

Aesthetic theories reflect community values, and thus vary greatly from culture to culture. For example, an exalted conception of Christianity dominated civic life during the Middle Ages in Europe. To express their faith, architects developed ingenious building strategies to create the soaring Gothic cathedrals we associate with that period (8.25). By contrast, intimacy and a sense of community were highly valued by the Unitarian congregation that commissioned Frank Lloyd Wright's

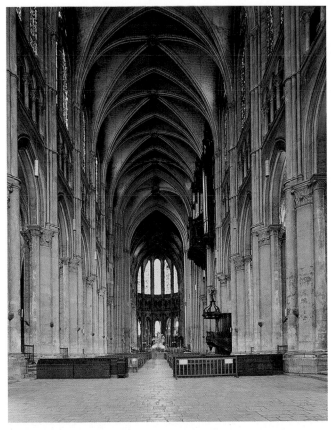

8.25 Notre-Dame Cathedral nave vaults, Chartres, 1194–1230.

8.26 Frank Lloyd Wright, Unity Temple interior, 1906. Oak Park, Illinois.

Unity Temple (8.26). The sanctuary is essentially a cube, with rows of seats facing inward from three sides. Congregants face each other while at the same time maintaining close contact with the minister. The Pompidou Center (8.27), by Renzo Piano and Richard Rogers, offers a third approach to public architecture. From the outside, it looks more like a roller coaster than a major art museum. To emphasize the importance of technology in contemporary life, the blue ventilation ducts, red elevators, and green water pipes are highlighted rather than being hidden. Because cultural values are so variable, before we conclude our discussion of meaningful design, we must delve into contemporary aesthetics.

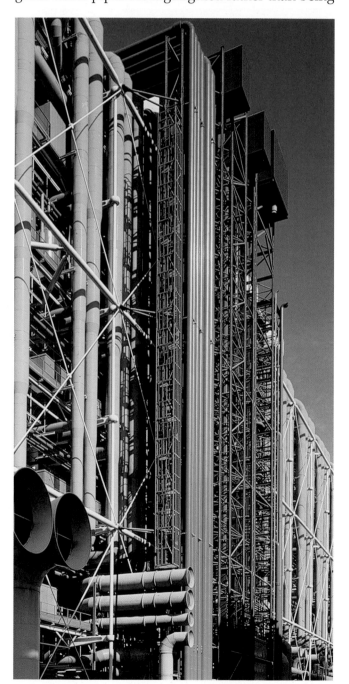

8.27 Renzo Piano and Richard Rogers, Pompidou Center, Paris, 1976.

Postmodernism

Contemporary art and design are widely categorized as **postmodernism.** This emphasizes the extent to which today's artists and designers seek solutions that challenge or exceed modernism. Thus, to understand contemporary aesthetics, we must first examine the basic characteristics of the previous aesthetic period.

In the arts, **modernism** is a general term that encompasses a wide range of individual movements. Beginning in Europe in the latter part of the nineteenth century, modernism became the dominant force in art and design from around 1915 to 1975.

In a sense, modernism rose from the ashes of World War I. After this devastating conflict, traditional attitudes and images seemed inadequate and out of date. Architects began to strip away traditional ornamentation to reveal the underlying structures and spaces in their buildings. Designers such as Marcel Breuer, Raymond Lowry, and Charles and Ray Eames used plastic, metals, and glass to massproduce objects and images for an expanding consumer market. Artists such as Wassily Kandinsky, Naum Gabo, and Piet Mondrian valued abstraction over traditional representation. The international art world became a hotbed of experimentation.

Many modernists shared four fundamental beliefs. First, they were fascinated by **form,** which may be defined as the physical manifestation of an idea. "Less is more" became a mantra for designers, while "the form is the content" became a catchphrase for many painters. Second, modernists readily embraced new materials and methods of production. Especially in architecture, traditional materials such as wood, brick, and stone began to be replaced by concrete, plastic, and glass. Third, the early modernists strongly believed in the social significance of the arts. They wanted to bring art and design to the general population, rather than working for an elite. Finally, many modernists sought to understand and express universal truths. No longer satisfied with a conventional representation of reality, they began to develop a new visual language based on distillation and abstraction.

These four fundamental beliefs stimulated innovation in all areas of art, architecture, and design, and an enormous amount of brilliant work was produced. Over time, however, many modernists became trapped by their own success. Constructed from hard, reflective materials and dominated by right angles, modernist buildings often seemed cold and monolithic. Based on an underlying grid and typographical conventions, modernist posters often seemed predictable. Reduced to the most essential forms, modernist painting and sculpture became detached from the chaos and complexity of contemporary life. It seemed that all the questions of modernism had been answered. Something had to change.

The 1966 publication of *Complexity and Contradiction in Architecture* set the stage for postmodern architecture. In it, architect Robert Venturi extolled the energy and ambiguities of renaissance architecture:

> I like elements which are hybrid rather than "pure," compromising rather than "clean," distorted rather than "articulated," perverse as well as impersonal, boring as well as "interesting," conventional rather than "designed," accommodating rather than excluding, redundant rather than simple, vestigial as well as innovating, inconsistent and equivocal rather than direct and clear. I am for messy vitality over obvious unity.

At the same time, philosophers Jean-Louis Lyotard, Jacques Derrida, Michael Foucault, and Roland Barthes began to expand our understanding of the process of communication. They argued that both knowledge and communication are impermanent and conditional: there *are* no universal truths. The audience rather than the artist ultimately creates the meaning of an artwork; thus, meaning changes constantly. Furthermore, they tended to see knowledge as cyclical rather than progressive. They argued that we are pursuing a complex path with multiple branches rather than a grand journey that will culminate in human perfection.

Influenced by these theorists and seeking fresh ideas and approaches, many contemporary artists and designers reject the central tenets of modernism. For the postmodernist, context and content are as important as pure form. Postmodern use of materials tends to be omnivorous and irreverent. An exhibition may be constructed from trash, and fiberglass may be manipulated to mimic metal.

Distinctions between "high art" (such as painting and sculpture) and "low art" (such as advertising and crafts) are considered artificial. And, since all aspects of visual culture are intertwined, the postmodernist may recycle images and ideas with impunity, "appropriating" them for use in a new context. Finally, for the postmodernist there are multiple rather than universal truths, and all truths are continually changing. As a result, where late modernism tended to be stable and reductive, postmodernism tends to be expansive and dynamic. As Venturi suggested, complexity and contradiction can be seen as strengths.

For the past 30 years, the collision between modernism and postmodernism has released an enormous amount of energy. Taboos have been broken repeatedly, and the criteria for excellence continue to evolve.

Visual Strategies

Five common characteristics of postmodern art and design follow.

Appropriation (the reuse of an existing artwork) is often used to create a connection between past and present cultural values. In *We Don't Need Another Hero* (8.28), Barbara Kruger borrowed a Norman Rockwell illustration in which a young girl admires her male counterpart's muscles. The emphatic text shifts the meaning from the original gender stereotype to a contemporary feminist statement.

Recontextualization is another postmodern strategy. Constructed from steel pins and placed in a gallery, Mona Hatoum's *Doormat* (8.29) forces us to rethink a commonplace object. As part of a series on racism, this artwork suggests that the opportunities

8.28 Barbara Kruger, *Untitled (We Don't Need Another Hero)*, **1987.** Photographic silksreen, vinyl lettering on Plexiglas, 109 × 210 in. (276.9 × 533.4 cm).

8.29 Mona Hatoum, *Doormat II*, 2000–01. Steel and rubber, 1 × 28 × 16 in. (2.5 × 71 × 40.6 cm).

offered by civil rights legislation may be as ironic as a welcome mat made of pins.

Layering is often used to create complex or even contradictory meanings. In *The Red Mean: Self-Portrait* (8.30), Jaune Quick-to-See Smith reinterprets Leonardo da Vinci's famous drawing of ideal human proportions (8.31). As a Renaissance man, Leonardo was fascinated by both perfection and the grotesque. In this drawing, he mapped out an idealized figure radiating out from the navel in the center.

Despite its superficial similarity, the aesthetic basis for Smith's self-portrait is entirely different. Her circular outline simultaneously suggests a target, negation, and the four directions emphasized in Native American spiritual practices. A sign proclaiming "Made in the USA" combined with the artist's tribal identification number covers the chest of the figure, and tribal newspapers fill the background. While the da Vinci drawing is simple and elegant, Smith's self-portrait provides a rich commentary on the complexities of her life as a Native American.

All of these examples demonstrate a fourth postmodern characteristic: words and images are often integrated in order to expand emotional impact or to create conflict. For the postmodernist, contradiction and complexity are celebrated as facts of life and sources of inspiration.

Finally, **hybridity** may be defined as the creation of artworks using disparate media and meanings to create a unified conceptual statement. In *I Wish I Could Help You* (8.32), Daniel Sutherland combined abstract painted shapes with a tiny, highly detailed figure and surrounded the entire image with a three-dimensional frame made of wood and hardware. For Sutherland, the deep frame is suggestive of both a shipping crate and a contemporary reliquary. Kathryn Frund combined government

8.30 Jaune Quick-to-See Smith, *The Red Mean: Self-Portrait*, 1992. Mixed medium.

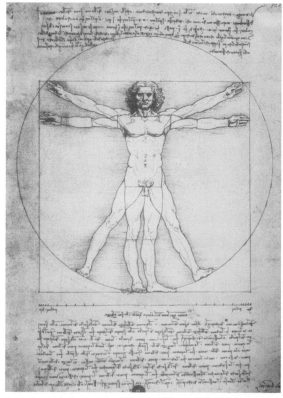

8.31 Leonardo da Vinci, *Proportions of the Human Figure* (after Vitruvius), c. 1485–90. Pen and ink, 13½ × 9¾ in. (34.3 × 24.8 cm).

8.32 Daniel Sutherland, *I Wish I Could Help You*, 1994. Oil on canvas on wood with hardware, 75 × 84 in. (190.5 × 213.4 cm).

documents and a carpenter's plumb bob with paint on aluminum to create *Radical Acts* (see figure 3.22, page 75). Jaune Quick-to-See Smith's *Self-Portrait* (8.30) is constructed from newspapers, posters, and identity cards as well as paint. And, as we will see in the interview at the end of this chapter, Roger Shimomura added Mickey Mouse ears to a pair of paintings dealing with racial stereotypes. For the postmodernist, visual impact and conceptual meaning are more important than technical purity.

DRAMA

Regardless of the medium used or the message conveyed, all communication can be strengthened through dramatic delivery. Even Martin Luther King Jr.'s "I Have a Dream" speech loses much of its power when delivered in a flat, monotonous tone of voice. Just as a playwright sets the stage for the story he or she seeks to tell, so an artist can set the stage for visual communication.

All of the elements and principles of design described in this book can be used to increase *compositional* drama. To increase *conceptual* drama, we can:

- *Personify the idea.* When we identify with a character in a play, we become more empathetic and involved in the story. Likewise, when we identify with a character in a painting or a poster, we are much more likely to remember the idea or emotion being conveyed.

- *Focus on essentials.* It has often been said that theater is "life with the boring parts left out." To be meaningful to an audience, the characters and events in a play must have a strong relationship to direct experience. However, a playwright rarely shows a character flossing his or her teeth. Too much detail clutters the composition, confuses the audience, and muddles the message. Including the right amount of information in just the right way can add drama to even the simplest idea.

- *Seek significance.* Any event, character, or time period can be used to create an effective play. Likewise, any object, event, or idea can be used in our quest for visual communication. A unique approach to a familiar subject or an insightful interpretation of personal and political events can add significance and increase impact.

SUMMARY

- A shared language is the basis on which all communication is built.

- Iconography (the study of symbolic visual systems) provides us with a way to analyze the meaning of images and objects.

- Just as films are targeted for specific audiences, so many forms of visual communication are designed for specific viewers.

- Immediacy is often highly valued in graphic design. By comparison, many paintings require extended viewer involvement and longer viewing time.

- A stereotype is a fixed generalization based on a preconception. Stereotypes can easily create a bridge between the image and the audience.

- A cliché is an overused expression or predictable treatment of an idea. Even the most interesting image will lose its power if overused.

- A shift in a stereotype or cliché challenges our assumptions and can increase impact.

- Artists and designers choose the style, iconography, and composition best suited to their purpose. A mismatch between the type of image and its purpose creates confusion.

- The visual and social context in which an image appears will profoundly affect its meaning.

- Analogies, similes, and metaphors are figures of speech that link one thing to another. Metaphors are especially widely used in visual communication.

- Appropriation, recontextualization, layering, word/image integration, and hybridity are five common strategies used to create postmodern meaning.

- Dramatic delivery of a message enhances meaning.

KEY TERMS

aesthetics	cliché	layering	postmodernism
analogy	form	metaphor	recontextualization
anesthetic	hybridity	metaphorical thinking	simile
appropriation	iconography	modernism	stereotype

STUDIO PROJECTS

To apply the concepts from this chapter in the studio, check out the Projects page in the Online Learning Center at www.mhhe.com/stewart4e. The following is a sample of the chapter-related assignments that are described in step-by-step detail.

Benign to Sublime. Transforming a benign still life into a compelling vehicle for the communication of an idea.

Build a Concept Generator. A basic cube turns into a conceptual toy.

Word/Image Synergy. Using Photoshop or photocopies to combine one or more images with a single word to create an unexpected message.

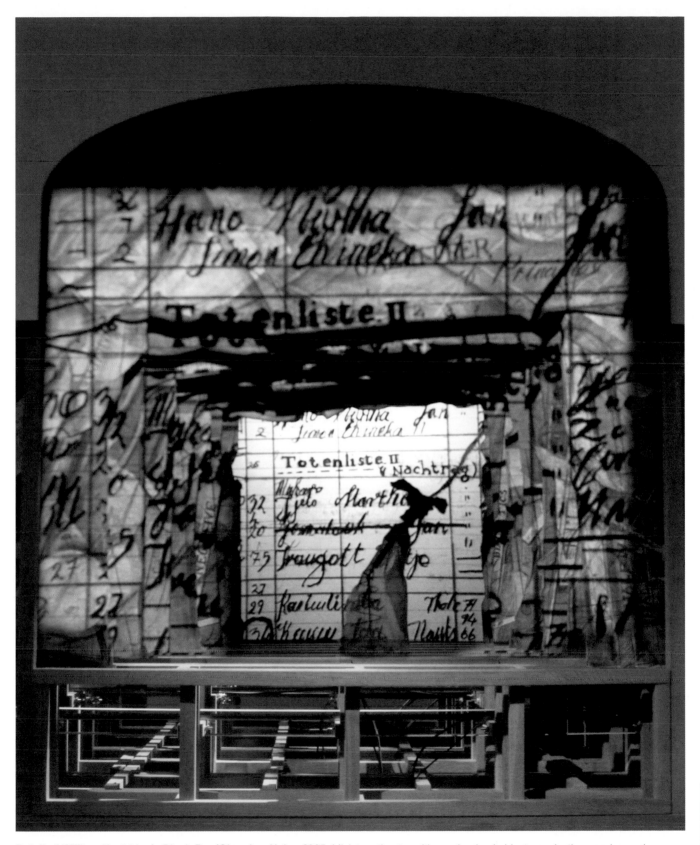

Detail of William Kentridge's *Black Box/Chambre Noire*, **2005.** Miniature theater with mechanized objects, projections and sound, dimensions variable.

Profile:
Roger Shimomura, Artist
Exploring Identity

Roger Shimomura's paintings, prints, and theater pieces address sociopolitical issues of Asian Americans and have often been inspired by 56 years of diaries kept by his late immigrant grandmother. He has had over a hundred solo exhibitions of his paintings and prints and has presented his experimental theater pieces nationally. Shimomura taught as a Distinguished Professor at The University of Kansas for 35 years and has been a visiting artist at over two hundred universities, art schools, and museums across the country. His work is found in nearly a thousand museums and private collections, including the Whitney Museum of American Art, Chicago Art Institute, Smithsonian, and Philadelphia Museum of Art.

MS: How do you define stereotyping, and why is it the focus of your artwork?

RS: Racial stereotyping is an oversimplified opinion or mental snapshot of members of that race. It's the focus of my artwork because it has caused harm to not only Asian Americans, but also every marginalized group in this country. This harm ranges from personal pain to larger legal actions that affect the entire community.

MS: What are the sources of your images?

RS: My sources range from old *Marvel* comic books to films by Kurosawa, from an image of Minnie Mouse to a geisha in an Utamaro print. Anything I see can generate an idea or become part of a composition.

Collecting objects and images that stereotype Japanese people is my current obsession. This includes Jap hunting licenses, slap-a-Jap club cards, postcards, ads, and movie posters featuring the buck-toothed, slant-eyed, yellow-skinned depictions of Asian people.

My collection of experiences is even more important. Following the Japanese attack on Pearl Harbor, my family was forcibly moved to Minidoka, a concentration camp in the southern Idaho desert. We were released two years later, when I was five years old. All through grade school and junior high, our favorite neighborhood game was not "Cowboys and Indians" but "Kill the Japs,"

bringing to life the values from the comics that I collected at that time. We reluctantly took turns being the "Jap," though we all preferred to be John Wayne, the most prolific Jap killer of the time. As a soldier during the Korean War, I was nicknamed "Pop-Up" because my fellow white officers thought I resembled the pop-up targets we used for target practice. All of these experiences feed into my exploration of stereotypes and racism.

MS: *Florence, South Carolina* is part of your "Stereotypes and Admonitions" series. Each painting in this series describes a single racist incident in a very straightforward, almost deadpan way. What is the advantage of this approach?

RS: It is the most direct and simplest way to tell a story of injustice. A verbal story accompanies the painting, making the content completely accessible. Hopefully, the work will resonate beyond the viewing, leading viewers to continue the conversation long after they leave.

MS: *Yellow Rat Bastard, Or How to Tell the Difference Between the Japanese and the Chinese* is much more complex. Can you talk us through this piece? What is the source and what do the various elements mean?

RS: *Yellow Rat Bastard* is a mixed media comparison between Roger (right panel) who is Japanese American, surrounded by his current family, with his friend, Norman Gee, who is a Chinese American painter.

It seems pretty simple. Each artist holds his respective country's chopsticks with either a short- or long-grained rice kernel, and is surrounded by appropriate cultural references. It gets complex when we look more carefully. Roger is married to a blonde-haired, blue-eyed Caucasian, has a daughter-in-law who is Filipina, and a grandchild that is half Filipino and half Japanese. Norman is married to a Japanese American (who studies Chinese Tai Chi). His children are half Chinese and half Japanese, as referenced by his daughter, who holds a bao (Chinese bun) in one hand and Makizushi (sushi roll) in the other.

Racist reminders are referenced by the WWII clichéd depiction of a *Yellow Peril Jap* looming behind Roger's portrait, while Fu Manchu peers out behind Norman's head. Both portraits are surrounded by contemporary pop icons from China and Japan.

Separating the two canvases is a shopping bag with the emblazoned words "Yellow Rat Bastard."

While this term was popularly used to describe the Japanese during WWII, it has been revived today, as the name of a trendy men's clothing store in New York City. Acting as a gesture to defuse the deadly yellow rat, the ears of a benign Mickey Mouse protrude out of the top of the bag. While non–Asian Americans continue to have difficulty distinguishing between the Japanese and Chinese, the unfortunate fact is that many still view Asians as a generically alien race in this country.

MS: You are renowned as a teacher as well as an artist. What advice can you offer to beginning students?

RS: When my students came up to me and said that they didn't know what to paint, I would tell them to take a hard look at themselves first. It is important to consider whether there is significant value in sharing what you are experiencing in life. Sometimes the simplest approach to making art ends up being the most poignant.

Roger Shimomura, *Yellow Rat Bastard*, 2006. Oil on canvas, 72 × 126 in. (182.9 × 320 cm).

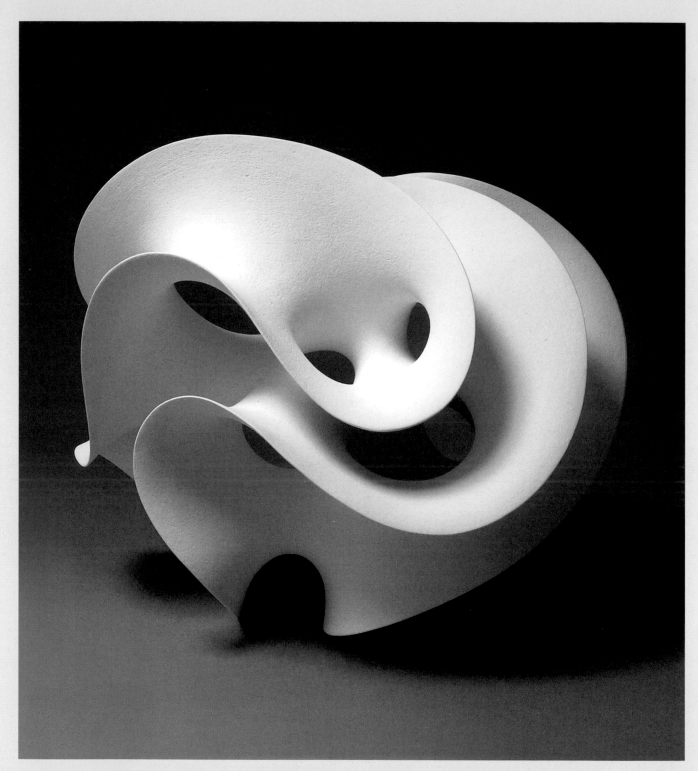

Eva Hild, *Lamella*, 2008. Stoneware, 26 × 23 × 22 in. (66 × 58 × 55 cm).

Three-Dimensional Design

As we begin our investigation of three-dimensional design, it is useful to consider both the similarities and differences between flat compositions and physical constructions. In both cases, the basic principles of design are used to create artworks that offer an effective balance between unity and variety. And, in both two- and three-dimensional design, concept development and critical thinking are complementary aspects of the creative process.

However, in two-dimensional design, we use our technical, perceptual, and conceptual skills to create flat visual patterns and convincing illusions. It is the viewer's *mental* response that gives the artwork meaning. In contrast, our experience in the three-dimensional world is more physical and direct. As we traverse an architectural space, we alter our perception with each step we take. When we circle a sculpture, we encounter new information on each side. The materials used in the construction of a three-dimensional object determine its aesthetic appeal as well as its structural strength.

This physical connection gives three-dimensional design inherent power. When we shift from an illusory world to a tangible world, a substantial shift in communication occurs. Confronted by the physical presence of a three-dimensional object, the viewer responds viscerally as well as mentally.

This section is devoted to the elements, organization, and implications of three-dimensional design. The basic building blocks are discussed in Chapter Nine. In Chapter Ten, the principles of three-dimensional design are described. The unique characteristics of various materials are considered in Chapter Eleven. Chapter Twelve is devoted to the ways in which artists have transformed their ideas into physical objects and to a discussion of differences between traditional and contemporary sculpture.

Part Three

Elements of Three-Dimensional Design

The chess pieces in Eddie Chui's *Let's Dance* (figure 6.5, page 135) rock back and forth on their curving bottoms. When the pieces are used in a game, their polished sides and hefty weight delight the players who hold them.

Beau Dick's *Mugamtl Mask* (*Crooked Beak*) (figure 5.10, page 116) embodies a powerful myth of deadly illness and glorious resurrection. When worn, it symbolically transforms an actor in costume into a man who can fly.

Xu Bing's *A Book from the Sky* (9.1) consists of printed volumes and scrolls containing thousands of "false" Chinese characters that he invented and then painstakingly hand-cut onto wooden printing blocks. Those who are not fluent in Chinese may admire the graceful characters and wonder at their meaning. Those who do know Chinese find that their familiar cultural references have turned into conceptual chaos. The 70-foot-long printed sheets of incomprehensible text mirror the books below and envelop the viewer in a world of mystery.

Our experience in the three-dimensional world is physical, cerebral, and emotional. While a painting or video can pull us into an imaginative world, a sculptural object offers a tangible presence that is powerful in itself. In the hands of a skillful artist or designer, this raw power is translated into insight and energy.

9.1 Xu Bing, *A Book from the Sky*, 1987–91. Hand printed books, ceiling and wall scrolls printed from wood letterpress type using false Chinese characters, dimensions variable.

Line, plane, volume, mass, space, texture, light, color, and time are the basic building blocks from which three-dimensional designs are made. In this chapter, we will consider the unique characteristics of each **element,** both individually and in combination with other elements.

FORM

As noted in Chapter Seven, **form** can be defined as the physical manifestation of an idea. **Content** refers to the idea itself, including the subject matter plus its emotional, intellectual, spiritual, and symbolic implications.

Form has an additional definition in three-dimensional design. In this context, *form* can refer to three-dimensionality itself. For example, a circle, a square, and a triangle are two-dimensional shapes, while a sphere, a cube, and a pyramid are three-dimensional forms.

Types of Form

- An empty three-dimensional form is generally

defined as a **volume,** while a solid form is generally defined as a **mass.**

- An effective three-dimensional composition balances **positive forms** (areas of substance) with **negative space.**

- **Organic forms** (forms that visually suggest nature or natural forces) create a very different effect than do **geometric forms,** which typically are based on cubes, spheres, and other simple volumes. **Mechanical forms,** such as belts and gears, can suggest an industrial source.

- The degree of actual or implied movement in a form can expand our vocabulary even further. **Static forms** appear stable and unmoving. Designed to last forever, the Great Pyramids at Giza exemplify stability and repose. **Dynamic forms** imply movement. *The Dance* (9.2), by Jean-Baptiste Carpeaux, is a highly dynamic form. Dominated by rotating figures and curving lines, this sculpture swirls with energy. **Kinetic forms** actually move. In Jean Tinguely's *Chaos 1* (9.3), a bowling ball on a track trips a series of movements in a massive mechanism.

9.2 Jean-Baptiste Carpeaux, *The Dance* **(after restoration), 1868–69.** Marble, 7 ft 6½ in. (2.3 m).

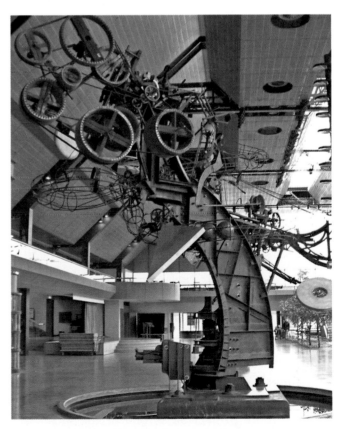

9.3 Jean Tinguely, *Chaos 1*, **1973–74.** Sculpture in Columbus Park. Metal construction with moving balls on tracks, electric motors, 30 × 28 × 15 ft (915 × 854 × 458 m).

Form and Function

Each artist seeks to express concepts and evoke emotions. Accordingly, a sculptor explores an idea, chooses materials, and develops a composition based on his or her aesthetic intention. Public art projects, such as Eero Saarinen's *Jefferson National Expansion Memorial* (9.4), and ritual objects, such as the Mugamtl mask, often commemorate historical events or express social values.

A designer uses the same mastery of concept, composition, and materials to create an object that is functional as well as beautiful. For example, when designing aquatic gear, designer Bob Evans carefully analyzes the needs of swimmers and then creates equipment to best meet those needs. The basic *Force Fin* (9.5A) provides the maneuverability needed for snorkeling. The *Multi Force Fin* (9.5B) was designed as a training device to strengthen a swimmer's legs, while the *Excellerating Force Fin* (9.5C) provides the extended power needed by scuba divers. For the designer, the form must fulfill a specific **function,** or purpose.

While an industrial designer has a different purpose than the sculptor, both use the same basic elements and principles of design. Both must organize line, plane, volume, mass, space, texture, and color into coherent form. The structural integrity of a sculpture is just as important as the structural integrity of a wheelchair, and a teapot that is both beautiful and functional is ideal.

Orthographic Projection

Height, width, and depth are the three dimensions in three-dimensional design. In computer-aided design, these three dimensions are defined using the x-, y-, and z-axes from geometry (9.6). Using the cube as a basic building block, we can create many variations on these basic dimensions. In figure 9.7A, the cube is modified through removal and displacement. In figure 9.7B and C, additional planes and unexpected intersections increase complexity.

There are many methods of depicting three-dimensional form on a two-dimensional surface. **Orthographic projection** is one of the most useful. Unlike perspective drawing, which relies on vanishing points to create the illusion of space,

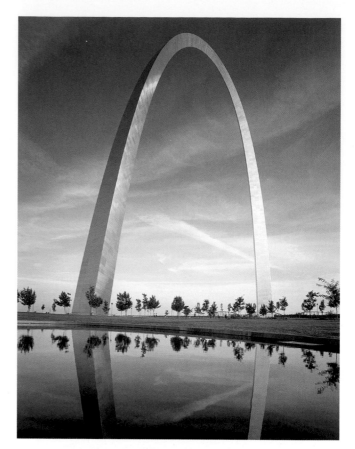

9.4 Eero Saarinen, *Jefferson National Expansion Memorial (Gateway Arch)*, St. Louis, 1966.

A Force Fin

B Multi Force Fin

C Excellerating Force Fin

9.5A–C Bob Evans, *Force Fin Variations*, 1990–present. Molded polyurethane, size variable.

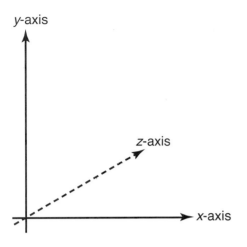

9.6 The three dimensions are defined through height, width, and depth.

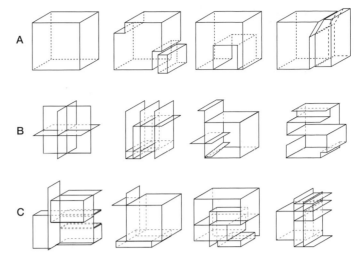

9.7A–C Variations on a cube.

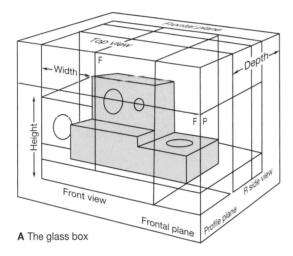

A The glass box

B Unfolding the glass box

orthographic projection uses parallel lines to define structural details. These details are essential to many types of construction.

An orthographic projection represents six views of a three-dimensional form. Imagine that your project is enclosed in a glass box (9.8A). As you look through the top, bottom, front, and back, then through the right and left sides, you can see six distinctive views. In effect, an orthographic drawing is created when you unfold and flatten this imaginary box (9.8B). Using orthographic projection, we can examine and record various surfaces of a three-dimensional object (9.8C).

C Rotating the object in space

9.8A–C Orthographic projection can be used to define structural details.

9.9 Robert Longo, *Corporate Wars* **(detail), 1982.** Cast aluminum, lacquer on wood relief, 7 × 9 × 3 ft (2.1 × 2.7 × 0.9 m).

Degrees of Dimensionality

Relief

When working in **relief,** the artist uses a flat backing (such as a wall or ceiling) as a base for three-dimensional forms. For example, Robert Longo's *Corporate Wars* (9.9) is like a sculptural painting. Using the boundaries created by the supporting wall and the four outer edges, it presents a group of white-collar warriors engaged in hand-to-hand combat. The figures are trapped, bound both to the backing and by their struggle for money.

Three-Quarter Works

A **three-quarter work,** such as Jean-Baptiste Carpeaux's *The Dance* (see figure 9.2) is more three-dimensional. We can walk around this piece, examining the front and two sides. As a result, the dancing figures create a vortex of implied motion. Based on the information we see, we assume that the dance continues into the wall.

Freestanding Works

Freestanding works are designed to be seen from all sides. When we circle Auguste Rodin's *The Kiss* (9.10A and B), we capture every nuance in the movement of the two figures. Details (such as the man's stroking hand and the woman's raised heel) bring life to the inanimate stone.

Environmental Works

An **environmental work** (or **environment**) presents a space that can be physically entered. Installations (which are usually presented indoors) and earthworks (which are usually presented outdoors) are two major types of environments. Such works often require active audience participation and may present a series of images, ideas, and experiences that unfold over time.

Installations

Typically, an **installation** is an ensemble of images and objects that are presented within a three-dimensional environment. Surrounded by information, we become emotionally and physically involved. For example, on entering Antoni Muntadas's *The Board Room* (9.11), the viewer confronts 13 chairs facing a long table. In a reference to the Last Supper described in the Bible, these chairs are accompanied by photographs of religious leaders, from Ayatollah Khomeini to Billy Graham. Inserted in the mouth of each man, a small video monitor plays a film clip showing him in action. In this installation, religion becomes an extension of both business and politics.

9.10A Auguste Rodin, *The Kiss*, 1886–98. Marble, over life size. Dramatic lighting accentuates form and can heighten emotion.

9.10B Auguste Rodin, *The Kiss*, 1886–98. Marble, over life size. A slight change in the viewer's position substantially changes the apparent orientation of the figures.

9.11 Antoni Muntadas, *The Board Room*, 1987. Installation at North Hall Gallery at Massachusetts College of Art, Boston. Thirteen chairs placed around a boardroom table. Behind each chair is a photo of a religious leader, in whose mouth a small video monitor shows the leader speaking. Subjects include Ayatollah Khomeini, Billy Graham, Sun Myung Moon, and Pope John Paul II.

The Board Room presents a series of clearly defined figures in a dark and dramatic setting. By contrast, Celotex panels covered with aluminum foil created a brightly lit and reflective space in Rudolf Stingel's installation (9.12). Visitors were invited to inscribe messages into the soft metal, creating overlapping layers of personal comments.

Earthworks

An **earthwork** is a large-scale outdoor installation. Often extending over great distances in time and space, earthworks may require substantial physical engagement by the artist, the audience, and inhabitants of the site. Robert Smithson's *Spiral Jetty* (9.13) is a classic example. This 1,500-foot-long coil of rock and earth extends from the shore into the water of the Great Salt Lake in Utah. For Smithson, the spiral created "a dot in the vast infinity of universes, an imperceptible point in a cosmic immensity, a speck in an impenetrable nowhere."[1] Remote and mysterious, this artwork evokes a cosmic connection that extends far beyond the walls of a museum or gallery.

9.12 Rudolf Stingel, *Untitled,* 2007. Chandelier and graffitied Celotex installation boards at the Whitney Museum of American Art.

9.13 Robert Smithson, *Spiral Jetty,* Great Salt Lake, Utah, 1970. Rock, salt crystals, earth, algae, coil, 1,500 ft (457 m).

9.14 Todd Slaughter, *Mano y Bola* **(details), 1997.** Aluminum and steel, hand 27 × 40 × 4 ft (8.2 × 12.2 × 1.2 m), ball 20 ft (6 m) diameter. Overlooking the Strait of Gibraltar.

Site-Specific Artwork

A **site-specific** artwork is designed for and installed in a particular place. Commissioned by the port city of Algeciras in Spain, *Mano y Bola* (9.14) rests on a bluff overlooking the Strait of Gibraltar. The 40-foot-long hand may be catching or throwing the 20-foot-tall ball positioned roughly 50 feet away. This artwork metaphorically alludes to the historical exchange of religion, power, and conflict between Europe and Africa. To heighten the metaphor, the hand has been designed to disappear when the wind blows. One thousand movable panels were covered with a photographic image of a hand. A brisk wind shifts the panels to a horizontal position, causing the image to dissolve visually into the surrounding sky.

Key Questions

FORM

- Experiment with organic, geometric, and mechanical forms. Which is best suited to the idea you wish to express?
- What proportion of static and dynamic forms is most appropriate for your artwork?
- Will the addition of a kinetic component add to or detract from the overall effect?
- When you are creating a freestanding artwork, how much similarity and how much contrast are needed on each side? What does the viewer gain by walking around the artwork?

LINE

In three-dimensional design, **line** can be created through the following:

- *A series of adjacent points.* The cars that make up Ant Farm's *Cadillac Ranch* (9.15) are distinct objects in themselves as well as the points that create a line of cars. Commissioned by a rancher in Texas, this sculpture has been described as a requiem for the gas-guzzling American automobile.[2]

- *A connection between points. Free Ride Home,* by Kenneth Snelson (9.16), was constructed using two types of line. The aluminum tubes provide a linear skeleton that becomes elevated when the connecting lines are attached. The resulting sculpture is compositionally dominated by diagonal lines that seem to defy gravity.

- *A point in motion.* A skater who wears the *Neon Skates* by Moira North and Rudi Stern (9.17) can literally create lines from a moving point of light. Because this artwork is dynamic, the simple skates become more dramatic.

9.15 Ant Farm (Chip Lord, Hudson Marquez, Doug Michels), Cadillac Ranch, 1974. Ten Cadillacs, Amarillo, TX.

9.17 Moira North and Rudi Stern, *Neon Skates,* 1986. Battery-operated neon skates for performance by The Ice Theater of New York, Moira North, director.

9.16 Kenneth Snelson, *Free Ride Home,* 1974. Aluminum and stainless steel, 30 × 30 × 60 ft (9.1 × 9.1 × 18.2 m). Storm King Art Center, Mountainville, NY.

Line Quality

Each line has its own distinctive quality. This quality is determined largely by the line's orientation, direction, and degree of continuity, as well as the material used.

Orientation

Orientation refers to the horizontal, vertical, or diagonal position of a line. Based on our experience in the natural world, we tend to associate horizontal lines with stability and diagonal lines with movement. Vertical lines tend to accentuate height and can make an object or an interior appear more formidable and imposing.

All three types of line are used in Mark di Suvero's *Ik Ook Eindhoven* (9.18) and Peter Pierobon's *Ladderback Chair* (9.19). The di Suvero sculpture is dominated by two horizontal I beams suspended from a nearly vertical support. The diagonal lines that are connected to this primary structure emphasize the weight of the artwork and add visual movement. On the other hand, it is the tall vertical back that transforms Pierobon's chair into a whimsical sculpture. Its exaggerated height pulls our eyes upward and provides support for the nine jagged lines that create the rungs of the ladder.

Curved lines can carve out complex patterns in space and may encompass an object to create a harmonious whole. For David Mach's *Eckow* (9.20), a full-size head was constructed from a collection of coat hangers. The undulating lines simultaneously define the form and create a vortex of energy.

9.18 Mark di Suvero, *Ik Ook Eindhoven,* **1971–72.** Painted steel, 24 × 24 × 33 ft (7.3 × 7.3 × 10 m).
In the background: *Are Years What?* **(for Marianne Moore), 1967.** Painted steel, 40 × 40 × 30 ft (12.2 × 12.2 × 9.1 m).

9.19 Peter Pierobon, *Ladderback Chair.* Firm &
Manufacturer: Snyderman Gallery.

9.20 David Mach, *Eckow,* **1997.** Coat hangers, 2 ft 2¼ in. ×
1 ft 11½ in. × 2 ft 5½ in. (67 × 60 × 75 cm).

9.21 Chris Burden, *Medusa's Head,* **1989–92.** Cement, wood, stone, train tracks, 16 ft (4.8 m) diameter, 5 tons.

Direction

Direction refers to the implied movement of a line. A line of consistent width tends to suggest equal movement in both directions. Varying line width can create a more specific sense of direction. For example, in *Jefferson National Expansion Memorial* (see figure 9.4, page 182), the massive lines at the bottom drive downward into the earth, while the tapered arch at the top lifts our eyes skyward.

Continuity

Continuity, or linear flow, can increase movement and accentuate form. In David Mach's *Eckow* (9.20), the smooth metal is both elegant and energetic. Continuity plays a very different role in Chris Burden's *Medusa's Head* (9.21). Here, a mad tangle of toy train tracks flows around and through the mass of stone, plywood, and cement. Representing the snakes that crowned the head of a mythical monster, these writhing lines accentuate the spherical mass and give us a fresh interpretation of an ancient Greek myth.

Actual Lines

Through their physical presence, **actual lines** can connect, define, or divide a design. *Laocoön and His Two Sons* (9.22) depicts a scene from the Trojan War. When the Greeks offer a large, hollow wooden horse to the Trojans, Laocoön warns against accepting the gift. The Greek goddess Athena then sends two serpents to attack and kill the seer, thereby gaining entry into Troy for the soldiers hidden in the horse. The writhing serpent compositionally connects the terrified men while adding emotional intensity to this depiction of Athena's wrath.

Implied Lines

Implied lines are created through mental rather than physical connections. *The Rape of the Sabine Women*, by Giovanni da Bologna (9.23), relies on a series of implied lines for its impact. Starting at the bottom and exploding upward, the repeated diagonals in the sculpture create a visual vortex as powerful as a tornado. At the bottom is the husband of the captured

9.22 Laocoön and His Two Sons. Marble, 7 ft (2.13 m).

9.23 Giovanni da Bologna, *The Rape of the Sabine Women,* **completed 1583.** Marble, 13 ft 6 in. (4.1 m).

9.24 Nancy Holt, *Sun Tunnels*, 1973–76. Great Basin Desert, UT. Four tunnels, each 18 ft long × 9 ft 4 in. diameter (5.5 × 2.8 m), each axis 86 ft long (26.2 m). Aligned with sunrises and sunsets on the solstices.

9.25 Steve McAllister, *Fencing Mask.*
Photograph.

woman. In the center, a standing Roman soldier is intent on stealing a wife for himself. The agitated movement culminates at the top with the extended arm of the embattled woman.

A **sight line** activates Nancy Holt's *Sun Tunnels* (9.24). At first glance, the four 22-ton concrete tunnels seem static. Upon entering each tunnel, the viewer discovers a series of holes that duplicate the size and position of the stars in four major constellations. The light pouring in through these holes shifts as the sun rises and travels across the sky. During the winter and summer solstices, the sculpture is further transformed as light from the rising and setting sun is framed by an alignment of the circular tunnels. Like a telescope, the massive cylinders are more important for the visions they create than as objects in themselves.

Line Networks

Both artists and designers use linear networks in many different ways. In figure 9.25, interlocking metal lines form the woven mesh on a fencer's mask. Due to its linear construction, it is light in weight and protects the athlete's face without blocking vision. As shown in Claire Zeisler's *Red Forest* (9.26), most fiber works are created through the organization of multiple lines of thread, yarn, or other materials. Single lines can bring a simple eloquence to a design, while multiple lines can be used to create strong, complex, and versatile forms.

Key Questions

LINE

- Vertical, horizontal, diagonal, and curving lines all have unique strengths. What can each type contribute to your design?
- What can line continuity or discontinuity contribute to your composition?
- What happens when you dramatically increase or decrease the number of lines?
- Can intersecting lines strengthen your design, both structurally and compositionally?

9.26 Claire Zeisler, *Red Forest*, 1968. Dyed jute, 8 ft 2 in. × 7 ft 4 in. × 2 ft (249 × 224 × 61 cm).

PLANE

A **plane** is a three-dimensional form that has length and width but minimal thickness. Depending on the material used, planes can be transparent or opaque, rigid or flexible, flat or curved. Complex surfaces and enclosures can be constructed using folded or bent planes, and when slotted together planes can be used to create a variety of sturdy forms (9.27). As demonstrated by Maya Lin's *Blue Lake Pass* (9.28), when modified incrementally and organized sequentially, planes can create forms that are as descriptive as a topographical map.

Alexander Calder was a master of planar construction. In his famous mobiles (9.29), he put simple planes in motion. Inspired by the delicate weights and balances he saw in the paintings of Piet Mondrian (see figure 3.32, page 80), Calder used these structures to represent the movement of heavenly bodies within the universe. Exquisitely balanced, the flat planes and curving lines can be activated by the slightest flow of air.

Finallly, intersecting planes can create large-scale structures that are remarkably strong. With outdoor sculptures, such as Alexander Calder's *La Grande Vitesse* (9.30), structural integrity is especially important. Located in a public plaza, the sculpture must withstand wind, rain, and snow while presenting minimal risk to pedestrians. Intersecting planes combined with a ribbed reinforcement at stress points create a durable structure.

9.27 *Scapes* cards. Artist: Darren Waterston. Designer: Ryan Burlinson. Art direction: Kurt Wolken. Client: Bellevue Art Museum. Wolken, Communica, Seattle, WA.

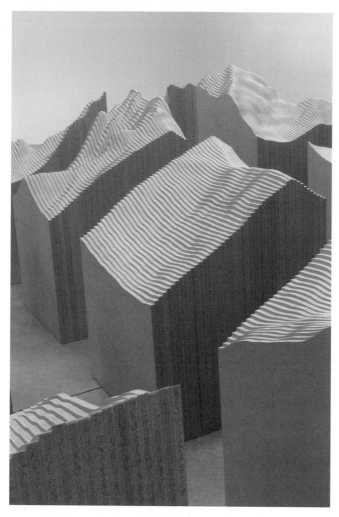

9.28 Maya Lin, *Blue Lake Pass* (detail), 2006. Duraflake particleboard, 20 blocks, approx. 5¾ × 17½ × 22½ ft (1.75 × 5.3 × 6.8 m).

9.29 Alexander Calder, *125,* also known as *Flight,* 1957. Painted aluminum and tempered steel, 300 in. × 540 in. × 204 in.

Key Questions

PLANE

- Consider the limitations of the material you are using. Can it be cut or scored and folded to create curving planes?

- What are the structural and compositional advantages of curved or twisted planes versus flat planes?

- What happens to your design when you pierce or slot together any or all of the planes?

VOLUME AND MASS

Volume

In general terms, volume is the amount of space an object occupies. In three-dimensional design, **volume** refers to an enclosed area of three-dimensional space.

Cubes, cylinders, cones, and spheres are among the most prevalent volumes found in both nature and architecture. Fascinated by such "biological structures," Kendall Buster has created entire exhibitions using large-scale, translucent volumes (9.31). By contrast, Xiao Min created his *Secret Room* series from elegant and seemingly weightless organic volumes. Using a twelfth-century Chinese sex manual as a source, he constructed a series of life-sized

9.30 Alexander Calder, *La Grande Vitesse*, 1969. Painted steel plate, 43 × 55 ft (13.1 × 16.8 m). Calder Plaza, Vandenberg Center, Grand Rapids, MI.

9.31 Kendall Buster, *New Growth*, 2007. Steel frame, cable ties, greenhouse shadecloth. Installation at Boise Art Museum. Size variable.

9.32 Xiao Min, *Secret Room #3*, 2008. Steel wire, 90 × 19 × 17 in. (127 × 48 × 43 cm).

couples embracing. Made from translucent sheets of steel wire, the suspended figures are both dreamlike and erotic (9.32).

Designers often create functional objects using **polyhedra,** or multifaceted volumes (9.33). Such volumes can be surprisingly strong. In an assignment at The Ohio State University (9.34), students used a variety of polyhedra to construct lightweight bristol board helmets.

The specific amount of enclosed space is especially important when we create any kind of container, from architecture to glassware. *The Ginevra*

Carafe, by Ettore Sottsass (9.35), easily holds a liter of wine. The elegant cylinder requires little table space, and an extra disk of glass at the base increases its weight and stability. An additional glass cylinder at the top ensures that the lid will remain firmly in place.

Linear networks, folding, and slotting are a few of the strategies artists and designers use to create volume. Defining an enclosed space while maintaining structural integrity is essential. If the structure fails, the volume will collapse and the space will be lost.

Each strategy has its advantages. As demonstrated by the fencer's mask in figure 9.25 (page 190), woven structures can be elegant, lightweight, and remarkably strong. On the other hand, package designers generally create volume through folding. The heavy paper used for this purpose can be printed while flat, then scored, cut, and folded. The patterns used are mathematically specific and often structurally complex. And surprisingly strong volumes can be created using slotted planes. Slotted structures can be used to protect and separate fragile contents (such as wine bottles) and hold them in a specific position.

9.34 **Charles Wallschlaeger,** professor emeritus, The Ohio State University, Department of Industrial, Interior, and Visual Communication Design. OSU students used a variety of polyhedra to construct bristol board helmets.

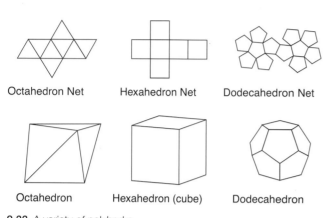

Octahedron Net   Hexahedron Net   Dodecahedron Net

Octahedron   Hexahedron (cube)   Dodecahedron

9.33 A variety of polyhedra.

Mass

A **mass** is a solid three-dimensional form. A massive object can be as dense and heavy as a bar of gold or as light and porous as a sponge.

Massive sculptures are often carved from a solid block of plaster, clay, or stone or cast using bronze, glass, or other materials. Solid and imposing, they tend to dominate the environment in which they are placed.

Just as Alexander Calder took advantage of the buoyancy of a thin plane to create his mobiles, so did Henry Moore take advantage of the power of mass when he created *Locking Piece* (9.36A). In such structures, the **primary contours** (or outer edges) are complemented by the **secondary contours** created by internal edges (9.36B). As the viewer circles the form, these contours visually alternate as the primary contours become the secondary contours and the secondary contours become the primary contours.

Massive forms tend to suggest stability, power, and permanence. A series of colossal heads produced by the Olmec people of ancient Mexico combine the abstract power of a sphere with the specific power of a human head (9.37). Tom Friedman produced a very different type of mass in figure 9.38. He cut hundreds of pencils at various angles, and then reconstructed them to create an energetic maze.

9.35 **Ettore Sottsass,** *Ginevra Carafe,* **1997.** Manufactured by Alessi, Crusinallo, Italy.

A

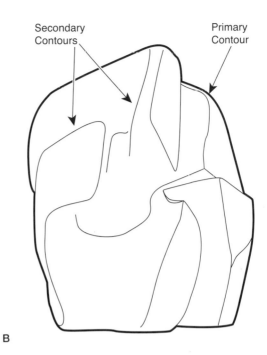

B

9.36A and B Henry Moore, *Locking Piece*, 1963–64. Bronze, 115 × 110¼ × 90½ in. (292 × 280 × 230 cm).

In diagram B, the labels read: Secondary Contours, Primary Contour.

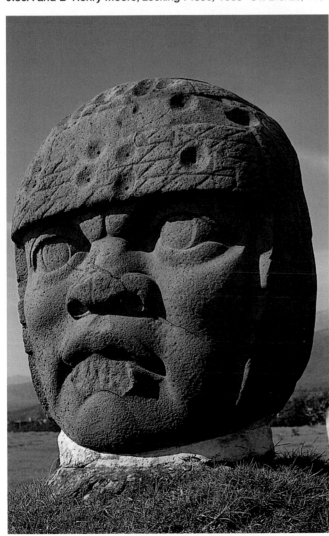

9.37 *Colossal Head*, 1300–800 BCE. Stone, 11 × 9⅝ × 9⅝ ft (3.4 × 3 × 3 m). Olmec culture, Jalapa, Veracruz, Mexico.

Key Questions

VOLUME AND MASS

- How can planar source materials (such as bristol paper and cardboard) be used to create sturdy volumes?

- What are the advantages of transparent versus opaque volumes?

- An enclosed volume can be filled with space, sand, marbles, or other materials. Experiment!

9.38 Tom Friedman, *Untitled*, 1995. Pencils cut at 45-degree angles and glued in a continuous loop, 11 × 14 × 11 in. (28 × 35 × 28 cm).

SPACE

In three-dimensional design, **space** is the area within or around an area of substance. A dialogue between a form and its surroundings is created as soon as an artist positions an object in space. Space is the partner to substance. Without it, line, plane, volume, and mass lose both visual impact and functional purpose.

The proportion of space to substance triggers an immediate response. The space in Alice Aycock's *Tree of Life Fantasy* (9.39) is defined by a filigree of delicate lines and planes. Inspired by the double-helix structure of DNA and by medieval illustrations showing people entering paradise through a spinning hole in the sky, Aycock combined a linear structure with a series of circular planes. The resulting sculpture is as open and playful as a roller coaster. By comparison, Burden's *Medusa's Head* (see figure 9.21, page 190) presents a relatively solid mass of tangled cement, wood, and metal. With sculptures of this kind, the *surrounding* space becomes more important than any enclosed space. Like a stone placed in a glass of water, the large, solid mass seems to displace the surrounding space, pushing it into the edges of the room.

Positive and Negative Space

The interrelationship between space and substance is demonstrated in every area of three-dimensional design. David Smith's *Cubi XXVII* (9.40) is dominated by a central void. The 10 gleaming geometric volumes are activated by the space they enclose. Space plays an equally important role in representational work. The open mouth in *Model of a Trophy Head* (9.41) really animates the mask. No facial expression, however extreme, would be as lively if this mouth were closed.

Negative space is especially noticeable in designs that are dominated by positive form. Karen Karnes's *Vessel* (9.42) is a functional pot, with its internal bottom placed just above the vertical slit. In effect, the lower half of the design serves as a pedestal for the functional container at the top. This narrow slit of negative space presents a strong contrast to the solidity of the cylindrical form and helps activate the entire form.

Compression and Expansion

Space is never passive or meaningless. It is just as important as the surrounding substance, and it can be manipulated very deliberately. The tangibility of space is especially apparent in the works of Richard

9.39 Alice Aycock, *Tree of Life Fantasy*, Synopsis of the Book of Questions Concerning the World Order and/or the Order of Worlds, 1990–92. Painted steel, fiberglass, and wood, 20 × 15 × 8 ft (6.1 × 4.6 × 2.4 m).

Serra and Walter de Maria. Using four enormous steel plates, Serra created a sense of spatial compression in figure 9.43. Upon entering the piece, the viewer immediately becomes aware of the weight of the tilted planes and of the support the compressed space seems to provide. The space in de Maria's *The Lightning Field* (9.44) is equally clearly defined yet is wonderfully expansive. Arranged in a grid over nearly 1 square mile of desert, 400 steel poles act as a collection of lightning rods. Impressive even in daylight, the site becomes awe-inspiring during a thunderstorm. Lightning jumps from pole to pole and from the sky to earth, creating a breathtaking pyrotechnic display.

Activated Space

The space in an artwork may be contemplative, agitated, or even threatening. For example, a Japanese Zen garden is usually made from an enclosure containing several large rocks surrounded by carefully raked white sand. A few simple objects

9.40 David Smith, *Cubi XXVII,* **March 1965.** Stainless steel, 111⅜ × 87¾ × 34 in. (282.9 × 222.9 × 86 cm).

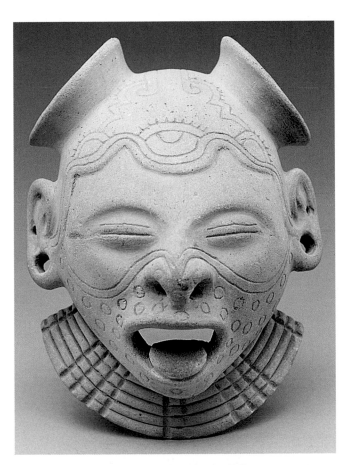

9.41 *Model of a Trophy Head,* **Ecuador, La Tolita, 600 BCE–AD 400.** Ceramic.

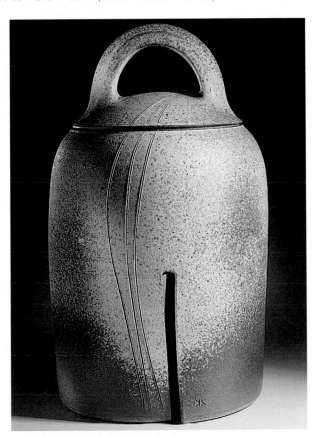

9.42 Karen Karnes, *Vessel,* **1987.** Stoneware, wheel-thrown, glazed, and wood-fired, 16½ × 10½ in. (41.9 × 26.7 cm).

9.43 Richard Serra, *Betwixt the Torus and the Sphere,* **2001.** Weatherproof steel, 142 × 450 × 319 in. (361 × 1,143 × 810 cm).

9.44 Walter de Maria, *The Lightning Field,* **1977.** Stainless steel poles, average height 20 ft 7½ in. (6.1 m), overall 5,280 × 3,300 ft (1,609.34 × 1,005.84 m). Near Quemado, NM.

are used to create a contemplative space. By contrast, the space in Anish Kapoor's sculptures is often disorienting. Placed at the entrance to Millennium Park in Chicago, *Cloud Gate* reflects the surrounding buildings while the lower "gate" section visually pulls the viewer into a reflective interior chamber (9.45).

Entering Space

Some sculptures are designed to be entered physically. Lucas Samaras's *Mirrored Room* (9.46) multiplies and divides the reflection of each visitor who enters. Other sculptures can be entered only mentally. *Subway with Silver Girders* (9.47), by Donna Dennis, re-creates in great detail the architecture and lighting we find in a subway station. Constructed at two-thirds the scale of an actual station,

the sculpture presents a magical entry into a prosaic place. This subway station provides transportation for the mind rather than the body.

Key Questions

SPACE

- What relationships between substance and space have you built into your design?

- What would happen if you substantially increased or decreased the amount of space? For example, would 70 percent space and 30 percent mass strengthen or weaken your design?

- How might space play a stronger conceptual and compositional role in your design?

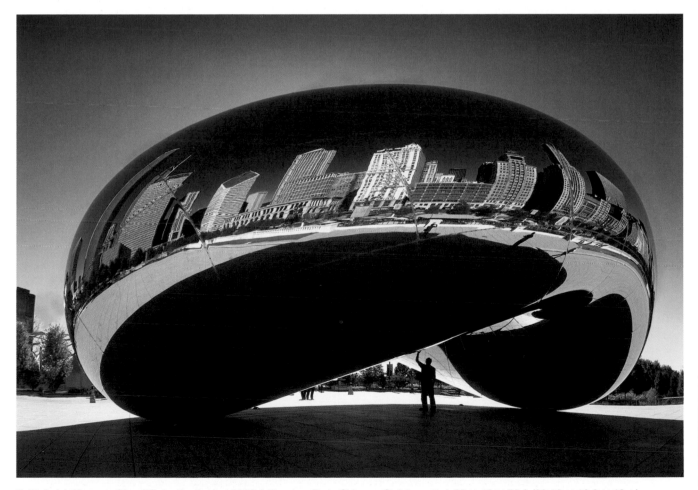

9.45 Anish Kapoor, *Cloud Gate*, Dedicated 2006. Millennium Park, Chicago. Stainless steel, 66 × 42 × 33 ft (20.12 × 12.8 × 10 m). Visitors and the surrounding city are reflected in the mirrorlike finish.

9.46 Lucas Samaras, *Mirrored Room,* **1966.** Mirrors on wooden frame, 8 × 8 × 10 ft (2.44 × 2.44 × 3 m).

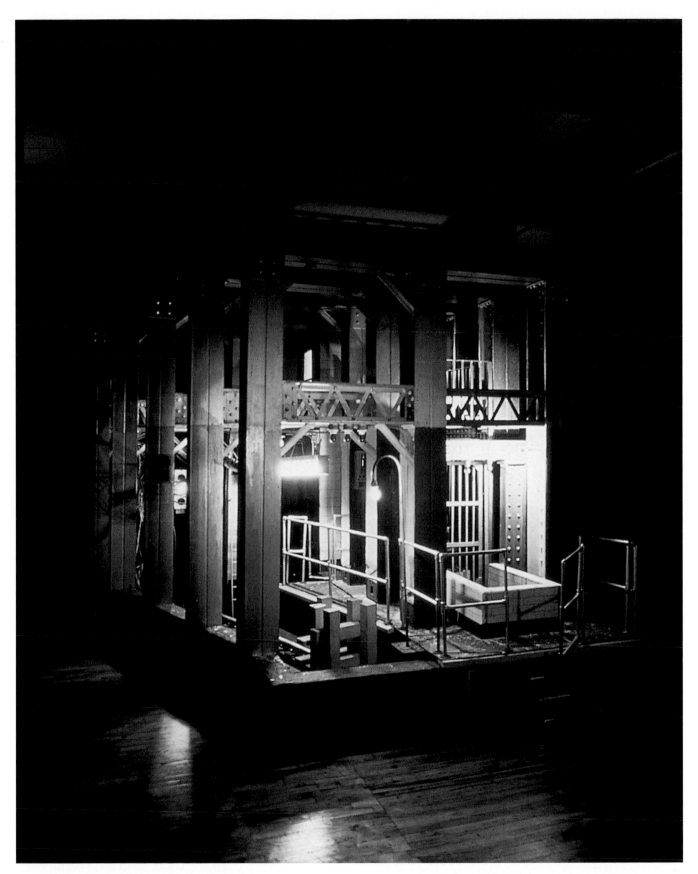

9.47 Donna Dennis, *Subway with Silver Girders,* **1981–82.** Wood, masonite, acrylic, enamel, cellulose compound, glass, electrical fixtures, and metal, 12 × 12 × 13.5 ft (3.6 × 3.6 × 4.11 m).

TEXTURE

Texture refers to the visual or tactile quality of a form. The increased surface area of a three-dimensional form heightens the impact of texture. The surface shifts and turns, presenting numerous opportunities for textural elaboration.

Degrees of Texture

Variations in the suface of a volume may be subtle or pronounced. In *Blackware Storage Jar*, by Maria Montoya Martinez and Julian Martinez (9.48), a burnished, shiny surface was combined with a subtle matte surface. The visual effect is dramatic despite the minimal textural variation. Geometric patterns enhance the surface of the jar but never compete with the purity of the graceful globe. On the other hand, Walter Oltmann's *Pillow* (9.49) is abuzz with texture. Hundreds of fragments of metal wire have been organized into a wide variety of textural units to create the oversized insect. In this case, the smoother areas on the extended legs contrast beautifully with the more compact textures on the wings and in the surrounding border. The result is a technical tour de force and a conceptual puzzle: Why is there a fly on my pillow?

9.48 Maria Montoya Martinez and Julian Martinez, *Blackware Storage Jar*, 1942. Hopi, from San Ildefonso Pueblo, NM. Ceramic, 18¾ × 22½ in. (47.6 × 57.1 cm).

9.49 Walter Oltmann, *Pillow*, 2004. Aluminum wire, 40.9 × 39 × 9 in. (104 × 101 × 23 cm).

Characteristic and Contradictory Textures

Every material has its own inherent textural properties. Clay, glass, and metal can be poured, cast, or pressed to create a wide variety of textures. Gold, which may occur in nature as dust, in nuggets, or in veins, can be cast, hammered, enameled, and soldered. Despite the adaptability of most materials, however, we are accustomed to their being used in specific ways. The reflective surface of a steel teapot, the transparency of glass, and the earthy functionality of clay fulfill our expectations.

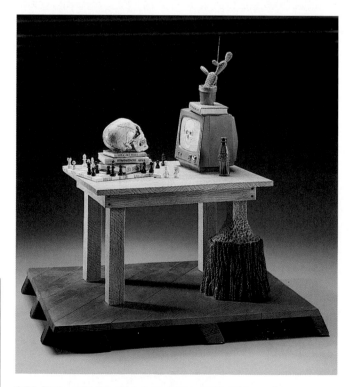

9.50 Richard Notkin, *Vain Imaginings*, 1978. White earthenware, glaze, brass, redwood, white cedarwood, 16 × 13½ × 16½ in. (40.6 × 34.3 × 41.9 cm).

9.51 **Globular vessel with inverted rim, tenth century, Igbo, Nigeria.** Terra-cotta, 16 in. (40.6 cm).

9.52 **Takako Araki, *Rock Bible*, 1995.** Ceramic, silkscreen, 8¼ × 23⅝ × 16½ in. (21 × 60 × 42 cm).

When a material is used in an uncharacteristic way or when strange textures are added to familiar forms, we must reappraise both the material and the object it represents. Except for the wooden platform and brass screws, Richard Notkin's *Vain Imaginings* (9.50) is made of clay. The textures of wood, plastic, glass, and bone have been skillfully imitated. Clay is very unlike any of these materials, and a purist might argue that such mimicry violates its inherent nature. On closer examination, however, we can see a perfect match between the image and the idea. The table, which symbolizes the world, supports a chess set, which suggests risk, and a television set, which presents an illusion. The ceramic skull is placed on top of four books titled *The Shallow Life, Moth and Rust, Vain Imaginings,* and *By Bread Alone.* The image on the screen repeats the skull. The clay itself suggests impermanence (as in "he has feet of clay") and mortality (as in "earth to earth, dust to dust," which is often said during funerals). In this masterwork of metaphor, ceramicist Richard Notkin has created a "fake" sculpture for a false world.

The Implications of Texture

On a compositional level, texture can enhance or defy our understanding of a physical form. In figure 9.51, the lines carved into the surface of the vessel increase our awareness of its dimensionality. Concentric circles surrounding the knobs at the base of each handle create a series of visual targets that circle the globe, while additional grooves accentuate the surface of the sturdy handles. On a conceptual level, texture can add layers of meaning to art and design. In *Rock Bible* (9.52), Takako Araki used three kinds of texture to animate the artwork and expand its meaning. The words on the pages of the Bible provide one texture, the rough surface of the disintegrating book provides a second, and the inherent texture of the clay provides a third.

In summary, texture can increase the surface area of an object, add contrast, and enrich our understanding of the physical and conceptual qualities of any three-dimensional object.

Key Questions

TEXTURE

- How many textures can be created with the material you are using?
- What happens visually when a surface gradually shifts from a polished, smooth texture to a very rough texture?
- Can contradictory texture enhance or expand the idea you want to convey?

LIGHT

Light can enhance or obscure our understanding of form. It can entice us to enter a room, heighten our emotions, and create a mystery. It can even become a sculptural medium in its own right. Often overlooked, light is actually a pivotal aspect of three-dimensional design.

9.53 Daniel Chester French, *Head of Abraham Lincoln* **(detail of seated figure), 1911–22.** Full-size plaster model of head of marble statue, Lincoln Memorial, Washington, DC, 1917–18. Head 50½ in. (128.3 cm), total figure 19 ft (5.8 m) h.

9.54 Stan Rickel, *Teapot Sketches,* **1991.** Mixed mediums, 12 × 12 × 12 in. (30.5 × 30.5 × 30.5 cm).

Value and Volume

A gradated series of highlights and shadows is produced whenever light pours across a surface. These values, or variations in light and dark, are our primary means of perceiving space. As demonstrated by two views of Daniel Chester French's *Head of Abraham Lincoln* (9.53), a surface that appears flat when lit from the front can become spatially rich when lit from the top or sides. Product designers are equally aware of the importance of light. A badly lit form will lack definition and impact, while even the simplest form will attract attention when it is dramatically lit. In figure 9.54, highlights, gradations, and shadows give definition to each of Stan Rickel's *Teapot Sketches.*

Striking a Surface

Light is strongly affected by the substance it strikes. As demonstrated by the teapots, light creates a continuous series of values when it strikes an opaque surface. Light behaves very differently when it strikes a **transparent** surface, such as clear plastic or glass. It is often **refracted** (or bent), creating a complex network of luminous shapes. **Reflective** surfaces can bounce light back into space. As a result, objects that are made from polished steel, mirrors, and other reflective materials can appear to emit their own light. A **translucent** surface is partially transparent. Neither fully opaque nor fully transparent, translucent surfaces can be mysterious and evocative.

Each type of surface can be used expressively. *The Dance* (figure 9.2) is dominated by the movement of seven opaque figures in and out of space. Light and shadow accentuate the action of the exuberant dancers. The same composition would dissolve into visual chaos if it were cast in transparent glass. Cast shadows further expand expressive potential. In Ruth Asawa's sculptures (9.55), suspended organic forms seem to float through the silent space. Spotlights illuminate the sculptures and create mysterious cast shadows.

Translucent materials can create even more complex effects. Robert Irwin's *Part II: Excursus: Homage to the Square*[3] (9.56) was installed at the Dia Center for the Arts in New York in 1998–99. This structure consisted of nine cubic rooms, defined by delicate walls of translucent cloth. The translucency of the fabric varied depending on the amount and location of the light. Two vertical fluorescent lights illuminated each cube, creating subtle changes in color from room to room.

Entering the installation was both inviting and disorienting. From any point, all of the rooms were visible yet veiled. The layers of fabric and the variations in light made the most distant rooms appear to dissolve. The vertical fluorescent lights, which always remained visible, read first as individual, then as mirror, images, creating a hallucinatory experience similar to a carnival funhouse. All activity within the space was created by the visitors themselves, who entered, explored, and left the installation like ghostly silhouettes.

9.55 Ruth Asawa, *Exhibition at de Young Art Museum in San Francisco*, 2005.

9.56 Robert Irwin, *Part II: Excursus: Homage to the Square³*. Installation at Dia Center for the Arts, New York, September 1998–June 1999.

Ambient and Directed Light

Ambient light encompasses an entire space or setting. For example, when we enter an open courtyard on a sunny summer afternoon, we are surrounded by warm ambient sunlight. Everything we see is colorful and brightly lit. **Directed light** is localized and focused, like a spotlight on a singer.

Exhibition designers are masters of light. They use directed light to focus the viewer's attention and increase visual drama. They use ambient light to create the underlying feeling. For example, the designers of a 1989 NASA exhibition used low ambient light to suggest the mystery of space travel. Bright pools of directed light were then used to emphasize individual displays (9.57).

Light as Sculpture

Many types of sculptural light are used by contemporary artists and designers. Some shape neon tubes into sculptural forms. Others use commercial lighting fixtures and illuminated signs to convey aesthetic meaning. Still others project light onto various shapes and surfaces, creating effects ranging from the humorous to the tragic to the bizarre.

Projection and containment are two common ways to create sculptural light. The neon tubes in Robert Irwin's *Excursus* emit light, while in Ruth Asawa's work light is projected to create expressive shadows. Stephen Knapp's light paintings (9.58) are created when light passes through shards of colored glass, creating a prismatic explosion. In all these cases, light is an essential component of the artwork.

The expressive possibilities increase when an image is projected onto a specific surface. On the anniversary of the bombing of Hiroshima, Krzysztof Wodiczko combined video interviews with a specific architectural structure—the A-Bomb monument, one of the few buildings that remained standing after the explosion (9.59). Standing near the epicenter, over 5,000 spectators heard the stories of Japanese and Korean survivors from World War II.

With the increasing use of new media, light has become an eloquent and versatile addition to the elements of three-dimensional design. Moving beyond its traditional role in accentuating form, it has become a sculptural medium in itself. For example, in *The Veiling* (9.60), Bill Viola hung thin sheets of translucent fabric on parallel lines across the center of a darkened room. An image of a man was projected from one end, while an image of a woman was projected from the opposite end. These projections became increasingly diffused as they passed through the multiple layers of cloth. Finally, the two figures merged on a central veil as pure presences of light.

9.57 NASA Exhibit at the 1989 Paris Air Show. Designers: Bill Cannan, Tony Ortiz, H. Kurt Heinz. Design Firm: Bill Cannan & Co.

9.58 Stephen Knapp installing *First Symphony.*

Key Questions

LIGHT

- How can lighting direction diminish or accentuate the dimensionality of your artwork?

- Does your artwork require special illumination, such as an internal light source, fiber optics, or a video screen?

- How can light enhance the expressive content of your artwork?

- Can your project be redesigned to use light and shadow more effectively? If so, how?

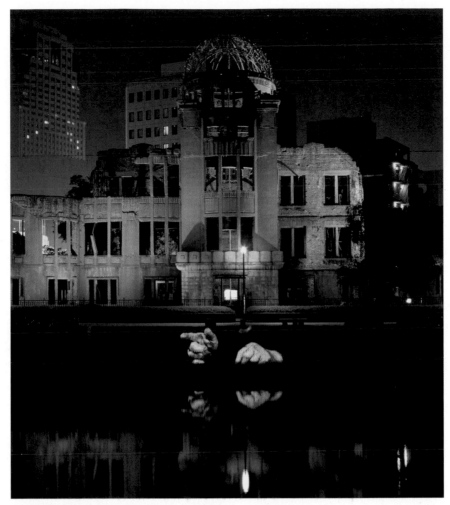

9.59 Krzysztof Wodiczko, *Hiroshima Projection,* **1998.** Public projection of video images at the A-Bomb Dome, Hiroshima, Japan.

9.60 Bill Viola, *The Veiling,* **1995.** Video/sound installation.

COLOR

Color definitions remain the same whether we are creating a three-dimensional or a two-dimensional composition. Each color has a specific **hue** (9.61A), which is determined by its wavelength. **Value** (9.61B), the lightness or darkness of a color, helps determine legibility. **Intensity,** or **saturation** (9.61C), refers to the purity of a color. **Temperature** (9.61D) refers to the psychological characteristics attributed to a color.

Degrees of Harmony

Selecting the right colors for a product and determining the degree of color **harmony** can make or break a design. The triadic harmony used in the Smartronics Learning System by Fisher-Price (9.62) creates an attractive educational toy for young children. The large red, yellow, and blue buttons are easy to push and invite even the most skeptical child to play. A very different type of harmony is offered in *Kita Collection,* by Toshiyuki Kita (9.63). These simple chairs with their removable seats can be color-customized to fit any interior. The buyer can create his or her own sense of harmony.

Analogous colors, such as green, blue, and violet, can be especially harmonious. In *Reflection* (9.64), Do Ho Suh used such colors to produce a mysterious mirrored image. The inverted gatelike form was combined with its reflected counterpart to create an installation that was both magical and meditative.

9.61A Hue.

9.61B Value.

9.61C Intensity.

9.61D Temperature.

Clashing colors can also be used effectively. In figure 9.65, Keith Edmier portrays his pregnant mother on the day President Kennedy was assassinated. She is wearing the same Chanel suit pattern that Jackie Kennedy wore, and she pensively rubs her glowing belly. The artist himself appears as a fetus in the womb. The orange-reds and purple-reds suggest traditional monochromatic harmony but seem skewed and off-key. While the surface of normalcy remained intact, the substance of American politics shifted after Kennedy's death. Likewise, while the artist's mother seems calm, the colors and materials used suggest an undercurrent of anxiety.

9.62 Smartronics Learning System by Fisher-Price.

9.63 Toshiyuki Kita, *Kita Collection* of chairs with removable seats for Stendig International Inc. Beechwood frame and upholstered seat.

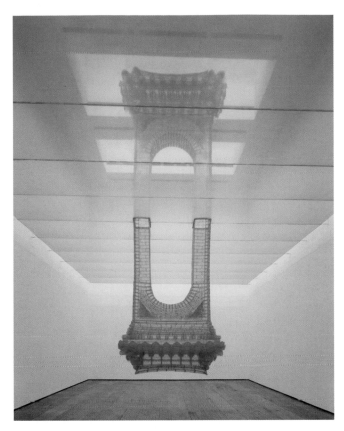

9.64 Do Ho Suh, *Reflection*, 2004. Nylon and stainless steel tubing, dimensions variable.

Contrast

Artists and designers often use contrasting colors to accentuate the function of a product or to create a distinctive image. Contrasting colors and contrasting materials distinguish Michael Graves's *Alessi Coffee Set* (9.66). The fragile, transparent glass is protected by metallic armor. These metal bands emphasize the cylindrical forms, while the blue handles and bright red accents further animate the set.

Using natural materials in natural settings, Andy Goldsworthy often creates intense areas of red, green, or gold to alert the viewer to junctions, boundaries, or unusual configurations between objects in the landscape. These accents of color are especially powerful when the surrounding colors are subdued. In figure 9.67, scarlet leaves dramatically distinguish the central stone from its somber gray neighbors.

Color and Emotion

The emotional implications of color can be demonstrated by a visit to any car dealership. Bright red, black, or silver sports cars are often marketed as

9.65 Keith Edmier, *Beverly Edmier, 1967*. Cast resin, silicone, acrylic paint, fabric.

9.66 Michael Graves, *Alessi Coffee Set.* Glass, silver, mock ivory, and Bakelite.

oversized toys for single drivers, while more subdued colors are often used for the minivans and station wagons favored by families. In figure 9.68, color is used to add a sporty look to quite a different vehicle. This children's wheelchair gives the user a psychological boost while encouraging the development of physical strength and dexterity. On the other hand, it is the absence of color that brings power to the life-size figures in George Segal's installations. Despite their proximity to the viewer and their large scale, the white figures in *Walk, Don't Walk* (9.69) are drained of color, alienated, and emotionally distant.

Symbolic Color

Symbolic color is culturally based. Because each culture is unique, color associations vary widely. For example, yellow signifies the direction north in Tibet but represents the qualities of light, life, truth, and immortality to Hindus.[4] Blue represents mourning in Borneo, while in New Mexico it is painted on

9.67 Andy Goldsworthy, Red Rock, 1989. Leaves and stones.

window frames to block the entrance of evil spirits. Blue represented faith and truth to the Egyptians yet was the color worn by slaves in Gaul.[5]

The blue face that dominates the mask of the Aztec god Tlaloc in figure 9.70 is both symbolically and visually appropriate. Symbolically, the blue represents sky and the rain that Tlaloc calls forth to nourish crops. Visually, the contrast between the warm, reddish clay and the sky-blue paint enhances the impact of the ferocious face.

Key Questions

COLOR

- Which will better communicate your ideas—a limited range of hues or a wide range of hues?

- Are all the colors in your design similar in intensity? What would happen if you combined low-intensity colors with high-intensity colors?

- What is the proportion of warm and cool colors in your design—is it around 50/50? 70/30? 20/80? What would happen if these proportions were changed?

- What are the conceptual or symbolic implications of the colors you have chosen?

9.68 Adele Linarducci, *Slingshot Wheelchair,* 1989. Polystyrene, vinyl, PVC, and other materials. A nonworking model created while the artist was a student at Rochester Institute of Technology.

9.69 George Segal, *Walk, Don't Walk,* **1976.** Museum installation, with viewer. Plaster, cement, metal, painted wood, and electric light, 104 × 72 × 72 in. (264.2 × 182.9 × 182.9 cm).

9.70 Ritual Vessel Depicting Mask of Tlaloc, Aztec, Mexico, **Tenochtitlán, 1400–1521.** Ceramic, 13.8 × 13.8 × 12.4 in. (35 × 35 × 31.5 cm).

TIME

Every object occupies a position in time as well as space. In some cases, the specific temporal location is of minor importance. For example, *Locking Piece* (see figure 9.36A and B, page 197) is as meaningful now as it was when constructed in 1963. Formalist in approach, it makes no specific reference to social or political events. Constructed from durable bronze, it has effectively withstood the test of time. In other cases, temporal location gives the object its meaning. As noted on page 192, Nancy Holt's *Sun Tunnels* creates a kind of celestial observatory. Light pours through the holes in the curving walls, creating projections that mark the movement of the planets. Without the element of time, the concrete tunnels would have no more meaning than drainage pipes at a construction site.

Two aspects of time are particularly important to sculptors. **Actual time** refers to the location and duration of an actual temporal event. For example, it takes less than a minute for the bowling ball to roll down the ramps in Tinguely's *Chaos 1* (see figure 9.3, page 181). By contrast, **implied time** is the suggested location or duration of an event. The traffic light in Segal's *Walk, Don't Walk* changes, but the sculptural figures never move.

Actual motion and implied motion are equally important. In a brilliant use of actual time, actual motion, and natural forces, Ned Kahn constructed *Wind Veil* (9.71) from 80,000 aluminum panels. Activated by each breath of wind, the wall shimmers with both energy and light. By contrast, *Shuttlecocks* (9.72), by Claus Oldenburg and Coosje van Bruggen, seems to capture the oversize game pieces just as they begin to hit the ground. In this case, the artwork depends on implied time and motion for its impact. A final example combines time and motion with anticipation. Positioned alongside Michigan Avenue in Chicago's Millennium Park, Jaume Plensa's *Crown Fountain* (9.73) attracts thousands of visitors each summer day. Smiling images of everyday people from various city neighborhoods are projected on the multiple video screens contained within each five-story tower. Every 15 minutes, the projected face purses its lips and a stream of water

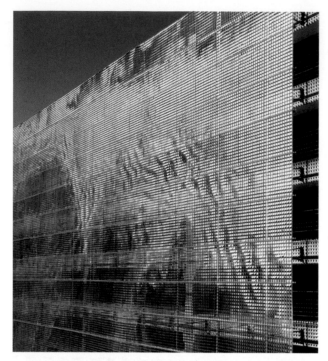

9.71 Ned Kahn, *Wind Veil*, 2000. 80,000 aluminum panels, total length 260 ft (79.25 m). Installation in Charlotte, North Carolina.

9.72 Claes Oldenburg and Coosje van Bruggen, *Shuttlecocks*, 1994. Aluminum, fiberglass-reinforced plastic, and paint. 230⁹⁄₁₆ × 191⅞ in. (585.63 × 487.36 cm).

9.73 Jaume Plensa, *Crown Fountain*, 2000–04. Glass, stainless steel, LED screens, light, wood, granite, and water, two 52½-ft-high towers, total area 7,217 ft² (2,200 m²).

bursts forth, drenching the delighted children waiting below.

Viewing time is a final basic consideration. The multiple surfaces presented by any three-dimensional object require extended analysis. We walk around Rodin's *The Kiss* (figure 9.10A and B, page 185), noting every nuance in form and texture; we rotate a ceramic vessel in our hands, savoring every detail. *The Board Room* (see figure 9.11, page 185), *Part II: Excursus* (see figure 9.56, page 207), and other installations require even more viewing time. To understand the artwork, the viewer must enter and fully explore the site.

Key Questions

TIME

- Is a "timeless" or a "timely" artwork more appropriate for the idea you want to communicate?

- What compositional choices can you use to increase timelessness?

- How can actual, implied, or viewing time expand meaning in your design?

SUMMARY

- *Form* may be defined as the physical manifestation of an idea. *Content* refers to the idea itself, including the subject matter plus its emotional, intellectual, spiritual, and symbolic implications.

- In three-dimensional design, *form* also refers to dimensionality itself. Thus, a circle is a shape, while a sphere is a form.

- The first step in creating a design is to understand its purpose. A sculptor seeks to convey ideas and express emotions. A craftsperson or designer is equally concerned with the function and the beauty of an object.

- Height, width, and depth are the three dimensions in three-dimensional design. Orthographic projection provides a means of clearly drawing these dimensions.

- Artworks can vary in dimensionality from relief, which uses a flat backing to support dimensional forms, to environmental works that the viewer can enter and physically explore.

- A line can connect, define, or divide a design. It can be static or dynamic, increasing or decreasing the stability of the form.

- A plane is a three-dimensional form that has length and width but minimal thickness.

- In three-dimensional design, *volume* refers to an enclosed area of three-dimensional space.

- A mass is a solid three-dimensional form. A massive object can be as dense and heavy as a bar of gold or as light and porous as a sponge.

- Space is the area within or around an area of substance. Space is the partner to substance. Without it, line, plane, volume, and mass lose both visual impact and functional purpose.

- *Texture* refers to the visual or tactile quality of a form. The increased surface area of a three-dimensional form heightens the impact of texture.

- Light can enhance our perception of a three-dimensional form, attract an audience, or be used as a material in itself. Light behaves very differently when it hits a reflective or translucent surface.

- Hue, value, intensity, and temperature are the major characteristics of color.

- Every object occupies a position in time as well as space. Actual time, implied time, actual space, and implied space can be combined in various ways to create compelling objects of great complexity.

KEY TERMS

actual lines	work (or	intensity	polyhedra	static forms
actual time	environment)	kinetic forms	positive forms	symbolic color
ambient light	form	line	primary contours	temperature
content	freestanding works	mass	reflective	texture
continuity	function	mechanical forms	refracted	three-quarter work
directed light	geometric forms	negative space	relief	translucent
direction	harmony	organic forms	saturation	transparent
dynamic forms	hue	orientation	secondary contours	value
earthwork	implied lines	orthographic	sight line	viewing time
elements	implied time	projection	site-specific	volume
environmental	installation	plane	space	

STUDIO PROJECTS

To apply the concepts from this chapter in the studio, check out the Projects page in the Online Learning Center at www.mhhe.com/stewart4e. The following is a sample of the chapter-related assignments that are described in step-by-step detail.

Calderesque Self-Portrait. A linear project using wire.
Spheres of Influence #1 and #2. Planar construction problems.
Discovering Mass. Modeling an object using foam rubber and carving a form from a plaster block.
Dominant and Subordinate. Exploring hierarchical composition.

Profile:
Todd Slaughter, Sculptor
Materials and Metaphors

Todd Slaughter was born in Memphis, Tennessee, in 1942. After majoring in chemistry and then in mathematics, he transferred into the art program at the University of Texas, where he earned a BSA (Bachelor of Science in Art) degree. He subsequently earned a master's degree in industrial design at Pratt, in New York City, and is now a professor in the sculpture program at The Ohio State University. He has had solo shows at the Wexner Center for the Arts, PS 1, and the Chicago Cultural Center, and his major commissions include *Mano y Bola* near Algeciras, Spain.

MS: Abstract forms dominated your early work. For the past 15 years, you have shifted more toward representational and narrative work. What is the advantage of each approach?

TS: There is a simple beauty in formal relationships. Like music, lines, planes, volumes and spaces can be organized into wonderful and expressive visual patterns. However, as I have gotten older, I have become more attuned to human relationships and more interested in the power of metaphor. Representational imagery helps the viewer understand the metaphor in a specific way.

MS: Your use of materials is especially distinctive. Many of your works have been constructed using graphite, sulfur, salt, paprika, and turmeric. Why use these unusual materials?

TS: They carry meanings and references that I want my artwork to reflect. I am especially interested in transience. Nothing is permanent; even the most massive chunk of steel changes over time. When I cast a thousand pounds of salt to create a full-sized sofa and then place it in a steam room, or set two opposing graphite fists in motion grinding each other to a powder (figure 12.28, page 275), the rate of change becomes accelerated and highly visible.

MS: I'm fascinated by your use of everyday objects, such as hats and domestic objects such as sofas, chairs, and houses.

TS: I want to create the strongest, most personal con-

nection possible between the audience and the artwork. Transforming known objects has become more effective for me than introducing forms that are outside of common experience. I am interested in exploring complex relationships within this world rather than in creating an escape into an alternative world.

MS: I'd like to highlight one of your most ambitious projects. Can you describe it to us?

TS: *Mano y Bola (Hand and Ball)* is a large-scale, permanent sculpture. It is installed on El Cabrito Ridge overlooking the Strait of Gibraltar and the coast of Morocco, Africa, seven miles from the Port of Algeciras, geographically the first Spanish port on the Mediterranean Sea. The sculpture was commissioned by the Port to mark its 200th anniversary, in conjunction with Galeria Magda Bellotti.

The hand is a double flat-sided structure, measuring 27 × 40 × 4 ft with a painted photographic image of an open hand on one side and its mirror image on the other. The surface of each side is made up of 1,116 movable panels that swing out horizontally when activated by a breeze. The ball is approximately 20 ft in diameter. It rotates very slowly, suggesting a line that is being drawn continuously.

MS: How did you develop the idea?

TS: In 1992 I was an artist in residence near the Strait of Gibraltar, in Manilva, Spain. The idea of a large artwork located within the landscape came to me as I was driving through southern Spain. To my surprise and delight at several locations, I came upon 30- to 40-ft-high, charging black bull silhouettes as I drove around a bend or over a rise. These were actually advertising signs with no text—the logo for a liquor company. While standing near the future site of my artwork and looking across the Strait at the city of Tangier, Morocco, my thought was to somehow create a temporary artwork addressing the historic and ongoing cultural, religious, and economic interaction of Europe and Africa in this region. The implied action of the hand—catching and throwing—metaphorically alludes to the history of exchange of religion, art, and power between the European and African continents.

MS: It seems remarkably dynamic for such a large sculpture.

TS: Yes, I hope so! During most day hours, the sculpture appears almost transparent and ephemeral due to its sky-blue color and the sky-revealing transformations of both hand and ball produced by variations in wind velocity. When backlit by the sun, the hand and ball become part of the silhouette of the ridge.

Todd Slaughter, *Mano y Bola* (details), 1997. Aluminum and steel, hand 27 × 40 × 4 ft (8.2 × 12.2 × 1.2 m), ball 20 ft (6 m) diameter. Overlooking the Strait of Gibraltar.

chapter ten

Principles of Three-Dimensional Design

Composition can be defined as the combination of multiple parts into a unified whole. In a well-composed design, all the elements work together as a team. A dialogue is created between positive and negative forms, and opposing forces add vitality rather than causing confusion. Each compositional part makes a positive contribution to the unified whole. Graceful metal lines have been combined with a series of contoured masses to create the elegant and utilitarian form of Niels Diffrient's *Freedom Chair* (10.1). In Alice Aycock's *Tree of Life Fantasy* (see figure 10.9, page 222), line, plane, and space have been combined to create an exuberant dance. Martin Puryear's *Seer* (10.2) consists of a closed volume at the top and an open volume at the bottom. The horn-shaped

10.1 Niels Diffrient, *Freedom Chair*, 1999. Die-cast aluminum frame with fused plastic coating; four-way stretch black fabric.

10.2 Martin Puryear, *Seer*, 1984. Water-based paint on wood and wire, 78 × 52¼ × 45 in. (198.2 × 132.6 × 114.3 cm).

top piece is powerful and imposing, while the open construction at the bottom invites us to enter and visually explore the structure. A series of curving vertical "ribs" unifies the top and bottom sections, while the contrast between open and closed forms adds a touch of mystery. In all three cases, every element is both dependent on and supportive of each other element.

The elements of design are the building blocks from which compositions are made. The principles of design describe the ways these building blocks can be combined.

UNITY AND VARIETY

Unity can be defined as similarity, oneness, togetherness, or cohesion. **Variety** can be defined as difference. Unity and variety are the cornerstones of composition.

Increasing Unity

We tend to scan an entire composition, then analyze the individual parts. A composition composed of units that are unrelated tends to appear random and unresolved. Evidence of deliberation and order tends to increase unity. As we will see in this section, grouping, containment, proximity, continuity, repetition, and closure are six common strategies for increasing order.

Grouping

When presented with a collection of separate visual units, we immediately try to create order and make connections. **Grouping** is one of the first steps in this process. As noted in the discussion of Gestalt psychology in Chapter Three, we generally group visual units by location, orientation, shape, and color. *Towards the Corner* (10.3), by Juan Muñoz, clearly demonstrates grouping by location. We first see a complete composition, comprised of seven figures. It is roughly triangular in shape, starting with the single seated figure on the right and extending to the standing figure at the far left. The division between the two sets of bleachers creates two subgroups, comprised of two figures on the right and five figures on the left. We can further group the three figures seated on the top bleachers and the three figures seated on the bottom, with the single standing figure providing a visual exclamation point for the sculpture as a whole.

10.3 Juan Muñoz, *Many Times*, 2000. Seven figures, wood, resin, and mixed mediums, 6¾ × 12½ × 3¾ ft (2.1 × 3.79 × 1.13 m).

10.4 Roni Horn, *How Dickinson Stayed Home,* **1993.** Installation. Solid aluminum and plastic. 26 cubes, each 3 × 3 × 3 in. (7.6 × 7.6 × 7.6 cm).

10.5A Louise Nevelson, *Wedding Chapel IV,* **1960.** Painted wood, height approx. 9 ft (2.7 m).

10.5B Line drawing of Figure 10.5A, showing containers in red and overall continuity in black.

10.6 Aaron Macsai, *Panels of Movement.* Bracelet, 18K gold, sterling, copper, ⅞ × 7 in. (2 × 18 cm).

Containment

Containment is a unifying force created by the outer edge of a composition or by a boundary within a composition. A container encourages us to seek connections among visual units and adds definition to the negative space around each positive form. The room itself provides the container for Roni Horn's *How Dickinson Stayed Home* (10.4). Letters from the alphabet are presented on 26 small cubes. Like Emily Dickinson's poetry, the installation is both economical and expansive. A minimal amount of information evokes a wide range of interpretations. Contained by the white walls and dark floor of the room itself, the blocks create a unified statement, despite their seemingly random distribution.

Proximity

In design, the distance between visual units is called **proximity.** Even the most disparate forms can become unified when they are placed in close proximity. For example, Louise Nevelson constructed *Wedding Chapel IV* (10.5A) from an improbable collection of wooden crates, staircase railings, dowels, chair legs, and other scrap. Organized into 14 rectilinear containers and placed in close proximity, the various pieces have become unified into a lively whole.

Continuity

Continuity can be defined as a fluid connection among compositional parts. When objects are placed in close proximity, continuity often happens naturally. As demonstrated by figure 10.5B, each form in *Wedding Chapel IV* touches several other forms. As a result, our eyes move easily from section to section, increasing the connections among the parts.

10.7 Zac Freeman, Detail of *Steve*, 2006. Found objects on board, 60 × 48 in. (152 × 122 cm).

Repetition

Repetition occurs when we use the same visual element or effect any number of times within a composition. In Aaron Macsai's *Panels of Movement* (10.6), similar lines, shapes, textures, and colors were used in each of the 10 panels from which the bracelet was constructed. A spiral shape, a wavy line, a sphere, and at least one triangular shape appear repeatedly. Despite their variations in size, texture, and location, these repeated forms create a strong connection from panel to panel.

Closure

Closure is the mind's inclination to connect fragmentary information to produce a completed form. In Zac Freeman's *Steve* (10.7), we must visually connect hundreds of washers, screws, and other hardware to create a man's face. Closure makes it possible to communicate using implication. Freed of the necessity to provide every detail, the artist or designer can convey an idea through suggestion rather than description. When the viewer completes the image in his or her mind, it is often more memorable than an explicit image.

Combining Unifying Forces

James Ingo Freed used all of these unifying forces to create the *Tower of Photos* in the Holocaust Memorial Museum in Washington, DC (10.8). His design team wanted to demonstrate the number of lives lost in one Polish village while honoring the individuality of the inhabitants. They collected and framed thousands of photographs, including groups of schoolchildren, weddings, and family snapshots. Placed in close proximity, the photographs personalize the victims while emphasizing their connection to the lost community. Based on the chimneys used to burn the bodies of the dead, the tower itself provides the dominant framework for the exhibition, both structurally and emotionally.

Increasing Variety

Difference in any aspect of a design increases variety. By reviewing the elements of design described in Chapter Nine and the principles of design described in this chapter, you can quickly create a checklist of areas for variation, such as

- *Line variation.* Lines of different diameter were combined with double linear "train tracks" in Aycock's *Tree of Life Fantasy* (10.9).

- *Variation in texture.* Combining smooth and textured surfaces can add energy and interest to even the simplest form.

- *Variation in pattern.* The Pacific island mask shown in figure 10.10 is unified through symmetrical balance. This underlying order freed the artist to experiment with many colors and patterns.

Degrees of Unity

As noted in Chapter Eight, our compositional choices must support our conceptual intentions. Some designs require a high level of unity. For example, Eva Hesse's *Accession II* (10.11) consists of a single cube. Dramatic contrast between the methodical exterior and the fiercely textured interior is the only significant variation. Other designs require a high level of variety. The lines, shapes, volumes, and masses in Judy Pfaff's *3-D* (10.12) ricochet off the floor, walls, and ceiling with an almost chaotic energy.

10.8 *Tower of Photos* from Ejszyszki, completed in 1993. United States Holocaust Memorial Museum, Washington, DC. James Ingo Freed, lead designer.

10.9 Alice Aycock, *Tree of Life Fantasy,* Synopsis of the Book of Questions Concerning the World Order and/or the Order of Worlds, 1990–92. Painted steel, fiberglass, and wood, 20 × 15 × 8 ft (6.1 × 4.6 × 2.4 m).

10.10 Mask (Wanis), New Ireland. 37 × 20⅞ × 19 in. (94 × 53 × 48.3 cm).

10.11 Eva Hesse, *Accession II,* **1967.** Galvanized steel, rubber tubing, 30.5 × 30.5 × 30.5 in. (77 × 77 × 77 cm).

10.12 Judy Pfaff, *3-D,* **1983.** Mixed mediums, installation in a 22 × 35 ft (6.71 × 10.67 m) room.

10.13 Leonardo Drew, *Number 56*, 1996. Rust, plastic, wood, 113 × 113 in. (287 × 287 cm).

10.14 Daniel Buren, *The Two Plateaus*, 1985–86. 1,000-square-foot sculpture for the Cour d'Honneur, Palais Royal, Paris. Black marble, granite, iron, cement, electricity, water.

Grid and Matrix

A **grid** is created through a series of intersecting lines. A **matrix** is a three-dimensional grid. Both can unify a design by creating containment, continuity, and proximity.

In *Number 56* (10.13), Leonardo Drew poured rust into hundreds of plastic bags, which were then connected to a wooden support. The rust and the methodically numbered plastic bags create a dialogue between the orderly grid and the decaying metal. This combination of order and disorder balances monotony with mystery.

Daniel Buren's *The Two Plateaus* (10.14) offers another variant on the grid. This public art project, located in the Palais Royal in Paris, covers a 1,000-square-foot plaza. The striped cylinders range in height from about 2 to 5 feet. Mimicking the columns in the building and organized on the pavement like players on a checkerboard, they bring both energy and humor to the site.

Key Questions

UNITY AND VARIETY

- What strategies have you used to unify your composition?

- What gives your composition variety?

- Is the balance between unity and variety appropriate for the ideas you want to express?

- What would happen if your composition were constructed using a grid or matrix?

- How can space be used to increase unity or increase variety?

BALANCE

Balance refers to the distribution of weight or force among visual units. Like physical balance, visual balance requires equilibrium in size, visual weight, and force. Visual balance can be created through the absence as well as the presence of form. And, as figure 10.15 demonstrates, balance and dynamism are interconnected.

There are three major types of balance. In **symmetrical balance,** forms are mirrored on either side of a central axis. The resulting form generally is physically and visually stable. The central face in figure 10.16A is an example of symmetrical balance.

With **radial symmetry,** design elements extend out from a central point, like the spokes of a wheel. Radiating in all directions while remaining anchored at the center, this type of balance tends to generate a great deal of energy while retaining a high level of unity. The outer ring in figure 10.16 is an example of radial balance. The diagram in figure 10.16B shows both of these forms of symmetry.

Asymmetrical balance creates equilibrium among visual elements that do *not* mirror each other on either side of an axis. Depending on the degree of asymmetry, the resulting design may be quite stable, very dynamic, or nearly chaotic.

10.16A Bella Coola Mask Representing the Sun, from British Columbia, before 1897. Wood, diameter 24¾ in. (63 cm).

10.16B Diagram of Bella Coola mask. The central face is symmetrically balanced. The outer ring is an example of radial symmetry.

10.15 Claes Oldenburg and Coosje van Bruggen, *The Typewriter Eraser,* 1998–99. MGM Mirage, Las Vegas. Aluminum, fiberglass, urethane paint, size variable.

A   B   C

10.17A–C Examples of asymmetrical balance.

Many strategies can be used to create asymmetrical balance:

- A large form is placed close to the fulcrum, while a small form is placed farther away. Just as a child at the end of a seesaw can balance an adult near the center, so large and small forms can be balanced in a design (10.17A).

- Multiple small forms can balance a single large form (10.17B).

- A small, solid form can balance a large, open form. The solidity and stability of the square give it visual weight as well as physical weight (10.17C).

10.18 Theodore Gall, *Plaza Facets,* **2001.** Cast bronze, 6 × 6 × 6 in. (15.2 × 15.2 × 15.2 cm).

Most artworks are constructed from multiple parts. Size variations among the parts affect both the physical balance and the expressive impact. A **dominant,** or primary, form is often balanced by one or more **subordinate,** or secondary, forms. For example, in Theodore Gall's *Plaza Facets* (10.18), the large head on the left is balanced by the column and fragmentary heads on the right. The seven smaller figures create yet a third compositional level. Using these compositional hierarchies, artists and designers can create unified designs from distinctly individual parts.

Two contrasting interpretations of a single figure further demonstrate the expressive power of balance. St. Bruno, an eleventh-century Catholic saint, is shown in figures 10.19 and 10.20. His followers, known as the Carthusian Order, lived in caves and devoted their time to manuscript transcription, meditation, and prayer.

The first statue, completed by Michel-Ange Slodtz in 1744, dramatizes a pivotal moment in Bruno's life. Preferring his contemplative existence to the power and prestige of a more public life, Bruno rejects promotion to the office of bishop. Slodtz used asymmetrical balance to express this dramatic moment. The small bishop's hat, offered by the angel in the lower-right corner, is the focal point of the entire sculpture. The much larger figure of St. Bruno recoils when confronted by this symbol of authority. As a result, the small hat matches the saint in compositional weight.

A very different interpretation of the life of St. Bruno is given in the second sculpture. Completed by Jean-Antoine Houdon in 1766, it emphasizes the contemplative nature of the Carthusian Order and its founder. Using symmetrical balance, Houdon presents a dignified, introspective man. If we divide the figure in half from top to bottom, the two sides basically mirror each other. This saint is a philosopher, very much at peace with the choices he has made. Just as asymmetrical balance is appropriate for the dramatic moment represented by Slodtz, so symmetrical balance is ideal for the serenity shown by Houdon.

10.19 Michel-Ange Slodtz, *St. Bruno*, 1744. Marble.

10.20 Jean-Antoine Houdon, *St. Bruno of Cologne*, 1766. Stucco.

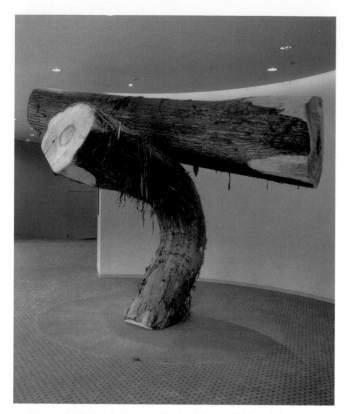

10.21 Chuichi Fujii, *Untitled*, 1987. Japanese cedar, 10 ft 6 in. × 13 ft ½ in. × 11 ft 6 in. (320 × 400 × 350 m).

Exaggerated weight or buoyancy can shift the balance in an artwork and expand meaning. In Chuichi Fujii's *Untitled* (10.21), a cedar log seems to have been crushed by the weight of a second log. At the other extreme, Patricia A. Renick's *Life Boats/Boats About Life* (10.22) seems to float on air, as weightless as a dream. Dramatic lighting and cast shadows heighten the magical effect. This artwork derives its power from the denial of gravity, while figure 10.21 derives its power from exaggerated gravity.

Key Questions
BALANCE

- Which form of balance is most appropriate to the ideas you want to express?
- Which is the dominant form in your composition? Is its dominance conceptually justified?
- What happens when an unexpected part of the design plays the dominant role?
- How does space affect compositional balance?

10.22 Patricia A. Renick, *Life Boats/Boats About Life,* 1979–80. 1 to 1½ ft high × 5 to 6½ ft long × 1 to 1½ ft deep (30.5 to 45.7 m high × 152.4 to 198.1 m long × 30.5 to 45.7 m deep).

SCALE AND PROPORTION

Scale

Scale commonly refers to the size of a form when compared with human size. Using our body as a constant, we can identify three major types of scale relationships. Small-scale objects can be **handheld,** while **human scale** refers to designs that are roughly our size. Very large objects and installations are **monumental** in scale.

Returning to Theodore Gall's sculpture (Figure 10.18, page 226), we can explore the implications of each scale type. The actual artwork is roughly 6 × 6 × 6 inches and can be handheld. At this scale, we are invited to enter and explore the artwork mentally rather than physically (10.23A). At triple this size (18 × 18 × 18 in.), the dominant head in the design would be about the size of our own head (10.23B). This would create a very different dialogue between the audience and the artwork. Expanded to monumental scale—say, 32 × 32 × 32 feet—the artwork would invite physical entry (10.23C). We could now stand beside the sculptural figures in the piece. Simply by changing the scale, the artist could create three very different responses to the same composition.

Proportion

Proportion refers to the relative size of visual elements *within* an image. When we compare the width of the head with its height, or divide a composition into thirds, we are establishing a proportional relationship.

In industrial design, changes in proportion can enhance or diminish function. The five gardening tools in figure 10.24 are all based on the same basic combination of handle, blades, and a simple pivot. Variations in proportion determine their use. The short-handled pruner in the lower-left corner is used to trim twigs and small branches from shrubs. It must fit comfortably in a single hand. The proportions of the lopper in the lower-right corner are much different. Its 20-inch-long handle provides the leverage needed to cut heavier branches from small trees. For the industrial designer, function often determines proportion.

In sculpture, variations in proportion can increase aesthetic impact. Three proportional variations on Constantin Brancusi's *Bird in Space* are shown in figures

A

B

C

10.23A–C Scale variations, from handheld to monumental.

10.24 Home Pro garden tool line. Designers: James E. Grove, John Cook, Jim Holtorf, Fernando Pardo, Mike Botich. Design Firm: Designworks/USA.

10.25 Constantin Brancusi, *Maiastra*, 1912. Polished brass, 29⅞ × 7¼ × 7½ in. (75.7 × 18.5 × 19 cm).

10.26 Constantin Brancusi, *Golden Bird*, 1919, Pedestal c. 1922. Bronze, stone, and wood, 37¾ in. (95.9 cm), base 48 in. (121.9 cm).

10.27 Constantin Brancusi, *Bird in Space*, 1928. Bronze (unique cast), 54 × 8½ × 6½ in. (137.2 × 21.6 × 16.5 cm).

10.25 through 10.27. In *Maiastra* (10.25), the abstract bird form is dominated by the egg-shaped torso, which tapers into the folded wings at the bottom and the raised head at the top. This bird is approximately 3 times taller than it is wide. Brancusi further abstracted *Golden Bird* (10.26) and elongated the body. The bird is now 7 times taller than it is wide, and an elaborate base adds even more height to the sculpture. With *Bird in Space* (10.27), Brancusi elongated the form even more and added an expanding "foot" below the folded wings. This bird is almost 10 times taller than it is wide. By lengthening the columnar structure in this final version and carefully tapering the sculpture near the base, Brancusi made this simple sculpture fly.

As with all design decisions, choosing the right scale and proportion greatly increases expressive power. Giovanni Bologna's *Apennine* (10.28) is scaled to overwhelm the viewer with a sense of the mountain spirit's presence. His human frame is monumental, and the surrounding trees and cliff appear to diminish by comparison.

Proportional extremes can be equally expressive. Less than 5 feet tall, Alberto Giacometti's *Chariot* (10.29) offers a somber analysis of the human condition. The solitary figure is delicately balanced on gigantic wheels, which rest on two small pedestals. The entire form is linear, as if distilled down to the barest essentials. Both the chariot and the life it transports are precariously balanced and seem fragile and vulnerable.

Key Questions
SCALE AND PROPORTION

- What would happen to your composition if you dramatically changed its scale?
- What would happen conceptually if you dramatically changed its proportions?
- Imagine that your design can be stretched or compressed in any direction. What are the advantages of a very tall, thin composition compared to a short, cubic composition?
- How does a change in proportion affect overall balance?

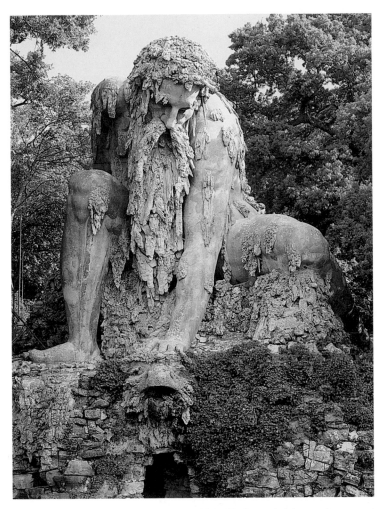

10.28 Giovanni Bologna, *Apennine*, 1580–82. Stone, bricks, mortar. Villa di Pratolino, Florence region, Italy.

10.29 Alberto Giacometti, *Chariot*, 1950. Bronze, 57 × 26 × 26⅛ in. (144.8 × 65.8 × 66.2 cm).

EMPHASIS

Emphasis gives particular prominence to part of a design. A **focal point** is a compositional device used to create emphasis. For example, the bishop's hat in Slodtz's version of St. Bruno (figure 10.19, page 227) is the focal point of the composition. Both emphasis and focal point are used to attract attention and increase visual and conceptual impact.

Emphasis by Isolation

Any **anomaly,** or break from the norm, tends to stand out. Because we seek to connect the verbal and visual information we are given, a mismatched word or an isolated object immediately attracts attention. In *I Never Liked Musical Chairs* (10.30), metalsmith Joana Kao established the norm through

10.30 Joana Kao, *I Never Liked Musical Chairs.* Bracelet, sterling, 24K, 2¾ × 1¾ in. (7 × 4 cm).

seven tiny chairs connected by a silver chain. The figure at the end of the chain breaks the pattern. This break conveys the isolation felt by a child who has been ejected from the game.

Emphasis Through Contrast

Contrast is created when two or more forces operate in opposition.

By reviewing the elements and principles of design discussed thus far, we can quickly create a long list of potential adversaries, including static/dynamic, smooth/textured, small/large, and curvilinear/rectilinear. When the balance is just right, powerful compositions can be created from any such combination. Many artists and designers devote most of their compositional area to one force and a much smaller amount to a contrasting force. The larger force sets the standard, while the smaller force creates the exception.

Contrast can appear in many forms and in varying degrees. In Arnaldo Pomodoro's *Sphere Within Sphere* (10.31), the imposing spherical form seems to have been eaten away by an external force, revealing a pattern of rectilinear teeth and a second sphere within. This creates a strong contrast between the massive structure and the invading space.

In *Plan, Prepare, Execute* (10.32A and B), Liza Lou also used contrast to suggest the metamorphosis

10.31 Arnaldo Pomodoro, *Sphere Within Sphere*, 1965. Bronze, 45 × 46½ × 47⅝ ft (114.2 × 118.1 × 121.0 m). Dublin, Ireland.

of an existing structure into a new configuration. It is hard to tell whether the dominant field of dark gray is "eating" or "being eaten" by the colorful patterns around the edge and the lines at the bottom. This uncertainty makes the artwork even more intriguing.

10.32A and B Liza Lou, *Plan, Prepare, Execute*, 2007–08. Glass beads on aluminum panel, 120 × 60 in. (305 × 152 cm).

A Full View

B Detail

Loops (10.33), by Mary Ann Scherr, presents a contrast between movement and constraint. A curving plane encircles the wearer's throat, providing protection but restricting motion. Below, the suspended rings sway with every movement of the body, creating a dynamic counterpoint to the constraining collar.

Water animates Pol Bury's *Fountains at Palais Royal* (10.34). The design relies on three major elements. The site itself is dominated by the regularly spaced columns so characteristic of neoclassical architecture. The polished steel spheres, poised within the bowl of each foundation, reflect these columns and the shimmering water, the third element in the design. In a sense, the spheres serve as mediators between the rigid columns and the silvery water. Like the columns, they are simple volumes arranged in a group. Like the water, they seem fluid as they reflect the rippling pool and the passing clouds. In this project, unity and variety have been combined to create an elegant and ever-changing sculpture.

10.33 **Mary Ann Scherr, *Loops*, 1988.** Sterling silver neckpiece, 8½ × 4¾ × 5 in. (21.6 × 12.1 × 12.7 cm).

Key Questions

EMPHASIS

- Is there a focal point in your composition? If not, should there be?

- What is the most prominent form in your composition? Is it the form you most *want* to emphasize?

- What would happen to your composition if you dramatically increased the amount of contrast?

10.34 Pol Bury, *Fountains at Palais Royal*, Paris, 1985.

REPETITION AND RHYTHM

10.35 David Watkins, *Torus 280 (B2)*, 1989. Neckpiece, gilded brass, 11 in. (28 cm).

As noted at the beginning of this chapter, repetition occurs when we use the same visual element or effect any number of times within a composition. **Rhythm** can be defined as the organization of these multiple elements or effects into a deliberate pattern. Just as a musician creates a deliberate pattern by connecting sound and silence, so the artist can create rhythm using positive form and negative space.

Percussive variations also create rhythm. For example, when every fourth beat is accented in a musical composition, a clear rhythm emerges. Repeated accents in an artwork have a similar effect. And the number of beats within a given space creates the **tempo,** or rate of change. In David Watkins's *Torus 280 (B2)* (10.35), the large circular shapes create a slow, regular pattern. Increasing the number of circles would accelerate the tempo.

Rhythm plays an even greater role in figure 10.36. The woven herringbone pattern at the bottom suggests first clockwise then counterclockwise visual movement. A similar pattern at the top accentuates spatial depth. Tapered rectilinear shapes create a border around both the interior and the exterior edges. Like a complex musical piece, three types of rhythm have been skillfully woven together.

The multiple views offered by physical objects accentuate the importance of rhythm. The movement of four women around an exuberant musician creates a joyous dance in Jean-Baptiste Carpeaux's *The Dance* (10.37). Our eyes follow the turning heads, clasped hands, and swirling arms as they move in, out, and around in space. A similar rhythm animates Steve Woodward's *Model of Proposal for Concourse Commission* (10.38). The plywood vortex seems to rise out of the floor to collect in a spinning disk at the top, and then descend again, in perpetual motion.

10.36 Tanija & Graham Carr, *Untitled*, 2001. Wet-formed leather, acrylic paint, 13¾ × 29¼ × 29¼ in. (35 × 74 × 74 cm).

10.37 Jean-Baptiste Carpeaux, *The Dance (After Restoration),* 1868–69. Marble, 7 ft 6½ in. (2.3 m).

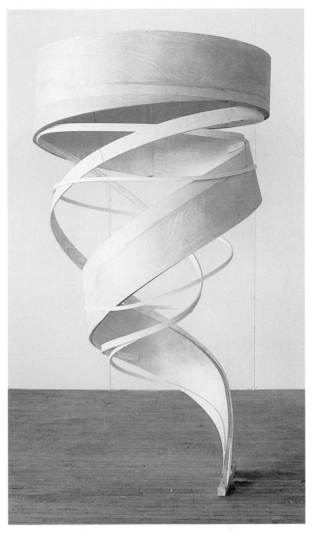

10.38 Steve Woodward, *Model of Proposal for Concourse Commission,* 1987. Wood, 13¾ × 8 × 7½ in. (34.9 × 20.3 × 19 cm).

10.39 Magdalena Abakanowicz, *Standing Figures (30),* 1994–99. Bronze, overall 54 ft 3 in. × 19 ft 8 in. (16.55 × 6 m).

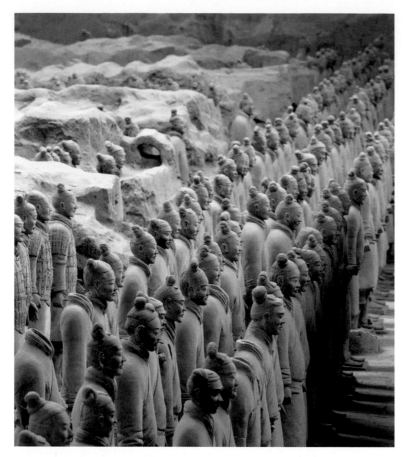

10.40 Tomb of Emperor Shih Huang Ti, 221–206 BCE. Painted ceramic figures, life-size.

When combined with the spinning effect, this up-and-down movement gives the design great vitality.

Repetition is often used to increase compositional unity. It can also be used to quantify an elusive idea. For example, the 30 statues in Magdalena Abakanowicz's *Standing Figures (30)* (10.39) are unified by their similarity in size, shape, and solemnity. Variations in each cast bronze surface provide a degree of individuality. Often interpreted as victims of war, the hollow, headless figures seem frozen in time, offering silent testimony to a tragic past. The 6,000 clay soldiers filling the tomb of Emperor Shih Huang Ti (10.40) demonstrate a different use of repetition. As he faced his death, the emperor may have sought companionship or protection from his army. Sherrie Levine's *La Fortune* (10.41) demonstrates a third use of repetition. Our sense of reality is challenged when we encounter these six pool tables. The identical arrangement of the balls seems impossible: the balls would be randomly distributed in six actual games. Here, a very ordinary scene becomes mysterious, even nightmarish, due to the inexplicable repetition.

Key Questions

REPETITION AND RHYTHM

- Try repeating any element in your design. What does this repetition contribute, conceptually and compositionally?

- What happens when simple repetition is changed to specific rhythm?

- Does the rhythm remain constant in your design, or is there a change in tempo? What is the advantage of each approach?

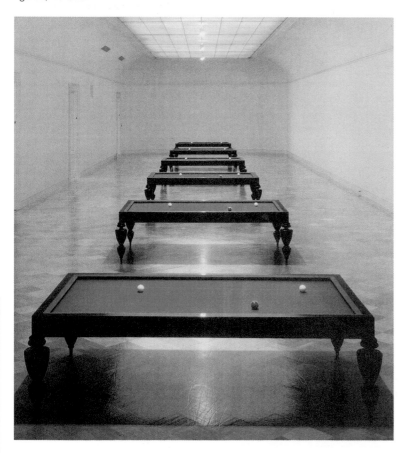

10.41 Sherrie Levine, *La Fortune (After Man Ray)* 1–6, 1990. Felt, mahogany, resin, 33 × 110 × 60 in. (84 × 280 × 153 cm).

SUMMARY

- Through composition, we can combine multiple parts to create a unified whole.

- Grouping, containment, proximity, continuity, repetition, and closure are six common strategies for increasing unity. Difference in any aspect of a design increases variety.

- A grid is created through a series of intersecting lines. A matrix is a three-dimensional grid.

- Symmetry, radial symmetry, and asymmetry are three common forms of balance. A dominant, or primary, form is often balanced by one or more subordinate, or secondary, forms.

- Scale and proportion are two types of size relationships. Proportion refers to size relationships within an image, while scale involves a size comparison with our physical size.

- Emphasis gives prominence to a specific part of a design. A focal point is a compositional device often used to create emphasis.

- Contrast is created when two or more forces operate in opposition. Many artists and designers devote most of their compositional area to one force and a much smaller area to a contrasting force. The larger force sets the standard, while the smaller force creates the exception.

- Repetition occurs when we use the same visual element or effect any number of times within a composition. Rhythm is the organization of these multiple elements or effects into a deliberate pattern. Just as a musician creates a deliberate pattern connecting sound and silence, so the artist can create rhythm using positive form and negative space.

KEY TERMS

anomaly	contrast	human scale	rhythm
asymmetrical balance	dominant	matrix	scale
balance	emphasis	monumental	subordinate
closure	focal point	proportion	symmetrical balance
composition	grid	proximity	tempo
containment	grouping	radial symmetry	unity
continuity	handheld	repetition	variety

STUDIO PROJECTS

To apply the concepts from this chapter in the studio, check out the Projects page in the Online Learning Center at www.mhhe.com/stewart4e. The following is a sample of the chapter-related assignments that are described in step-by-step detail.

Negative and Positive. Creating a dialogue between substance and space.

Three-Dimensional Balancing Act. Increasing compositional complexity, using curvilinear and rectilinear forms.

Myths and Masks. Working with many elements of 3-D design to create a wearable mask for a new ceremonial occasion.

Profile:
Marilyn da Silva, Metalsmith
Metals and Metaphors

Professor Marilyn da Silva is program chair of the Jewelry/Metal Arts Department at California College of the Arts in Oakland. She was selected as "Master Metalsmith 1999" by the National Ornamental Metal Museum in Memphis, Tennessee, and her work has been displayed nationally and internationally, including at the Victoria and Albert Museum in London and the National Gallery of Australia.

MS: What is it that attracts you to metal?

MdS: I really love the resistance and permanence of metal. It only changes when I work it very deliberately: this gives me more control. If dropped, it will dent, but it will not break. It is inherently a "cool" medium, but using patinas and colored pencils, I can make metal appear "warm."

MS: How did you get started in this field?

MdS: From a very young age, I was always making things, such as furniture and clothing for my dolls. Working with my hands just came naturally. Other children enter into art through drawing; I entered through construction.

MS: You studied with Alma Eikerman, a particularly renowned metalsmith. What did you learn from her?

MdS: Alma emphasized both excellent craft and excellent design. She expected impeccable work: there were no excuses for weaknesses in either area. In one assignment, we made a black paper silhouette of our teapot body shape. We then designed 20 variations on handles and spouts using black paper. We then tried different combinations of handles, spouts, and pots, seeking the best solution. It sounds simple, but by generating dozens of variations, we were able to find the ideal combination.

MS: Your designs are charged with meaning. Please take us through your conceptual and compositional development of *Reap What You Sow.*

MdS: I designed this piece for a show devoted to pillboxes. The concept was based on three premises: (1) my recent discovery that I was allergic to penicillin, (2) the alarming amount of antibiotics in the foods we eat every day, and (3) the need for many to go over the border to acquire affordable prescriptions.

I did many drawings and decided to have a bird land on furrows found in fields. The bird would either be stealing a pill in its mouth or be placing it in the furrow. On all of my book pieces, the "leather" of the book turns into something else. In this case, it becomes the dirt and furrows of a field. I then selected the barn swallow as the bird of choice. It was an obvious solution because of its name "swallow" and the fact that this bird often builds its nest in barns, placing it in a farm environment.

The furrows have young plants sawed out of copper. If you look closer, you can see that the leaves look like small hands. The shadows of the hands are grasping at pills lying on the ground.

The book is made from heavy-gauge copper that has been hammered to give it texture. I used red oak flooring for the pages. The bird is carved out of basswood and has wings, feet, eyes, and beak made of metal. All of the metal parts of the book are colored with gesso and colored pencil. The title of the book, *Reap What You Sow: A Prescription for Life*, is etched into a brass plate and riveted to the book spine. Finally, an antique silver spoon with the name "Grove" on it props up the book in the corner. You know, "just a spoon full of sugar helps the medicine go down . . . ."

MS: Conceptually, what do you seek in your work?

MdS: My artworks are layered with meaning. The viewer first sees the basic form and may respond to the beauty of the metal. Upon reflection, he or she may be drawn in by the storytelling and conceptual associations inherent in the work. For example, my *Rock, Paper, Scissors* refers to a children's game that is based on power dynamics and unpredictability. Likewise, *Reap What You Sow* can be read on many personal and environmental levels.

I avoid in-your-face polemics. It is better for viewers to respond to the work on the basis of their own experiences, and then return to the work for a second viewing.

Marilyn da Silva, *Reap What You Sow: A Prescription for Life,* **2004.** Copper, sterling silver, brass, wood, plastic, gesso, colored pencil.

Materials and Methods

An incredible range of materials and methods can be used to produce three-dimensional objects. Paper, metal, fibers, clay, and plastic are among the most versatile materials used by artists and designers; folding, casting, carving, weaving, and stamping are just a few of the production methods. A separate course specifically devoted to materials would be needed if we were to explore this subject in depth.

The purpose of this chapter is more pragmatic. As a beginner, you need both practical advice and a basic introduction to the aesthetic implications of various materials. We begin with a discussion of the essential characteristics of all materials, then consider ways in which contemporary artists use both traditional and nontraditional materials. The last section provides an overview of basic materials commonly used in three-dimensional design courses.

CHOICE OF MATERIALS

Each material has specific strengths and limitations. For example, rubber cement is a temporary adhesive for ordinary paper, while white glue is a permanent adhesive for heavier paper and cardboard. Carpenter's glue works well for wood, while hot glue is an effective adhesive for assemblage materials. Misuse of any material can ruin a great design. By understanding the physical characteristics of common materials, we can produce better work in less time and at less cost. The following considerations are crucial:

- *Strength.* How much weight can a given material support? What is its breaking point when it is twisted, folded, or bent?

- *Workability.* How difficult is it to alter the shape of a material? Does it cut and bend easily? Can it be melted and cast or dripped to create a new form?

- *Durability.* What range of forces can this material withstand and for how long? Is it impervious to heat, water, wind, and ultraviolet light?

- *Weight.* A material that is too light for a given purpose can be as problematic as a material that is too heavy. What is the function of the project, and how can material weight best serve that function?

- *Cost.* Can the material chosen be obtained easily and at a reasonable cost? If your budget is limited, you may have to remove expensive materials from consideration.

- *Toxicity.* Many plastics produce toxic gases when they are cut, etched, or burned. Paints and solvents may require the use of masks and gloves and often present significant disposal problems. Is the ventilation of your workplace appropriate for your work process? Are less toxic materials available? How will you dispose of toxic waste?

- *Function.* How appropriate is a given material for a particular purpose? A teapot will be useless if the material used is porous, and a chair that is too difficult to construct can never be mass-produced. The material chosen must serve the structural and aesthetic needs of the object you design.

Increasing Material Strength

Composites

A **composite** is created when two or more materials of differing strengths are fused together. Fiberglass (which combines glass filaments with plastic resin) and ferro-concrete (which is made from metal mesh embedded in concrete) are familiar examples. Foamcore (which is made from a sheet of polystyrene sandwiched between sheets of coated paper) and duct tape (constructed from three layers of "skin") are composites that are commonly used in three-dimensional design classes. Composites are often used when light weight, low cost, and increased strength are required.

Structural Strength

After millions of years of experimentation, nature has developed an amazing array of effective structures. Two major types are skeletons and exoskeletons. A **skeleton** (or **endoskeleton**) provides the internal structure needed by mammals and fish, while insects and many sea creatures rely on an external **exoskeleton** for support.

Architects are masters of both skeletal and exoskeletal structures. In *Guggenheim Museum Bilbao* (11.1), architect Frank Gehry created a complex "skeleton" to support the building's gleaming titanium skin. The Gothic cathedral in figure 11.2 demonstrates the use of an exoskeleton. To increase building height while reducing mass, medieval

11.1 Computer-generated Catia image used for the Solomon R. Guggenheim Museum Bilbao, finished 1997.

CATIA
DASSAULT SYSTEMES

1 Bay
2 Nave
3 Side aisle
4 Nave arcade
5 Clerestory
6 Cluster pier
  with colonettes
7 Triforium
8 Buttress
9 Flying buttress
10 Wooden roof

11.2 Perspective diagram and cross-section of Chartres Cathedral, 1145–1220.

11.3 Shoji Design. Three Japanese floor lamps. Steel, bamboo, paper, size variable.

11.4 Alexandre-Gustave Eiffel, diagram of the construction of the Statue of Liberty.

architects developed the **flying buttress** used in hundreds of cathedrals throughout Europe.

Artists and designers often use an **armature** to create internal structure. For example, a wire or wooden armature is often used to support the cloth or paper in lampshades. Designers from around the world have created an amazing range of variations on this simple object (11.3). Engineer Alexandre-Gustave Eiffel developed a much more elaborate armature to support Auguste Bartholdi's *Statue of Liberty* (11.4). Standing over 150 feet tall and weighing 225 tons, this monumental sculpture has to withstand wind, rain, and brisk sea winds. Without a strong internal structure, the statue could never have been built.

Distributing Force

As shown in figure 11.5A–E, the five major forces are compression, tension, bend, torque, and shear. **Compression** occurs when a material is pushed inward; **tension** occurs when a material is pulled outward; direct pressure at one point causes a material to **bend; torque** is a twisting motion; **shear** can occur when force is applied to the opposite sides of a material.

The equilateral triangle is the linear shape that best resists deformation caused by each of these forces, and the tetrahedron, or pyramid, is the strongest three-dimensional form. A triangular support, such as a corner brace on the back of a painting, can distribute force effectively and greatly increase strength. On a larger scale, a network of crossbeams in Thorncrown Chapel (11.6) adds both strength and beauty to a sacred space.

11.5A–E Major physical forces.

11.6 E. Fay Jones & Associates, Thorncrown Chapel, Eureka Springs, Arkansas, 1981.

11.7 R. Buckminster Fuller, U.S. Pavilion, Expo-67, Montreal, 1967.

11.8 Joseph Cornell, *Untitled (Medici Princess)*, c. 1948. Construction, 17⅝ × 11⅛ × 4⅜ in. (44.8 × 28.3 × 11.1 cm).

R. Buckminster Fuller's geodesic dome (11.7) expands this idea even further. Typically constructed using hundreds of tetrahedrons, the dome is relatively easy to build and creates a large volume using a minimal amount of mass. A model of beauty and efficiency, the geodesic dome has been widely used for large, open buildings such as greenhouses and exhibition spaces.

Methods of Construction

Compositional choices are strongly influenced by the method of construction. The two most common methods are addition and subtraction.

In **additive sculpture,** the artwork is created from separate parts that have been connected, usually using glues, joints, stitching, or welds. **Assemblage** is one additive method. Using objects and images originally designed for another purpose, Joseph Cornell created a whole series of evocative box structures (11.8). Many of these assemblages were designed to honor specific people, past and present. **Modeling** is an additive process often used by ceramicists. Pinching and pushing the pliable clay, skillful ceramicists can make both functional and sculptural objects of great complexity. To create his *Head Series* (11.9), Jean-Pierre Larocque stamped slabs of clay with various textures from cloth, then modeled and carved a head that is both activated and imposing.

In **subtractive sculpture,** the artist removes materials from a larger mass. Carving, drilling, cutting, and turning on a lathe are all subtractive processes. The Tlingit man shown in figure 11.10 follows a methodical process, beginning by drawing on the cedar pole, making a rough cut, then refining and finishing the totem pole.

Plastic and metal forms are often produced using two additional methods. In **solidification,** a liquid material is poured into a mold or extruded through a pipe, then allowed to harden. For example, when we squeeze cake frosting through a shaped nozzle, we can create a wide range of extruded forms. This same basic principle can be applied to materials that are more permanent and less tasty. In **displacement,** a solid material is physically forced into a new configuration. The stamping process used to mint coins is a familiar example of displacement.

Key Questions

CHOICE OF MATERIALS

- Test the limits of the materials you plan to use. Note especially their strength, workability, toxicity, and cost.

- Are there "greener" materials that you might use for your project?

- Make a model from an unfamiliar material. Does it offer any conceptual or technical advantages over the material you usually use?

11.9 Jean-Pierre Larocque, *Untitled (Head Series),* **2002.**
Stoneware, 36¾ × 21 in. (93.3 × 53.3 cm).

11.10 Tlingit totem carver, 1996. Southeast Alaska.

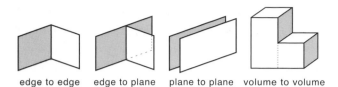

edge to edge   edge to plane   plane to plane   volume to volume

edge to edge   edge to plane   plane to plane   mass to mass

11.11A Examples of connections through contact.

11.11B Examples of connections through junctions.

ball and socket   hinge   pivot

11.11C Examples of connections through joints.

CONNECTIONS AND TRANSITIONS

Connections

Physical and visual connections are equally important in three-dimensional design. Visual connections compositionally unify multiple surfaces, while physical connections can increase strength, flexibility, functionality, and stability. Most commonly, connections are made

- Through *contact* (11.11A)
- Through *junctions* (11.11B)
- Through *joints* (11.11C)

Physical connections are especially important to woodworkers. Carpenters and furniture designers learn dozens of specific joints, hinges, and splices. Mary Miss's *Staged Gates* (11.12A) was largely constructed using three types of joints (11.12B). The use of nails, screws, bolts, or glue is required when lap or butt joints are used. Interlocking joints can often create a simple connection without such additional reinforcement.

11.12A Mary Miss, *Staged Gates,* **1979.** Wood, 12 × 50 × 120 ft (3.6 × 15.2 × 36.6 m).

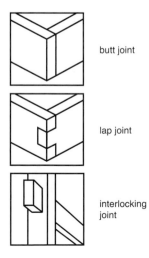

butt joint

lap joint

interlocking joint

11.12B Three types of joints.

11.13 Katherine Wetzel (photo), Elizabeth King (sculpture), *Pupil* from *Attention's Loop,* **1987–90.** Porcelain, glass eyes, carved wood, brass, one-half life size.

Employed to create functional objects, industrial designers pay particular attention to all types of connections. Because of the various joints used in its construction, a simple camera tripod can be expanded or collapsed, and the top can be rotated and reoriented. A sculpture based on the human figure (11.13) presents an even wider array of possibilities. Ball-and-socket joints at the shoulders and hips create rotating forms, while hinge joints in the fingers, knees, and elbows permit a folding and unfolding movement.

Visual connections are just as important as physical connections. A split yellow-orange circle dominates the center of John Okulick's *Wind Wizard* (11.14). Through closure, we mentally connect the halves, despite their physical separation. A second broken circle echoes the interior circle and creates a dynamic boundary for the composition as a whole. The two gold spheres at the upper left and lower right seem poised for movement. Every form is connected to at least one other form, enhancing overall continuity in the design.

Transitions

Many types of transitions can be created in three-dimensional design. The various angles and joints in Eduardo Chillida's *Asbesti Gogora III* (11.15)

11.14 John Okulick, *Wind Wizard,* **1987.** Painted wood, gold leaf, oil stick, 22 × 25 × 6 in. (55.9 × 63.5 × 15.2 cm).

11.15 Eduardo Chillida, *Asbesti Gogora III,* 1962–64. Oak, 81½ × 136⅜ × 73⅛ in. (207.3 × 346.4 × 184.2 cm).

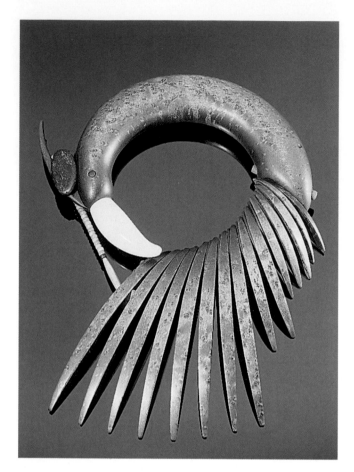

11.16 Liv Blåvarp, *Bird*, 1991. Neckpiece, bird's-eye maple, satinwood, whale tooth, 12½ × 10¼ in. (32 × 26 cm).

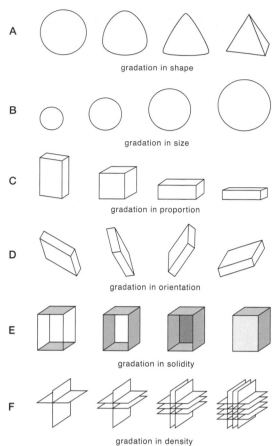

11.17A–F Examples of gradation.

create an abrupt transition from surface to surface, while a fluid transition helps unify the various sections of Liv Blåvarp's *Bird* (11.16). Fluid transitions are often created through gradual change from one form or surface to another. Such **gradation** creates sequential change within a consistent pattern. Examples of gradation are shown in figure 11.17A–F.

Key Questions

CONNECTIONS AND TRANSITIONS

- How can physical and visual connections enhance the strength of your artwork?

- Which type of transition is most appropriate to the idea or emotion you wish to convey?

- What happens when two or more types of transitions are used in a single artwork?

TRADITIONAL AND TRANSFORMATIVE MATERIALS

Stone

Limestone, basalt, marble, and other dense, fine-grained stones have been used since prehistory to create durable and imposing objects. Handheld stone amulets have been worn to ward off evil, while monumental sculptures, such as Mount Rushmore and the pyramids at Giza, have been constructed to commemorate political and spiritual figures as well as religious beliefs. Using chisels, mallets, and rasps, stone carvers can create remarkably delicate forms with an amazing array of textures.

In *Blind Man's Bluff* (11.18), Louise Bourgeois used traditional methods to make a very contemporary statement. Spherical and cylindrical forms seem to bubble up from the lower half of the sculpture. They are capped by a block of rough stone.

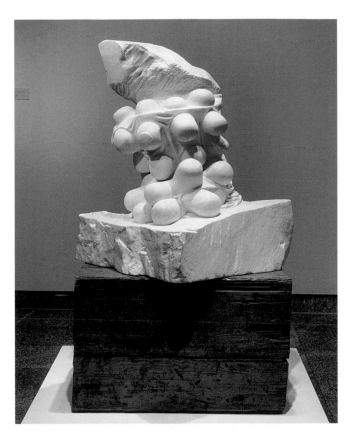

11.18 Louise Bourgeois, *Blind Man's Bluff*, 1984. Marble, 36 × 35½ × 25 in. (91.4 × 90.2 × 63.5 cm).

This contrast, which Bourgeois describes as "polarization," creates tension between the animated and sexually suggestive forms and the intractable stone cap. Surrounded by sexual promiscuity as a child, Bourgeois has often described the emotional blindness she developed as a coping strategy.

Clay

Clay is perhaps the most basic and versatile of all materials. Essentially made from refined earth, it can be hand-formed using coil, slab, and carving techniques; poured into molds; and "thrown," using a potter's wheel. When fired, it becomes extremely durable and can be decorated with beautiful colored glazes.

All of these qualities are fully exploited by contemporary ceramicists. Born into a family of traditional Cochiti potters, Virgil Ortiz began making pottery at the age of six. Creating a fusion between traditional Native American methods and contemporary life, Ortiz combines bold surface decoration with animated figurative forms (11.19). The malleability of clay is strongly evident in Jean-Pierre Larocque's *Head Series* (see figure 11.9, page 245). Adding and subtracting textural layers, Larocque combined the fluidity of gesture drawing with the solidity of fired clay. Carving into "leather-hard" clay, David MacDonald (see Profile, page 260) activates his simple forms with parallel and intersecting bands of texture.

Metals

Bronze casting, refined during the Renaissance, has traditionally been used for large-scale sculptures of all kinds. Gold, silver, copper, pewter, and brass are more commonly used for jewelry and utensils. Most metals can be cast, forged, soldered, etched, and stamped.

Mariko Kusumoto used copper, nickel silver, sterling silver, resin, bronze, and brass to create *Tansu no Oku* (11.20). A lotus blossom, seashells, butterflies, and an open hand extend out from an etched sheet of

11.19 Virgil Ortiz, *Untitled*, 2002. Cochiti red clay, white and red clay slip, black (wild spinach) paint, 28 × 29 in. (71 × 74 cm).

11.20 Mariko Kusumoto, *Tansu no Oku.* Copper, nickel silver, sterling silver, resin, bronze, and brass, 15½ × 14 × 14 in. (39.4 × 35.6 × 35.6 cm) open.

turn-of-the-century advertisements. A plastic resin adds color and sparkle to the butterflies. The structure is based on a children's pop-up book, while the images recall the Victorian fascination with mechanical and natural objects.

John Paul Miller's *Dung Beetle Pendant Brooch* (11.21) was also inspired by nature. Both the lowly beetle and its ball of dung are transformed by exquisite construction and the extensive use of gold.

Wood

Traditional cultures worldwide use wood to create functional structures, such as buildings, furniture, and utensils, as well as sculptural objects,

11.21 John Paul Miller, *Dung Beetle Pendant Brooch,* 1984. Gold fabricated, granulated, and enameled, 2¾ × 1¾ × ⅝ in. (7 × 4.5 × 1.5 cm).

such as masks, ancestor poles, and walking sticks. Readily available in most areas, wood is inherently beautiful, easily painted, relatively lightweight, and surprisingly versatile. It can be carved, steam-formed, and assembled using various hinges and joints. Traditional examples of wood sculpture are shown on pages 246, 247, and 248. Figure 11.22 demonstrates the power of wood in a nontraditional setting. Constructed from pliable strands of bamboo, Patrick Dougherty's large-scale artwork seems to arise directly from nature.

Glass

Glass, which is made primarily from silica, has been used for containers of all kinds since the time of the pharaohs. It can be transparent or opaque and, with the addition of copper, cadmium, cobalt, and other materials, can take on a complete range of colors. In its molten state, it can be poured, blown, pressed into molds, drawn into threads, stamped, and extruded.

The transparency of glass is emphasized in Eric Hilton's *Innerland* (11.23). Constructed from 25 cubes of clear glass, the sculpture appears to shift with each change in the viewer's position. Hilton combined the transparency and brilliance of glass with its density and mass to create an evocative artwork.

Gene Koss's *Hay Loader* (11.24) transforms a piece of farming equipment into a sculpture that is both fragile and imposing. Because we know that the heavy sheets of glass will shatter if the tower topples, the entire sculpture is charged with energy.

Fibers

The term *fibers* covers a wide range of linear materials, including strips of willow, bamboo, and reeds, as well as the more familiar cotton, linen, silk, and wool. Like the other traditional materials, fibers have been used for basketry, quilts, clothing, and other commonplace objects, as well as for prayer rugs and ritual clothing from shrouds to wedding dresses. Most fibers can be painted or dyed and can be worked in many ways, including weaving, braiding, knotting (as with macramé), knitting, and felting. Nick Cave's *Soundsuit* (11.25) combines technical

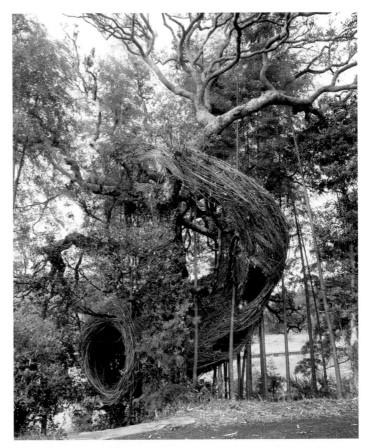

11.22 Patrick Dougherty, *Untitled*, 1992. Bamboo, height 25 ft (7.6 m), diameter 10 ft (3 m). Temporary installation.

11.23 Eric Hilton, *Innerland*, 1980. Engraved by Ladislav Havlik, Lubomir Richter, Peter Schelling, and Roger Selander, cut by Mark Witter. Cast, cut, engraved, sandblasted, and polished, 3⅞ × 19⅜ × 19⅜ in. (9.9 × 49.3 × 49.3 cm).

mastery with whimsical inventiveness. Used in both solo and group performances, it creates various sounds as the dancer moves.

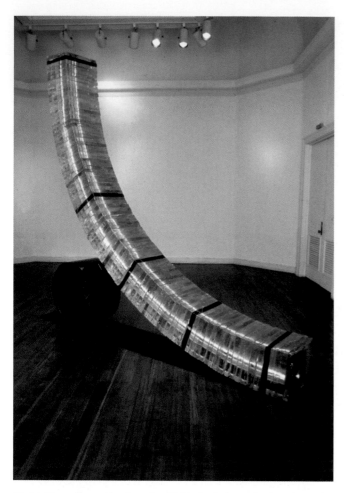

11.24 Gene Koss, *Hay Loader*, 2006. Cast glass, steel, and neon, 13 × 2 × 10 ft (4 × 0.61 × 3 m).

11.25 Nick Cave, *Soundsuit*, 2009. Mixed mediums, 90 × 40 × 32 in. (229 × 102 × 81 cm).

Three qualities most distinguish contemporary fibers. First, the traditional separation between sculpture and fiber arts has largely disappeared. As demonstrated by *Red Forest* (see figure 9.26, page 193), fibers are often used for large-scale designs. Second, the definition of *fibers* has become increasingly broad. For example, Cathy Strokowsky wove together glass, wire, artificial sinew, and horsehair to create *Glass Pod with Hair,* shown in figure 11.26. Third, the relationship between fiberworks and the human body continues to evolve through performance art and installations.

Plastics

Transparent, translucent, or opaque, plastics can be formed into sheets and then cut and assembled. Many types of plastic can also be extruded, cast, vacuum-formed, and stamped. Lightweight, varied in color, and relatively cheap to produce, plastics have fueled a revolution in the design and distribution of household products.

Using a variety of plastics, Ron Mueck has created many large-scale sculptures of human figures. One of the most compelling is *The Boy* (11.27), installed in London's Millennium Dome. The crouching adolescent boy seems vulnerable and defensive, despite (or perhaps because of) his enormous size. As with all of Mueck's work, the details are astounding: every hair is defined, and the eyes seem to glisten with moisture as well as apprehension.

Ephemeral Materials

One of the most notable characteristics of postmodern art is its emphasis on concept combined with a de-emphasis on traditional materials and methods. Many artists today deliberately use **ephemera** (materials that rapidly decay) or trash (which is already in a state of decay). In some cases, the transient nature of the material is part of the concept; in other cases, conceptual punch simply trumps material value.

11.26 Cathy Strokowsky, *Glass Pod with Hair,* 2001. Blown glass, sandblasted, woven artificial sinew, wire, horsehair, 4¾ × 12½ × 4¾ in. (12 × 31.75 × 12 cm).

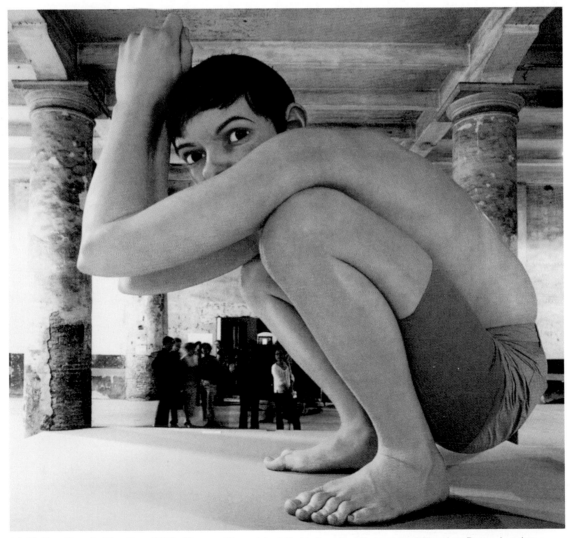

11.27 Ron Mueck, *The Boy,* 1999. Site-specific work installed in the Mind Zone at the Millennium Dome, London, United Kingdom. Mixed media, 16.8 × 16.8 × 7.9 ft (490 × 490 × 240 cm).

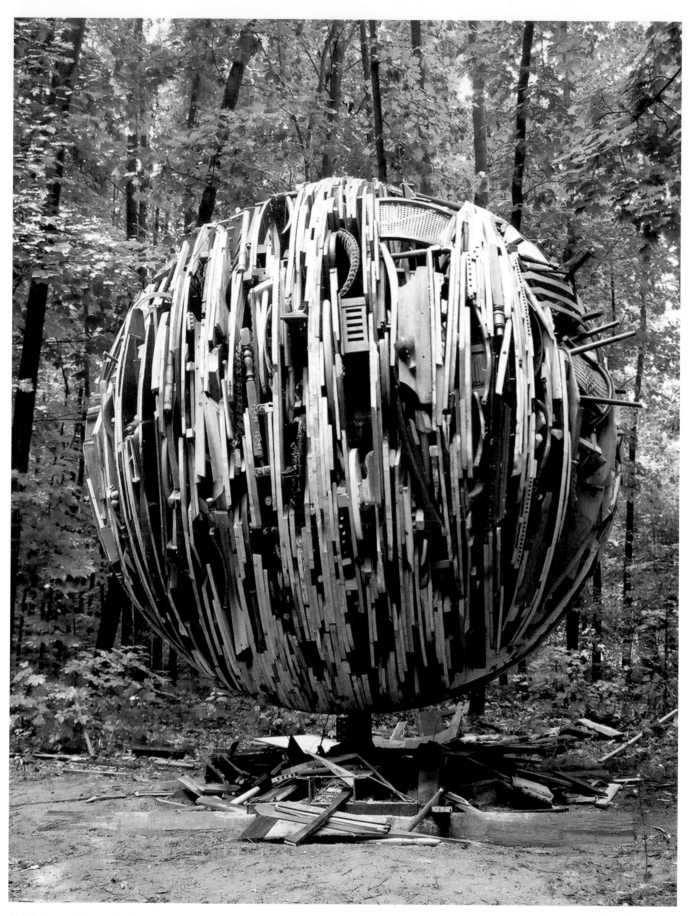

11.28 Ernest Daetwyler, *Time Bomb (Im Hölzernen Himmel),* **2008.** Old furniture parts, steel substructure, 11.8 ft (3.6 m) diameter.

Time Bomb (11.28) by Ernest Daetwyler is a dramatic example. Constructed from fragments of broken furniture supported by a steel armature, the nearly 10-foot-tall sphere is ominous and imposing. Precariously balanced and displayed in a lovely forest, this time bomb seems on the verge of exploding.

Tara Donovan uses commonplace materials in a very different way. From hundreds of mass-produced cups, drinking straws, plastic forks, and other lightweight materials, she creates elegant structures and installations that seem to defy their humble origins. The installation shown in figure 11.29 suggests both cloud formations and biological structures.

Rick Paul also used nonprecious materials in many of his installations. *Querschnitt* (11.30) was made from an especially strong type of foam board and translucent fabric supported by a wooden armature. Filling a room nearly the size of a basketball court, this temporary artwork had to be both strong and inexpensive to produce.

Key Questions

TRADITIONAL AND TRANSFORMATIVE MATERIALS

- Research the material you plan to use. How has it been used traditionally? Do contemporary uses expand its physical and conceptual potential?

- What are the conceptual and environmental advantages of ephemera? What are the challenges in terms of construction and longevity?

11.29 Tara Donovan, *Untitled* (Styrofoam Cups), 2008. Styrofoam cups and glue. Installation dimensions variable. Installation view, The Institute of Contemporary Art, Boston.

11.30 Rick Paul, *Vessel at Rest*, 1994. Installation, Gatorfoam™, wood, fabric, 24 ft × 12 ft (7.31 × 3.6 m).

STUDENT MATERIALS

To minimize cost and expedite exploration, three-dimensional design projects are often constructed from common materials, such as bristol board, corrugated cardboard, plywood, wire, plaster gauze, and plaster. This section describes the characteristics of the most basic types of boards and adhesives.

Boards

As noted in our discussion of 11.30 on the previous page, many types of board are remarkably strong as well as inexpensive. *Bristol board* is like thick, stiff paper. It is available in various thicknesses from 1-ply (similar to drawing paper in weight) to 5-ply (similar in weight to illustration board). A *cold-pressed* (or vellum) surface is slightly textured, while a *hot-pressed* (or plate) surface is very smooth. The vellum surface is best for graphite, charcoal, pastels, and colored pencils. The smooth surface is good for felt markers and for pen and ink. Either can be used for model building, book arts, and planar structures.

Chipboard is a dense, gray, uncoated board made from recycled paper. Most drawing pads have a chipboard backing. Single-thickness chipboard can be cut with an X-Acto knife or a heavy-duty paper cutter; use a utility knife to cut all heavier board.

Foamcore is light, strong, and rather unforgiving. It must be cut with a very sharp X-Acto knife or a scroll saw, and dents in the surface or cutting errors are difficult to repair.

Corrugated cardboard is strong, lightweight, cheap, and amazingly versatile. It is often used for large-scale projects. Through careful planning, you can use the grain (corrugation direction) to create curving planes or even expose it to add texture.

Glues

White glue is nontoxic and water-soluble when wet. It can be used with most porous materials, including all the boards described previously. It is not suitable for paper-to-paper adhesion, as most papers will buckle as they dry.

Glue stick is water-soluble, acid-free, and nontoxic. Designed as an adhesive for thin paper, glue stick generally is ineffective for gluing any kind of board.

Rubber cement is a traditional paper adhesive that can be "erased" when misapplied. However, because rubber cement is highly toxic, flammable, and impermanent, it has limited use in three-dimensional design classes.

Hot glue is a wax-based, translucent material that is heated in a gun and applied as a hot, viscous fluid. It is most effective in adhering nonporous materials, and it provides a quick way to create an assemblage. It can also be used to tack cardboard structures together while the white glue dries.

Dry mounting tissue is distributed in sheets of thin, clear plastic. Adhesion occurs when this material is heated, either in a drymount press or using an iron. This is an excellent adhesive for most papers and lightweight cloth, and it is widely used in photography and book arts.

Tapes

Transparent tape ("Scotch tape") is an all-purpose, lightweight, temporary adhesive for paper. It is not an effective adhesive for boards.

Masking tape is tough, flexible crepe-paper tape. It is designed to mask off unpainted areas, as when painting a car. It is a good temporary adhesive for boards, especially during the model-building stage.

Drafting tape and *artist's tape* are like masking tape but have less glue. They can be removed without damaging the surface to which they are applied.

Double-sided encapsulating tape has acrylic adhesive on both surfaces. A layer of thin paper protects one side until the tape is applied. An archival version of this material is sold by bookbinding stores, and it can be used for well-crafted final projects.

Key Questions

STUDENT MATERIALS

- Why did you choose a particular material for your project? Considering its strength, workability, and cost, is it really the best material for your purpose?
- How would a change in material affect the meaning of your project?
- What nontraditional materials might you use? How can they expand meaning?

11.31 Michele Oka Doner, *Terrible Table,* **1988.** Bronze and glass, 16½ × 26 × 22 in. (42 × 66 × 56 cm).

MEANINGFUL MATERIALS

The materials used in most three-dimensional design classes are inexpensive, can be easily manipulated, and are conceptually neutral. As you begin to expand your ideas through more advanced assignments, you can more fully explore the meaning of materials.

Every material has unique psychological associations as well as physical properties. Mirrors are fragile, reflective surfaces commonly used for observation of the self and others. A pile of autumn leaves suggests decay and exudes an earthy aroma. Powdered turmeric spice is pungent and suggests both cooking and travel.

Whether we are creating a sculpture or designing a product, materials have meaning. For example, the thorny branches at the base of Michele Oka Doner's *Terrible Table* (11.31) are sure to change the emotional atmosphere of any room this table occupies. The wood and wire Deborah Butterfield used to create *Large Horse #4* (11.32) force us to reconsider our understanding of both horses and nature. A love of materials and an understanding of their characteristics are essential aspects of all three-dimensional work.

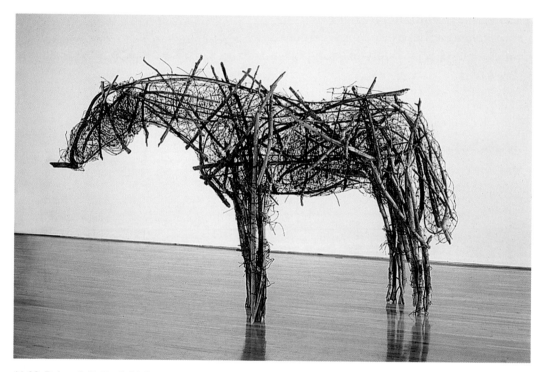

11.32 Deborah Butterfield, *Large Horse #4,* 1979. Steel, wire, sticks, 77 × 124 × 33 in. (195 × 315 × 84 cm).

SUMMARY

- Choice of material substantially affects both the structure and the meaning of a three-dimensional object.

- Strength, workability, durability, weight, cost, toxicity, and function are major considerations when an artist or a designer chooses a material.

- Materials can be strengthened by using composites, by using skeletons or exoskeletons, and by distributing force.

- Common construction methods include addition, subtraction, solidification, and displacement.

- Connections and transitions can increase visual impact as well as structural strength.

- Traditional materials, such as stone, wood, metal, clay, glass, fibers, and plastics, are used by contemporary artists to express a wide range of ideas.

- Ephemeral materials can expand meaning, reduce cost, and minimize environmental impact.

- Student materials, including various types of boards and adhesives, work best when used for the intended purpose.

KEY TERMS

additive sculpture	compression	gradation	solidification
armature	displacement	modeling	subtractive sculpture
assemblage	ephemera	shear	tension
bend	exoskeleton	skeleton (endoskeleton)	torque
composite	flying buttress		

STUDIO PROJECTS

To apply the concepts from this chapter in the studio, check out the Projects page in the Online Learning Center at www.mhhe.com/stewart4e. The following is a sample of the chapter-related assignments that are described in step-by-step detail.

Wooden Wizardry. Transforming a standard wooden plank into an extraordinary wizard's staff.
Book Transformed. Transforming an old or used book into a new content-based sculpture.

Profile:
David MacDonald, Ceramicist

A Passion for Pottery

Internationally renowned ceramicist David MacDonald is best known for his work with utilitarian vessels. His work has been included in over 60 exhibitions, including the Torpedo Factory Art Center in Alexandria, Virginia; the Studio Museum in Harlem; and the Afro-American Historical and Cultural Museum in Philadelphia. He is also a renowned community leader, having worked in an adult literacy program, in a summer ceramics intensive program for high school students, and with inmates at the Green Haven Maximum Security Correctional Facility in New York State.

MS: How did you start making art?

DM: Initially, it was a way to create some private space. As the third in a family of nine children, I always shared a bedroom with at least three of my brothers. I would help my parents unpack the groceries, then unfold the paper bags so that I could use the inside as drawing paper. Through hours of drawing, I was able to create my own little world.

MS: In our conversations and in viewing your work, I am struck by your passion for ceramics in general and functional vessels in particular. What is special about clay?

DM: I was introduced to ceramics during my second year in college. I was immediately fascinated by clay: it is responsive to the slightest pressure and can record the finest impression. After my first mug came out of the kiln and I made my first cup of tea, I was hooked. The idea of turning a lump of dirt into a useful object amazed me. Since I grew up with very little material wealth, I loved the idea of transforming nothing into something.

Now, I am drawn to functional ceramics because I like playing with the interaction between the object and the user. Having to produce a functional object makes the creative act much more interesting and challenging for me. When a teapot has just the right weight, balance, and proportions, it makes the act of pouring tea a celebration of the physical world.

MS: What is the source of your ideas?

DM: Anything can become a conscious or unconscious inspiration. I can get lost in the produce section of the supermarket: the shapes and colors of the vegetables give me all sorts of ideas.

On a more scholarly level, I was influenced by Japanese and Chinese ceramics during college, and for the past 30 years I have been strongly influenced by African art and culture.

MS: Yes, I notice that a dramatic change in your work occurred around 1978. Before that time, your work was sculptural, representational, and highly charged politically; afterward, it became more utilitarian and abstract. What happened?

DM: At the opening for a solo show in Syracuse, I was asked a question by an elderly white woman that dramatically changed my attitude about my work. She innocently asked if there was anything positive about being black in America or was it just one frustration and humiliation after another. The question haunted me for months afterward. I realized that my creative work had been based on anger and a feeling of victimization. As I matured as an individual, I realized that my experiences weren't limited to anger—there is much more to my life than that! I then decided to tap the rich and varied cultural and artistic tradition to which I am heir. Now I am most interested in expressing the magnificence and nobility of the human spirit and in celebrating my African heritage.

MS: What distinguishes a great pot from a mundane pot?

DM: There is no simple answer to this question. We can talk endlessly about form, surface, line, and so forth and still not gain any real insight into what makes one pot great and another mundane, yet we immediately feel it when the mixture of physical elements is just right. Out of the 30 similar bowls a potter produces, two or three always seem to stand apart, as something special.

The search for this elemental quality makes my art magical and compels me to make the next piece. Ironically, if I ever identify exactly what it is that makes an exceptional piece, the excitement will be sucked out of the creative process. The search is as compelling as the solution.

MS: Tell me about the vessel pictured here.
DM: *Carved Stoneware Storage Jar* was inspired by the bulbous form of a melon or gourd. The body is full and round and the lid handle is suggestive of a stem. I like the sense of an internal force or energy stretching the outer shell almost to the point of bursting.

First, I considered the function of the jar. To a large extent, the function determines the form. A certain size range facilitates everyday use. If the size is increased, the object is more suitable for ceremonial use, or as a decorative object. Certain shapes offer more storage capacity and better accessibility to whatever is being stored. Finally, the base must be big enough to provide stability.

The surface was carved when the jar was leather-hard, a couple of days after being thrown on the potter's wheel. A form this large can "carry" a fairly complex pattern, composed of smaller shapes in combination with larger design areas. By leaving some areas uncarved, I was able to create an overlapping effect and increase the illusion of space. The slashing diagonal lines help to unify the design and move the viewer's eye around the form, reinforcing the spherical volume.

MS: What were the most valuable lessons you learned from your teachers?
DM: From Joseph Gilliard at Hampton University, I learned the history and technique of ceramics and gained greater patience and self-control. I developed my self-awareness and passion for communication through my work with Robert Stull at the University of Michigan. From Henry Gernhardt, my Syracuse University colleague for 24 years, I learned that teaching is also an art. In nearly 40 years of teaching, Henry's commitment to his art and his students never faltered.

MS: Is there any advice you would like to give to my students?
DM: An artist has to believe in him- or herself. The dedication, courage, and energy my students bring to the classroom are more important than anything I can offer. If you want to stand above the crowd, your passion for your art must be manifest through a willingness to work harder than anyone else. The students who succeed see their art as a way of life and not simply as a way of earning a living. My job as a teacher is to help my students realize their potential and to bring eloquence to their unique voice.

David MacDonald, *Carved Stoneware Storage Jar*, 1997. 15 in. (38.1 cm).

Physical and Cerebral

What is the difference between the pile of wood in figure 12.1 and the sculpture in figure 12.2? The size, orientation, and location of the pile of wood are based on its purpose. It provides the raw material needed for building a house. Positioned at the edge of a construction site, the boards are arranged in a roughly parallel position so that workers can easily grasp and remove individual planks. The pile of wood is purely functional. Its organization has no aesthetic intention.

At first glance, figure 12.2 may seem very much like a pile of wood. The rough planks are clustered together, in close proximity to the house and in a parallel position. On closer examination, we see the perpendicular boards that elevate the structure. Balanced on stilts, the mass of wood seems suspended and in transition. It continues around the house and into the windows. Is the house expelling or inhaling the boards? The entire structure seems poised, ready to shift at any moment.

How and why was this sculpture made? Artist Tadashi Kawamata begins by collecting scrap wood from demolished buildings. He then constructs temporary installations, which he describes as "cancers," on conventional buildings. With no predetermined end point, the structures grow like weeds, often enveloping the building. When the exhibition ends, Kawamata continues onward, dismantling the construction to create another sculpture elsewhere.

12.1 Pile of wood at a construction site.

12.2 Tadashi Kawamata, *Tetra House N–3, W26 Project,* Sapporo, Japan.

Using scrap material to build temporary structures, his work demonstrates the fluidity and circulation of urban structures. His design is based on aesthetic rather than functional criteria.

All three-dimensional work gains power through its physical presence. Sculpture, however, is much more than brute force. It is through the transformation of tangible material into ideas and emotions that a sculpture gains significance. The planks in figure 12.1 begin and end as physical material. A pile of wood is just a pile of wood. By contrast, sculpture, such as *Tetra House N–3, W26 Project*, uses physical material to explore and express ideas.

CONSTRUCTED THOUGHT

From Life to Art

Contemporary sculpture is made from a wide range of materials, including ice, fire, blood, spools of thread, and crushed automobiles. In her *Ceremonial Arch* (12.3), Mierle Ukeles combined the metal and wood used in traditional sculpture with gloves, lights, metal springs, and asphalt to create an artwork that is both visually exuberant and structurally sound. Sculpture is now shown in parks, subway stations, and public plazas, in addition to galleries and museums. Because contemporary sculpture is so reliant on everyday materials and public settings, the relationship between art and life has become especially close.

This can be an advantage or a disadvantage. Connection to life gives art its vitality. Authenticity is essential. For example, when a play expresses actual feelings in a compelling way, it connects to our personal experience. Too direct a connection is deadly, however. A pile of wood is just a pile of wood. For art to have meaning, commonplace

12.3 Mierle Laderman Ukeles, *Ceremonial Arch Honoring Service Workers in the New Service Economy*, 1988. Steel arch with materials donated from New York City agencies, including gloves, lights, grass, straps, springs, and asphalt; overall structure 11 ft × 8 ft × 8 ft 8 in. (3.35 × 2.43 × 2.44 m), plus glove branches ranging from 2 to 4 ft (61 to 122 cm) long.

experiences must be distilled, reexamined, or transformed. It has often been said that a play is "life with the boring parts left out." A play that simply replicates everyday experience can never transport an audience beyond the commonplace. Likewise, sculpture requires a heightened experience *beyond* everyday life. Through a combination of insight and hard work, the sculptor transforms even the most resistant material into compelling communication. When all elements in a sculpture support the central concept, the viewer is simultaneously connected by the reality of the material and transported by the power of the idea.

Degrees of Representation

Representational artworks often depict persons or objects in such exquisite detail that they seem to come to life. Michelangelo's *Pietà* (12.4) is a good example. In this massive sculpture, Mary grieves as she cradles the dead Jesus. Every crease in the fabric is defined, and every nuance of gesture is deliberate. Mary's right hand extends Jesus' flesh as she gently lifts his right shoulder. She tilts her head slightly, and her left hand echoes the position of his feet. Sculptures such as the *Pietà* seem to embody life. They engage our thoughts and emotions through their compelling realism and narrative implications.

Nonobjective artworks can be appreciated for their pure physical beauty. For example, the simple metal rings Sandra Enterline constructed for her *Caged Sphere Bracelet Series* (12.5) work beautifully as ends in themselves. We can appreciate their economy and grace without knowing a story or pursuing any additional ideas they may suggest.

Most sculptural objects fall somewhere between these two extremes. These **abstract artworks** have been distilled down from a recognizable source. Myra Mimlitsch-Gray's *Timepiece* (12.6) simultaneously suggests the mechanism and movement of a clock, a pendulum, and a musician's metronome. By reducing

12.4 Michelangelo, *Pietà*, 1498–1500. Marble, 5 ft 8 in. × 2 ft 3 in. (1.74 × 0.69 m).

these familiar timepieces to their essential form, she was able to create an economical design that conveys a universal sense of time.

Each approach has its advantages. Nonobjective forms are often used in situations that require universality or simplicity. Barnett Newman's

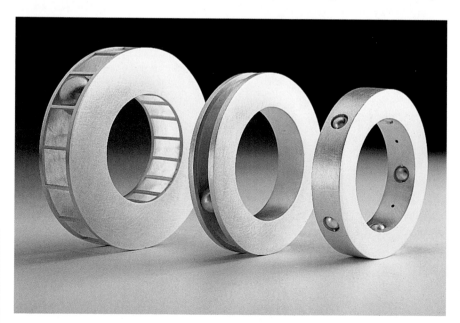

12.5 Sandra Enterline, *Caged Sphere Bracelet Series*, 1992. Sterling silver, 18-karat gold, hollow-formed, fabricated. Left to right: 5 × 5 × 1⅛ in. (12.7 × 12.7 × 3 cm), 4 × 4 × ¾ in. (10.2 × 10.2 × 1.9 cm), 4 × 4 × ¾ in. (10.2 × 10.2 × 1.9 cm).

12.6 Myra Mimlitsch-Gray, *Timepiece*, 1988. Kinetic brooch, 14-karat gold, lens, diamonds, abrasive disk. Fabricated, 2¼ × 1½ × ¼ in. (6 × 4 × 0.5 cm).

12.7 Barnett Newman, *Broken Obelisk,* **1963–67.** Cor-Ten steel, 26 × 10½ × 10½ ft (66 × 26.7 × 26.7 m).

12.8 Walter Martin and Paloma Muñoz, *Of Bodies Born Up by Water,* **1987.** Plaster, oil paint, sheet metal, wood, 111½ × 20 × 16½ in. (283 × 51 × 42 cm).

Broken Obelisk (12.7) is a monochromatic structure constructed from a simple pyramid and an inverted obelisk. The point of contact between the two sections becomes charged with energy, as the top half seems to balance on the top of the pyramid. Caught in this moment of equilibrium, the sculpture is as carefully balanced as a ballerina on her toes.

On the other hand, a representational approach can stimulate the imagination by providing a fresh interpretation of a familiar object. In *Of Bodies Born Up by Water* (12.8), Walter Martin and Paloma Muñoz used a similar structure to create a very different effect. The poised obelisk is now a grandfather clock. When it topples, time, memory, and family history may be erased.

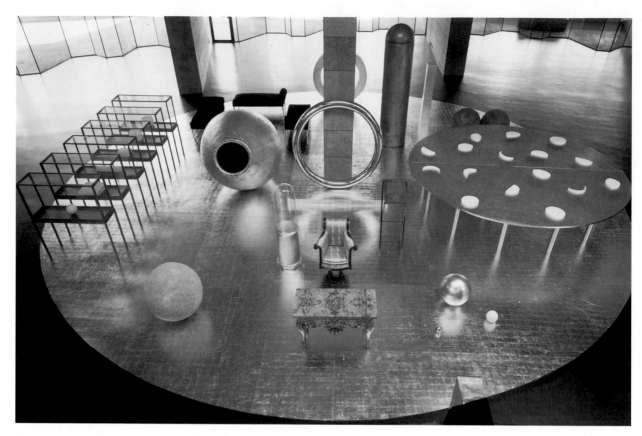

12.9 James Lee Byars, *The Perfect Thought,* 1990 (installation shot). Various objects covered with gold leaf, composed in one of two circles of gold leaf, large circle 40 ft (12.2 m) diameter, small circle 27 ft (8.2 m) diameter.

Boundaries

Because the art/life connection is so important, sculptors must be especially attentive to the physical and psychological boundaries in each piece. As a dividing line between objects, images, or experiences, the boundary is charged with energy. It can serve three major purposes.

Boundaries Can Connect

A simple shape can create a boundary. To define *The Perfect Thought* (12.9), James Lee Byars placed two gold-leaf circles on the floor. The larger circle enclosed 23 separate works from earlier exhibitions, while the smaller circle remained empty. This simple strategy unified a collection of individual artworks while leaving a second space open, to be filled by the viewer's imagination.

Dwelling (12.10) by Yong Soon Min, deals with psychological boundaries. Born in Korea and raised in the United States, Min explores issues of alienation and disorientation in her artwork. In *Dwelling*, she combined a brightly lit Korean dress with a pile of maps, photographs, and books. A fragment of poetry, inserted in the dress, describes the loss of identity. In this type of sculpture, boundaries between the personal and the public begin to blur.

Boundaries Can Separate

Constructed from nine 12-foot-wide bushes within the median of a busy highway, Maya Ying Lin's *Topo* (12.11) uses a boundary to separate as well as to connect. Enclosed within the mile-long median, the bushes provide a series of visual stepping-stones, inviting us to move down the line diagonally. Shifting circles at either end of the sculpture appear to rotate the last two bushes, directing our attention back down the line. This illusion of perpetual motion activates the simple design.

Psychological separation adds power to George Segal's *The Subway* (12.12). This artwork replicates a commonplace setting, using actual subway seats, handrails, and a window, which flashes with the lights of "passing" trains. The ghostly white plaster figure seems familiar but remains distant, the shell of a living, breathing person. In this installation, a psychological boundary transforms the commonplace into an expression of isolation.

12.10 Yong Soon Min, _Dwelling_, 1994. Mixed mediums, 72 × 42 × 28 in. (183 × 107 × 72 cm).

12.11 Maya Ying Lin, _Topo_, 1991. 1,600 × 40 ft (487.7 × 12.2 m).

12.12 George Segal, _The Subway_, 1968. Plaster, metal, glass, rattan, electrical parts with lightbulbs, map. 7 ft 4 in. × 9 ft 5 in. × 4 ft 2 in. (2.25 × 2.88 × 1.3 m).

12.13 Susan Trangmar, *Blue Skies*, 1990. Installation view, size varies.

12.14 Olafur Eliasson, *The Parliament of Reality*, 2006–09. Concrete, stone, stainless steel, water, trees, other plants. Dimensions variable. Installation at The Center for Curatorial Studios (CCS Bard), New York. The Center for Curatorial Studies and the Luma Foundation. © 2006 Olafur Eliasson.

Boundaries Can Enclose

Increasingly, sculptors are using every square inch of gallery space and surface to create complex installations. In *Blue Skies* (12.13), Susan Trangmar used the gallery walls as four large projection surfaces. Surrounded by the projections and by his or her own cast shadow, the viewer becomes a participant in the installation.

The sculpture itself can also envelop the viewer. Olafur Eliasson's *The Parliament of Reality* (12.14) is composed of multiple units, including a man-made island surrounded by a circular lake, grasslands, and two dozen trees. Shown here is a 20-foot-long bridge loosely enclosed by latticework. As visitors cross the bridge, they become part of the sculpture.

Bases and Places

Traditional sculpture is generally mounted on a **plinth,** which provides a horizontal base, or on a **pedestal,** which provides a vertical base. Either can serve three purposes:

- To physically separate the sculpture from the surrounding space
- To provide strength and structural stability

12.16 Edgar Hilaire Germain Degas, *Horse Galloping on Right Foot,* **c. 1881.** Bronze cast of wax model, 11⅛ in. (30 cm).

12.17 Benvenuto Cellini, *Perseus and Medusa,* **1545–54.** Bronze, 18 ft (5.5 m) h.

12.15 Barbara Chase-Riboud, *Malcolm X #3,* **1970.** Polished bronze and silk, 118 × 47 × 10 in. (300 × 120 × 25 cm).

• To elevate an object psychologically, distinguishing it from its surroundings and increasing its impact

Seemingly insignificant, the plinth or pedestal is actually a crucial component of sculpture, both physically and aesthetically. In figure 12.15, the marble base adds elevation as well as a marked contrast in material. As a result, Barbara Chase-Riboud's *Malcolm X #3* now has a solid platform from which to speak. The plinth in *Horse Galloping on Right Foot* (12.16), by Edgar Degas, provides a visual context for the galloping horse, as well as physical stability. The sculpture would collapse, physically and aesthetically, if the base were removed. The pedestal for Benvenuto Cellini's *Perseus and Medusa* (12.17) elevates the heroic statue and creates an architectural connection to the surrounding buildings.

For Constantin Brancusi, the base was an aesthetic element rather than a passive support. He used a specific pedestal form to enhance the power and grace of each of his variations on birds (figures 10.25, 10.26, and 10.27, page 230). Seeking dynamism rather than stability, Umberto Boccioni split the base in half

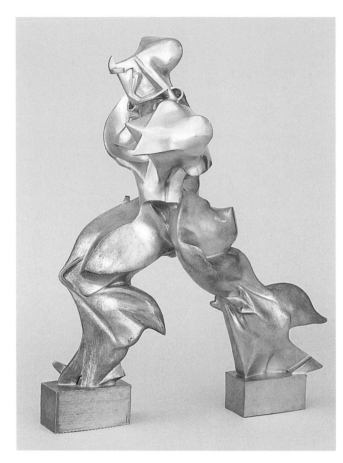

12.18 Umberto Boccioni, *Unique Forms of Continuity in Space,* 1913. Bronze (cast in 1931), 43⅞ × 34⅞ × 15¾ in. (111.2 × 88.5 × 40 cm).

when he composed *Unique Forms of Continuity in Space* (12.18). The abstracted figure strides forward in space, too energetic to be constrained by conventional boundaries.

In contemporary sculpture, the base often extends to include an entire architectural site. Resting directly on the surface of the plaza, the granite boulders in Elyn Zimmerman's *Marabar* (12.19) are intended to suggest continents, while the channel of water suggests the ocean. Combining large scale with a "baseless" design, the artist has dissolved the traditional boundary between the stones and the surroundings. The entire plaza is transformed into a sculptural site.

Key Questions

CONSTRUCTED THOUGHT

- How is your artwork similar to everyday life? How is it different?
- What can a boundary or base contribute to your design?
- How will the meaning change if your project is placed in a specific setting?

12.19 Elyn Zimmerman, *Marabar,* 1984. Boulders (natural cleft and polished granite) and water. Plaza: 140 × 60 ft (42.7 × 18.3 m).

12.20 Dennis Oppenheim, *Device to Root Out Evil*, 1997. Galvanized structural steel, anodized perforated aluminum, transparent red Venetian glass, concrete foundations, 20 × 15 × 8 ft (6.1 × 4.57 × 2.44 m).

12.21 Antony Gormley, *Learning to Think*, 1991. Lead, fiberglass, air, five figures, each 68 × 41¾ × 122 in. (173 × 106 × 310 cm).

PHYSICAL FORCES

Weight and Gravity

Of the forces of nature, gravity is the most immediately noticeable when we begin to construct a three-dimensional structure. Lines, spaces, and volumes must be organized according to the laws of physics while simultaneously meeting our aesthetic objectives. Balance is a structural necessity as well as a compositional force. After watching several prototypes collapse, it is easy to conclude that gravity is our enemy, to be conquered at all costs. But is it?

When we begin to analyze the uses of gravity in sculpture, we soon find that it is an asset rather than a liability. Just as a ballet dancer relies on gravity to provide a solid launching pad for each leap and a predictable support for each landing, so the sculptor uses gravity to express ideas and generate emotions.

Downward gravity animates *Device to Root Out Evil* (12.20). The inverted church structure seems to have been propelled aloft, finally driving into the ground upon landing. As noted by sculptor Dennis Oppenheim, this inversion of a familiar structure creates a reversal of content. The steeple is now pointing to hell rather than to heaven. Even without any cultural associations, however, we would still respond to the improbable balance and intense color in this large piece.

A combination of weight and weightlessness gives Antony Gormley's *Learning to Think* (12.21) its impact. Constructed from a mold made from the artist's own body, the hollow lead figures are basically identical. Hovering 10 feet off the ground, they seem weightless. At the same time, because they are suspended from the ceiling, each figure seems as heavy as a convict at the end of a hangman's noose. This paradox gives the sculpture great physical force

12.22 John Chamberlain, *The Hedge*, 1997. Painted milled steel, chromium-plated steel, stainless steel; overall installed 44½ in. × 44½ in. × 46 ft 4 in. (113 cm × 113 cm × 14.12 m); 16 units, each 44½ × 44½ × 12 in. (113 × 113 × 30.5 cm).

and communicates an elusive concept. Clearly, the knowledge embodied in this sculpture is not easy to attain!

Compression and Expansion

Most materials tend to compress as weight increases. As shown in figure 10.21 (on page 228), physical compression can be used to evoke a visceral response. We feel the pressure as the top log pushes down on the log below. Compression plays an especially important role in the works of John Chamberlain, who began making sculptures from crushed automobiles in the 1960s. In *The Hedge* (12.22), crushed pieces of metal have been transformed into an improbable garden. The contradiction between the materials and the meaning suggests a new definition of nature.

Expansion is an equally compelling force. Constructed from the charred fragments of a church that had been struck by lightning, Cornelia Parker's *Mass* (12.23) seems to present the event in suspended animation. Supported by fine steel wire and cotton thread, the hovering sculpture appears weightless, caught at the moment of explosion.

12.23 Cornelia Parker, *Mass (Colder Darker Matter)*, 1997. Charcoal retrieved from a church struck by lightning, suspended from steel wire and cotton thread, 10 × 10 × 10 ft (3.5 × 3.5 × 3.5 m).

Tension and Torsion

Tension can be used to stretch or bend an object, while torsion creates a twisting movement. Either can add physical and cerebral strength to a sculpture. Stretched taut, the steel cables in Kenneth Snelson's *Free Ride Home* (see figure 9.16, page 188) provide the force needed to elevate the aluminum tubes that dominate the sculpture. Tension is equally important for the designer. It is the tension in the bent metal rods that creates the structure in the Peregrine Tent from The North Face (12.24). In Maren Hassinger's *12 Trees No. 2* (12.25), cables and wires have been twisted together, then clamped at the top. Based on our experience in the physical world, we can feel the force in the twisted strands and imagine the explosive result if this power were released.

Presence and Absence

Presence is another important aspect of physicality. When we confront a massive sculpture, like the Olmec portrait on page 197 (figure 9.37), it exudes a strength that is far beyond anything a small photograph can convey. Equally, the space surrounding a sculpture or the absence of an anticipated object can have great impact.

Many sculptors have used this quality of presence and absence to explore the passage of time and the nature of memory. British sculptor Rachel Whiteread explores presence and absence in many of her works. Using hundreds of gallons of cement to create a solid cast from an empty house, she accentuated absence by making the space within the house

12.24 Peregrine Tent by The North Face, San Leandro, CA.

12.25 Maren Hassinger, *12 Trees No. 2*, 1979. Galvanized wire rope, 10 × 150 × 5 ft (3.1 × 45.7 × 1.5 m).

very solidly present (12.26). In *The Writing on the Wall* series, Shimon Attie used slide projections to remind us of shops and families destroyed during the Holocaust. Figure 12.27 shows one of the many slides from the 1930s that he projected onto various buildings in Berlin. The actual bookstore depicted disappeared long ago.

Process and Product

In the past 50 years, sculptors have expanded their choice of materials to include many physical and chemical processes:

- *Friction.* The graphite hands in Todd Slaughter's *Grinding Knuckles* (12.28) slowly rotate, grinding the sculpture away every time this artwork is displayed.

- *Condensation.* Sealed inside the Hans Haacke *Weather Cube* (12.29), water evaporates or condenses based on the

12.26 Rachel Whiteread, *House,* **1993.** Commissioned by Artangel Trust and Beck's (corner of Grove Rd. and Roman Rd., London, destroyed 1994).

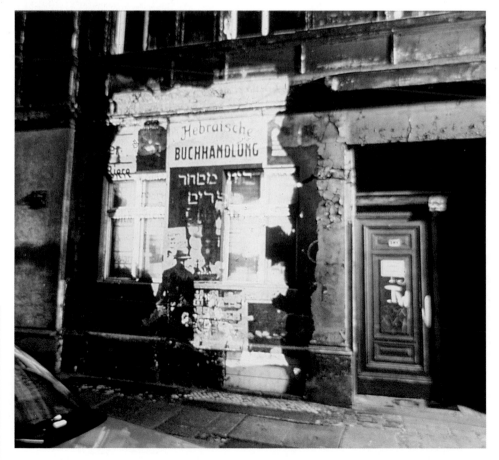

12.27 Shimon Attie, *Almstadtstrasse 43 (formerly Grenandierstrasse 7): Slide Projection of Former Hebrew Bookstore, Berlin,* **1930, from the series** *The Writing on the Wall,* **1992.** Ektacolor print of site-specific slide-projection installation, 20 × 24 in. (50.8 × 60.9 cm).

12.28 Todd Slaughter, *Grinding Knuckles,* **1993.** One RPM graphite and motors, 12 × 20 × 12 in. (30.5 × 51 × 30.5 cm).

ambient temperature inside the gallery.

- *Oxidation.* Ronald Dahl transformed the familiar ladder when he placed his sculpture in the Nevada desert and set it aflame to create *Seven Windows to a Sky on Fire* (12.30).

- *Filtration.* Located next to a wastewater treatment plant, Lorna Jordan's *Waterworks Gardens: The Grotto* (12.31) purifies up to 2,000 gallons of oil-laced storm water per minute. The 8-acre site includes stone mosaics, natural filtration systems, and colorful bands of sedges, yellow irises, and red-twig dogwoods.

12.29 Hans Haacke, *Weather Cube,* **1963–65.** Acrylic plastic, water, climate in area of display, 12-in. (30.5-cm) cube.

12.30 Ronald Dahl, *Seven Windows to a Sky on Fire,* 1982. Wood/flame, 9 × 12 × 3 in. (22.7 × 30.5 × 7.6 cm).

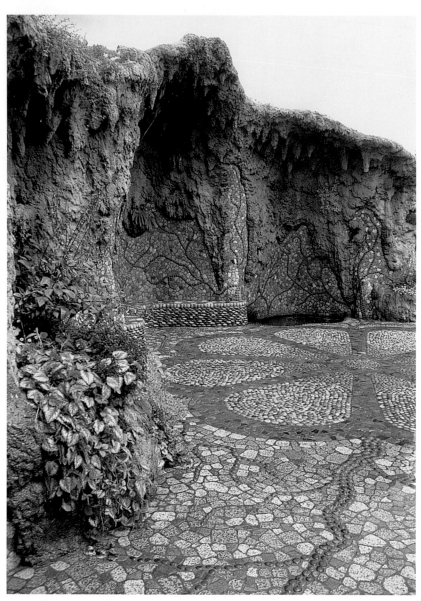

12.31 Lorna Jordan, *Waterworks Gardens: The Grotto,* 1996. Third of five public garden rooms in King County East Division Reclamation Plant, Renton, WA.

Key Questions

PHYSICAL FORCES

- How can weight or gravity add meaning to your artwork?

- What are the compressive and expansive limitations of the material(s) you are using? How might these forces enhance your concept?

- Tension and torsion create pent-up energy, like a spring ready to be released. How might these forces add meaning or a sense of suspense?

- What happens when the absence of an object or the residue after an event becomes the artwork?

- All materials and actions eventually decay. Can this process of decay become part of your concept?

12.32 Covered Effigy Jar with Removable Head. From Teotihuacán, Mexico. Ceramic, 10¾ in. (27.3 cm).

12.33 Raymond Duchamp-Villon, *The Great Horse*, 1957 version of a 1914 work. Bronze, 39¼ × 24 × 36 in. (99.7 × 60.9 × 91.4 cm).

CONTEMPORARY QUESTIONS, CONTEMPORARY ANSWERS

Building on a Tradition

Traditional sculpture has been characterized by four qualities. First, mass, or solid substance, rather than open space, is the primary concern. Traditional sculptures, such as Michelangelo's *Pietà* (see figure 12.4, page 262), are relatively solid. In this masterpiece, a sense of profound resignation is created through the use of gravity. The mother has fully accepted her grief. The position of the limbs and the folds in the fabric create a dynamic surface on a stable pyramidal mass. Second, the human figure is the primary subject. Sculptors have long sought to capture in wood, metal, or stone the vitality of a living person. Third, as a means to this end, traditional sculpture is overwhelmingly representational. Indeed, attention to detail and the ability to animate marble have long been the hallmarks of Western sculpture, from the Renaissance to Romanticism. Even an expressive pre-Columbian effigy jar (12.32) gains eloquence from the use of representation.

Finally, traditional sculptures often tell stories. Public monuments have frequently been commissioned by kings or by communities of ordinary people to tell national stories. For example, the Statue of Liberty was designed to embody the democratic ideal shared by France and the United States. It was financed through a public lottery, theatrical events, and even prizefights. The poem describing "huddled masses yearning to breathe free," combined with the heroic figure, distills the history of immigration to America into a few words.

Reinventing Sculpture

In Europe, the four qualities of traditional sculpture reached their climax during the nineteenth century. Seeking fresh ideas and new approaches, artists in Russia, Italy, and France then began a process that would transform sculpture forever.

Four major changes followed. First, space became a major concern. Sculpture began to be developed from the inside out, rather than being carved from the outside in. Second, abstraction and transformation became more important than description and representation. For example, Raymond Duchamp-Villon's *The Great Horse* (12.33), constructed from a mix of organic and mechanical parts, bears little resemblance to an actual horse. Third, while the human figure continued to dominate early-twentieth-century sculpture, by mid-century almost any subject matter could be used. Indeed, many significant artworks from this period, including Mark di Suvero's *Ik Ook Eindhoven* (see figure 9.18,

page 189), are nonobjective, having no external subject matter. Weight, balance, and the dynamics of space are the only content such works require. Most important, sculptors began to break down the traditional separation between art and life. Commonplace objects, such as Marcel Duchamp's *Bicycle Wheel* (12.34), were placed in galleries and defined as art. Finding a sculptural idea became as important as forming a sculptural object.

Contemporary Directions

The evolution of sculpture has accelerated in the past 30 years. Earthworks, which transform natural sites into sculptural settings, have become a powerful force in both art and ecology. An installation, which may combine time, space, and sound, can present both artist and audience with new opportunities for communication and expression. Performance art (which is discussed at greater length in Chapter Fifteen), combines art, technology, and theater. The traditional has become the transformative. Four of the manifestations of this change are described next.

Sculpture as Place

Traditionally permanent, sculpture has always been placed in a wide variety of significant settings. Stonehenge (12.35), constructed from massive limestone blocks weighing up to 50 tons, may have been used as a gigantic sundial by its Neolithic builders. The avenue approaching the stone circle is carefully aligned to the summer solstice, while stones within the circle are aligned with the northernmost and southernmost paths of the rising moon.

Likewise, contemporary sculptors add meaning to their work by exploring the physical, psychological, and temporal characteristics of each site. Glen Onwin's *Nigredo* (12.36) is one of four works in a series titled *As Above, So Below*. Placed in an abandoned chapel, this concrete pool, filled with water, black brine, and wax, seems especially ominous in the once-sacred site. In a very different investigation of place, David Adjaye's *Europolis* (12.37) traces transportation networks between the various capitals of Europe. Sandwiched between panes of glass, the brilliant red lines resemble both pulsating blood vessels and a teeming microscopic world.

12.34 Marcel Duchamp, *Bicycle Wheel,* **1951.** (Third version, after lost original of 1913.) Assemblage, metal wheel, 25½ in. (63.8 cm) diameter, mounted on painted wood stool 23¾ in. (60.2 cm) h.; overall 50½ × 25½ × 16⅝ in. (128.3 × 63.8 × 42 cm).

12.35 Stonehenge (aerial view), Salisbury Plain, England, c. 2800–1500 BCE.

12.36 Glenn Onwin, _Nigredo_, 1992. Installation view of exhibition _As Above, So Below_, at the Square Chapel, Halifax, May 9–June 15, 1992. Exposed timbers of the roof reflected in an artificial concrete pool filled with black brine and wax.

12.37 David Adjaye, _Europolis_, 2008. Metallic foil laminated in clear float glass, 6 ft × 4 ft × 2 ft.

12.38 Karin Giusti, *White House/Greenhouse,* **New York City, 1996.** Recycled steel beams, vinyl, Plexiglas, and rosebushes, 40 × 15 × 14 ft (12 × 4.5 × 4.3 m).

The personal and the political were combined in Karin Giusti's *White House/Greenhouse* (12.38). Placed in Battery Park in New York City, the transparent one-quarter scale model of the White House had both Wall Street and the Statue of Liberty in the background. Made of recycled steel beams, clear vinyl, and large paintings on Plexiglas, the structure presented a scathing commentary on American politics while providing a greenhouse for 200 rosebushes.

Sculpture as Journey

As sculptures have expanded in size, the manner in which the viewer enters, exits, and explores the site has become increasingly important. When the audience participates, a sculpture can be transformed from an object into an experience.

Christopher Janney's *Sonic Plaza* (12.39) at Eastern Carolina University is an especially enticing example. Composed of four distinct sculptures, the site offers a variety of sensory experiences. Various melodic sounds greet participants at the *Sonic Gates*. The 64 water jets on the *Percussion Water Wall* spew forth complex patterns of water to a percussive accompaniment. Four smaller sculptures emerge from the large doors of the *Media Glockenspiel* each day. Finally, a cloud of water vapor created by *Ground Cloud* hovers over the plaza, responding to pedestrian movement and wind direction.

12.39 Christopher Janney, *Sonic Plaza,* Eastern Carolina University, 1998. Sound, light, water, and interactive elements, total length 400 ft (122 m). Top: *Sonic Gates;* middle row left to right: *Media Glockenspiel* and *Percussion Water Wall;* bottom, *Ground Cloud.*

Sculpture as Time

A fascination with time pervades contemporary sculpture. Many sculptures demonstrate the changes that occur as time passes. The amount, frequency, and means of change vary widely. Placed atop the corporate offices of a lighting company, Fumaki Nakamura's *Light Communication* (12.40) presents a simple metamorphosis in a spectacular way. The 88 neon poles gradually illuminate the interior of the structure in three 30-second cycles. The beauty of the light, combined with the hypnotic sequence of change, animates and illuminates the night sky.

Christian Marclay often combines sound with sculpture to expand our experience and understanding of time. In *Amplification* (12.41), he installed large-scale translucent reproductions of six anonymous flea-market photographs in San Stae, a Baroque church in Venice, Italy. Each photograph captures a nonprofessional musical performance. An old woman plays a piano; a small girl plays a recorder; a group of men on various instruments comprise an informal band. Fragments of audio recordings combined with the muted footsteps of each visitor create a somber evocation of the past while simultaneously emphasizing the present.

Sculpture can also demonstrate the impermanence that is an essential characteristic of time. To create *curcuma sul travertino* (12.42, on page 284), Shelagh Wakely covered the entrance hall to a British school with a thin layer of yellow turmeric spice. As visitors passed through the room, they gradually erased the dust. Thus, during the week-long exhibition, visitors were marked by their passage through the room, and, with spice on their shoes, subsequently marked each new room they entered.

12.40 Fumaki Nakamura, *Light Communication,* **Ohyama Lighting.** Installed at Ginza 4-chome (main intersection). Eighty-eight poles on a box frame with 400 flashing lamps and projection lights underneath, front 26 ft 3 in. × 19 ft 8 in. × 29 ft 4 in. (8 × 6 × 12 m), neon tube total length 546 ft 2 in. (1,500 m).

12.41 Christian Marclay, *Amplification,* 1995. Mixed mediums with six found prints and six photographic enlargements on cotton scrim, size varies.

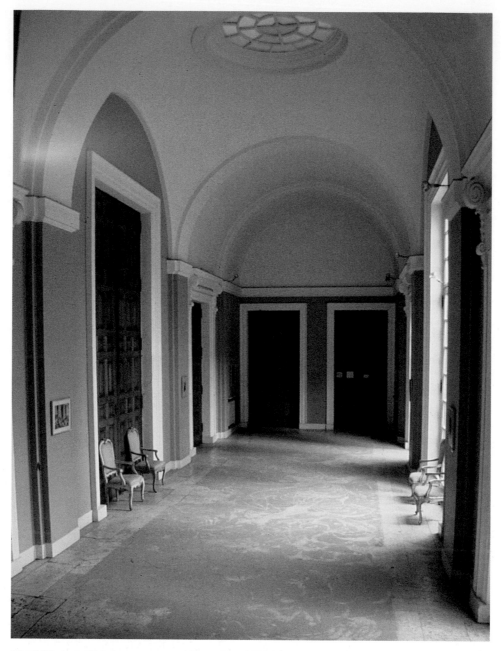

12.42 Shelagh Wakely, *curcuma sul travertino*, 1991. Turmeric powder on travertine marble floor (smell of turmeric filled the space), swept up after three weeks, 46 ft × 11 ft 6 in. (14 × 3.5 m).

Sculpture as Self

It has often been said that all artwork is autobiographical. This is especially true of sculpture. As the physical manifestation of thought, sculpture has an immediacy similar to that of a living person.

Both traditional and contemporary sculptors have explored this theme in many marvelous ways. The indigenous people of New Zealand, the Maori, have often combined sculpture with architecture to create a genealogical self-portrait. The face of a prominent ancestor is placed on the front gable of the sacred meeting house (12.43). The ridge at the top of the roof is the ancestor's backbone, the rafters form his ribs, and the four corner posts represent his arms and legs. Faces of other ancestors are carved on the exterior of the building and on interior posts. Finally, carvings of the Earth Mother and Sky Father are placed over the porch. Through a combination of representation and symbolism, every aspect of the building is designed to honor the past and inspire the present people.

Attention's Loop (12.44), by Elizabeth King, offers another type of self-portrait. In this installation, six highly detailed mannequins are presented in a variety of poses. Carefully articulated arms and hands in three additional display cases line the back wall of the gallery, while an 11-minute video loop shows the mannequins moving. The combination of supreme craftsmanship, robotic machinery, and fluid animation communicates a complex range of ideas. The mannequins are both fascinating and disturbing. Human consciousness seems to be trapped in a sculptural form.

Kiki Smith infused her *Virgin Mary* (12.45) with a very different energy and insight. Completed during a tragic period in her life that included the death of both her sister and her father, the figure appears flayed and exposed. Built from wax, cheesecloth, and wood, the woman is physically and emotionally fragile.

Eva Hesse's *Laocoön* (12.46) is a more abstract self-portrait. As noted in Chapter Nine, the ancient Greek sculpture *Laocoön and His Two Sons* (see figure 9.22, page 191) depicts a scene from the Trojan War. Laocoön warns against accepting the large wooden horse the Greeks offer as a gift. The Greek goddess Athena sends two serpents

12.43 *Maori Meeting House,* called "Rautepupuke," New Zealand, 1881. 56 ft × 13 ft 10 in. (17 × 4 m).

to attack and kill Laocoön, thereby gaining entry into Troy and victory for the Greeks hidden in the horse. Like the snakes that bind Laocoön and his sons, the cords in Hesse's sculpture are messengers of death. They choke the ladder structure and foreshadow Hesse's own death at age 34 from a brain tumor. As she noted, "My life and art have not been separated."

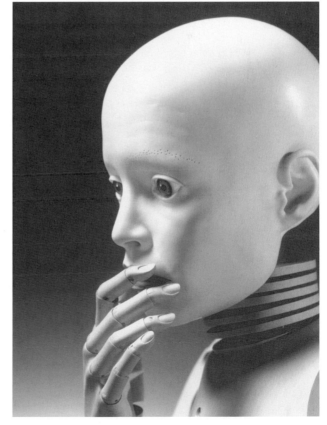

12.44 Katherine Wetzel (photo), Elizabeth King (sculpture), *Pupil* from *Attention's Loop,* 1987–90. Porcelain, glass eyes, carved wood, brass, one-half life size.

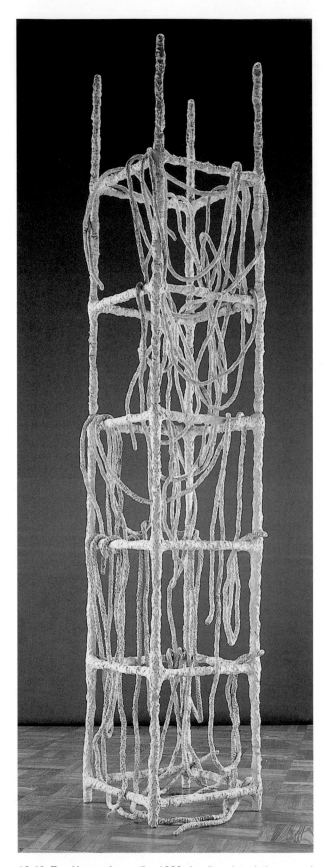

12.45 Kiki Smith, *Virgin Mary,* **1992.** Wax, cheesecloth and wood with steel base, 67½ × 26 × 14½ in. (171.5 × 66 × 36.8 cm).

12.46 Eva Hesse, *Laocoön,* **1966.** Acrylic paint, cloth-covered cord, wire, and papier-mâché over plastic plumber's pipe, bottom 130 × 23½ × 23 in. (330.2 × 59.7 × 58.4 cm), top 130 × 21½ × 21½ in. (330.2 × 54.6 × 54.6 cm).

Ideas in Physical Form

The combination of tangible material and aesthetic complexity gives sculpture a unique power. Like an alchemist, the sculptor transforms ordinary materials into conceptual gold. Tadashi Kawamata's pile of wood becomes a metaphor for urban change. In Mierle Ukeles's *Ceremonial Arch,* the gloves and lightbulbs used by sanitation workers are transformed into a sculpture. A burning ladder becomes a metaphor for a spiritual passage in Ronald Dahl's *Seven Windows to a Sky on Fire.* Through a miracle of invention, the best sculptures simultaneously embrace and transcend their physical nature.

Key Questions

CONTEMPORARY QUESTIONS, CONTEMPORARY ANSWERS

- What are the historical antecedents for your idea?
- How can contemporary materials and methods strengthen your idea?
- What does your artwork reveal about yourself and the world around you?

SUMMARY

- A pile of wood at a construction site is stacked for convenience and accessibility. A pile of wood in a sculpture is designed to communicate ideas and emotions.

- Art gains power from its connection to life. Through art, commonplace experiences are distilled, reexamined, and transformed.

- Physical and psychological boundaries can connect or separate art and life.

- A base can separate a sculpture from its surrounding space, provide structural stability, and expand aesthetic content.

- Physical forces, such as gravity, compression, expansion, tension, and torsion, can be used to express ideas while providing structural strength.

- The materials a sculptor selects can heighten and deepen the meaning of the artwork.

- Traditional Western sculpture is massive, representational, figurative, and narrative.

- Contemporary sculpture is often more spatial, abstract, and nonfigurative than traditional sculpture. It often breaks down the traditional separation between art and life.

- Many contemporary sculptors use specific sites, audience participation, temporal change, and explorations of the self to create powerful artworks.

KEY TERMS

abstract artworks	**pedestal**	**representational artworks**
nonobjective artworks	**plinth**	

STUDIO PROJECTS

To apply the concepts from this chapter in the studio, check out the Projects page in the Online Learning Center at www.mhhe.com/stewart4e. The following is a sample of the chapter-related assignments that are described in step-by-step detail.

Becoming Borg. The skin and skeleton of human and machine.
Time Piece. Expanding upon kinetic time.

Profile:
Samuel Yates, Artist
One Man; 17,860 Parcels

Samuel Yates is known for creating large-scale conceptual art projects that combine performance and minimalism with the structures of government. His artwork is included in numerous public collections, including the San Francisco Museum of Modern Art, Berkeley Art Museum, di Rosa Preserve (Napa, CA), and Ballett Frankfurt (Frankfurt, Germany).

"The Color of Palo Alto" is a public art project commissioned by the City of Palo Alto. The project incorporates technology, contemporary art, environmental protection, and public service into one award-winning public art project. It created a free lexicon of sustainable color and the nation's first photo-assisted 9-1-1 emergency response system.

MS: How did "The Color of Palo Alto" begin?

SY: In the summer of 2001, I installed a seven-story-tall file cabinet sculpture in Napa Valley for a private collector. I had shredded an MG sportscar into tiny pieces, steamrolled each piece flat, and filed the pieces by weight in milligrams from heaviest to lightest inside the cabinet. A public art commissioner from the City of Palo Alto saw the sculpture and invited me to apply for a rotating public art grant, sited in their Civic Center Plaza. I applied for and was awarded the $10,000 grant.

Rather than simply installing a pre-made sculpture in Civic Center Plaza and then taking it away—a practice often called "Plop Art" where you "plop" an existing sculpture in a public space to have it function as "public art"—I tried to consider the concept of public art as an academic exercise or problem to be solved. The fundamental question revolved around the collective group of Palo Alto residents who were funding the project with their taxes: Was there a way to design a public art project that could serve and involve this entire public?

The initial solution I developed, and later expanded, was to digitally photograph all 17,860 parcels in Palo Alto—the entire property tax base—and use the photographs to compute the average color of each parcel, street, and neighborhood, creating "The Color of Palo Alto." On a very basic level, each parcel would contribute one "vote" of color toward the final color of the city; the project would therefore

involve the entire public: every resident would necessarily have a relation to the final colors.

MS: How did you expand the public art concept in this project?

SY: I first considered whether I could make the project more public by installing an office in the plaza to function both as a sculpture and as my project headquarters. Many questions emerged: Would this transform my behind-the-scenes studio practice into a public performance and add a layer to the project's "public-ness"?

Next, what if I installed all of the photographs on the front of City Hall for every person in Palo Alto to find their parcel and see their public contribution to the color of their city? City Hall represents the entire city, could we represent the entire city on City Hall? What if my office was solar- and wind-powered so that all the energy I used was renewable, including the energy I used to power my electric scooter around the city every day? Could the project formally promote the city's environmental initiatives?

And, what if the colors could be mixed at any paint store, printed from any computer, or used in any design to freely spread this environmental awareness? What if people could post photographs on a Web site showing how they used the colors, thereby contributing to a larger social canvas—a giant pointillist painting—as a larger public artwork? What if I tied the photographs into the City of Palo Alto database of parcels for use by city staff in planning, public works, emergencies, etc.?

As the project developed, the possibilities appeared endless and taking photos would simply be the beginning.

MS: How do you sustain your interest in the same project year after year to bring them to completion?

SY: I try to keep evolving my projects until hopefully I no longer recognize them, they are something I have never seen before, or they present something I have never thought about before. When I have an idea, I tend to ask myself, "And then what? How can I take this farther? How can I make this more interesting? What can I do to change it? How can I recontextualize it?" Then I ask, "What relation do those changes have to contemporary art discourse? How might those changes affect its possible interpretations and meanings?" Finally, when I come up with the next evolution of that idea, I ask myself the same questions all over again, "And then what?" I try not to settle on an idea for an object too soon.

MS: Are there any pitfalls to this strategy?

SY: Yes and no. I am extremely careful and methodical about my work. Although I work diligently every day, it takes me a tremendous amount of time to complete a project, sometimes years. Some people produce a lot of work very quickly, which is fine. I am not that type of person and I have tried to turn my methodical nature—a trait that could be perceived as a weakness—into a strength.

MS: The whole thing seems so improbable. You were only 26 years old when you began, had little money, and had never done anything on this scale before. Was the sheer size of the project the most difficult part?

SY: Although I generally worked from around 7 A.M. to midnight six or seven days a week, from January to December, the most difficult part was funding the project, rather than executing it. I had to start from scratch, and the $3,000 upfront budget did not begin to cover the expenses. For example, I did not own a computer when I started the project, and I couldn't afford to buy one. Everything had to be donated in one way or another. Leading up to the installation, I lived in my car for over a year (a car donated by a host family), and I stayed with six different host families over five years. It truly was a grassroots, group effort that happened only from sheer force of will.

MS: What advice can you offer to beginning students?

SY: First, I have reached many goals simply by being persistent and consistent. For example, it took

The "portable solar garage" in the Civic Center Plaza served as both a sculpture and "The Color of Palo Alto" headquarters. The garage powered an electric scooter, a digital camera, a GPS, and other computer equipment, turning the colors of the city into intrinsic symbols of ecological awareness because they were generated using renewable energy.

months, and in some cases years, to get permission to do certain projects. When people see that you are serious and committed, they may be more willing to help. I try not to take "no" for an answer and instead try to figure out some alternate route. Ironically, the more difficult path often leads to more interesting and surprising results than the easier path. Second, I try to bite off more than I can chew, so to speak; that is to say, I know that I will be able to finish a project—I am confident that I have the ability—but it will challenge me more in the meantime. It can be good to be naive and not know that something is impossible because you end up doing it anyway. Third, I try not to underestimate my source material. Anything can be material: plumbing, gardening, video games, etc. It just requires noticing it and committing to it. Fourth, if you ever have to sleep in your car, buy a car cover. If you put a cover on your car and then crawl inside, no one can tell you're in there sleeping and you can roll down the windows for air more safely. It's like an urban tent!

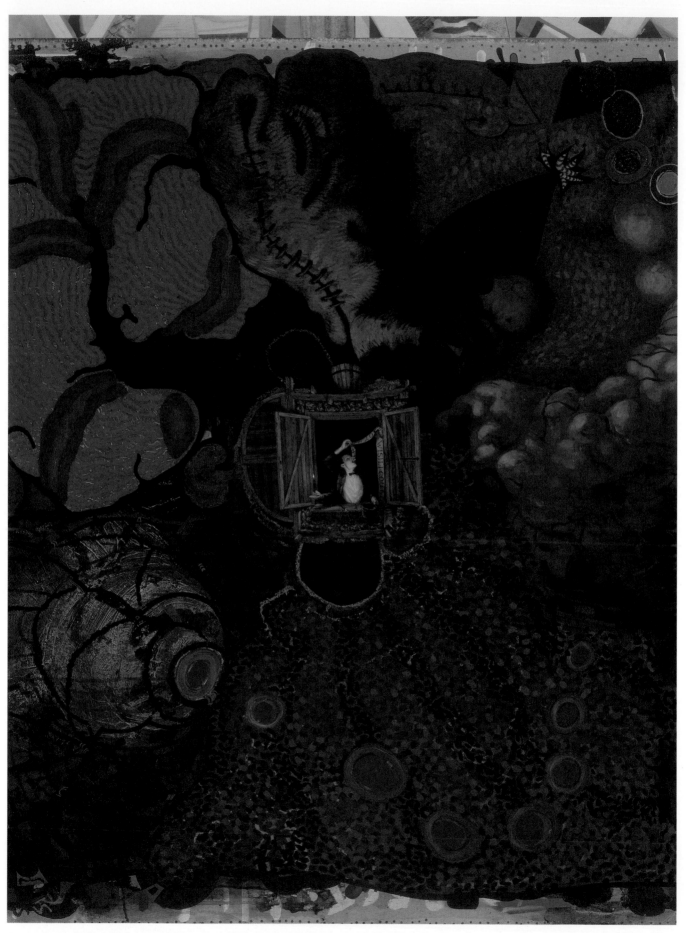

Daniel Sutherland, *I Wish I Could Help You,* **1994.** Oil on canvas on wood with hardware, 75 × 84 in. (190.5 × 213.4 cm).

Creativity

Bohm, David. *On Creativity.* New York: Routledge, 2000.

Briggs, John. *Fire in the Crucible: Understanding the Process of Creative Genius.* Grand Rapids: Phanes Press, 2000.

Csikszentmihalyi, Mihaly. *Creativity: Flow and the Psychology of Discovery and Invention.* New York: HarperCollins, 1996.

Dewey, John. *Art as Experience.* New York: Capricorn Books, 1958.

Gardner, Howard. *Art, Mind and Brain: A Cognitive Approach to Creativity.* New York: Basic Books, 1982.

Gardner, Howard. *Creating Minds: An Anatomy of Creativity Seen Through the Lives of Freud, Einstein, Picasso, Stravinsky, Eliot, Graham, and Gandhi.* New York: Basic Books, 1993.

Gardner, Howard. *Frames of Mind: The Theory of Multiple Intelligences.* New York: Basic Books, 1985.

Lamott, Anne. *Bird by Bird: Some Instructions on Writing and Life.* New York: Anchor Books, 1998.

Le Boeuf, Michael. *Imagineering.* New York: McGraw-Hill, 1980.

Prince, George. "Creativity and Learning as Skills, Not Talents," *The Philips Exeter Bulletin,* 1980.

Shekerjian, Denise. *Uncommon Genius: How Great Ideas Are Born.* New York: Penguin Books, 1991.

Wallace, Doris B., and Howard E. Gruber, eds. *Creative People at Work.* New York: Oxford University Press, 1989.

Concept Development

Adams, James L. *Conceptual Blockbusting.* Reading, MA: Addison-Wesley, 1986.

de Bono, Edward. *Lateral Thinking.* London: Ward Educational Limited, 1970.

Grear, Malcolm. *Inside/Outside: From the Basics to the Practice of Design.* New York: Van Nostrand Reinhold, 1993.

Johnson, Mary Frisbee. *Visual Workouts: A Collection of Art-Making Problems.* Englewood Cliffs, NJ: Prentice Hall, 1983.

Kelley, Tom. *The Art of Innovation: Lessons in Creativity from America's Leading Design Firm.* New York: Doubleday, 2001.

Lakoff, George, and Mark Johnson. *Metaphors We Live By.* Chicago: University of Chicago Press, 1981.

Shahn, Ben. *The Shape of Content.* Cambridge, MA: Harvard University Press, 1957.

Von Oech, Roger. *A Kick in the Seat of the Pants.* New York: Harper and Row, 1963.

Von Oech, Roger. *A Whack on the Side of the Head.* New York: Harper and Row, 1986.

Wilde, Judith and Richard. *Visual Literacy: A Conceptual Approach to Graphic Problem Solving.* New York: Watson-Guptil, 2000.

Critical Thinking

Barrett, Terry. *Criticizing Photographs: An Introduction to Understanding Images,* 4th ed. New York: McGraw-Hill, 2006.

Barrett, Terry. *Interpreting Art.* New York: McGraw-Hill, 2003.

Tucker, Amy. *Visual Literacy: Writing About Art.* New York: McGraw-Hill, 2002.

Three-Dimensional Design

Andrews, Oliver. *Living Materials: A Sculptor's Handbook.* Berkeley: University of California Press, 1988.

Bachelard, Gaston. *The Poetics of Space,* trans. Maria Jolas. Boston: Beacon Press, 1969.

Beardsley, John. *Earthworks and Beyond: Contemporary Art in the Landscape.* New York: Abbeville Press, 1998.

Ching, Frank. *Architecture: Form, Space, and Order,* 2nd ed. New York: Van Nostrand Reinhold, 1996.

de Oliveira, Nicolas, Nicola Oxley, and Michael Petry. *Installation Art.* Washington, DC: Smithsonian Institution Press, 1994.

Dormer, Peter, and Ralph Turner. *The New Jewelry: Trends and Traditions.* London: Thames and Hudson, 1985.

Frantz, Suzanne. *Contemporary Glass: A World Survey from the Corning Museum of Glass.* New York: Harry N. Abrams, 1989.

Koplos, Janet. *Contemporary Japanese Sculpture.* New York: Abbeville Press, 1991.

Lane, Peter. *Ceramic Form: Design and Decoration,* rev. ed. New York: Rizzoli, 1998.

Lewin, Susan Grant. *One of a Kind: American Art Jewelry Today.* New York: Harry N. Abrams, 1994.

Lidstone, John. *Building with Wire.* New York: Van Nostrand Reinhold, 1972.

Luecking, Stephen. *Principles of Three Dimensional Design.* Upper Saddle River, NJ: Pearson Education, 2002.

Lynn, Martha Dreyer. *Clay Today: Contemporary Ceramicists and Their Work.* Los Angeles: Los Angeles County Museum of Art; and San Francisco: Chronicle Books, 1990.

Manzini, Ezio. *The Material of Invention: Materials and Design.* Cambridge, MA: MIT Press, 1989.

Miller, Bonnie J. *Out of the Fire: Contemporary Glass Artists and Their Work.* San Francisco: Chronicle Books, 1991.

Nunley, John W., and Cara McCarty. *Masks: Faces of Culture.* New York: Harry N. Abrams in association with the Saint Louis Art Museum, 1999.

Penny, Nicholas. *The Materials of Sculpture.* New Haven, CT: Yale University Press, 1993.

Selz, Peter Howard. *Barbara Chase-Riboud, Sculptor.* New York: Harry N. Abrams, 1999.

Wallschlaeger, Charles, and Cynthia Busic-Snyder. *Basic Visual Concepts and Principles for Artists, Architects and Designers.* New York: McGraw-Hill, 1992.

Williams, Arthur. *Sculpture: Technique, Form, Content.* Worcester, MA: Davis, 1993.

Wong, Wucius. *Principles of Form and Design.* New York: Van Nostrand Reinhold, 1993.

Wyatt, Gary. *Spirit Faces: Contemporary Native American Masks from the Northwest.* San Francisco: Chronicle Books, 1994.

Chapter Five Works Cited

1. Keith A. Smith, *Structure of the Visual Book* (Fairport, NY: The Sigma Foundation, 1991), pp. 17–18.

Chapter Six Works Cited

1. Mihaly Csikszentmihalyi, *Creativity: Flow and the Psychology of Discovery and Invention* (New York: HarperCollins, 1996), pp. 55–76.

2. George Prince, "Creativity and Learning as Skills, Not Talents," *The Philips Exeter Bulletin*, June–October, 1980.

3. Anne Lamott, *Bird by Bird: Some Instructions on Writing and Life* (New York: Anchor Books, 1998), pp. 18–19.

Chapter Eight Works Cited

1. Henry M. Sayre, *A World of Art*, 3rd ed. (Upper Saddle River, NJ: Prentice Hall, 2000), p. 496.

Chapter Nine Works Cited

1. John Beardsley, *Earthworks and Beyond: Contemporary Art in the Landscape* (New York: Abbeville Press, 1998), p. 31.

2. Jonathan Fineberg, *Art Since 1940: Strategies of Being* (Englewood Cliffs, NJ: Prentice Hall, 1995), p. 383.

3. Alexander Theroux, *The Primary Colors: Three Essays* (New York: Henry Holt and Company, 1994), p. 86.

4. Theroux, p. 6.

notes

Glossary by
Mary Stewart and Peter Forbes

A

abstract artwork; abstract form 1. an artwork or form derived from visual reality that has been distilled or transformed, reducing its resemblance to the original source. 2. a multiple image structure, such as a film, in which the parts are related to each other through repetition and visual characteristics such as shape, color, scale or direction of movement.

abstract shape a shape that is derived from a visual source, but is so transformed that it bears little visual resemblance to that source.

abstraction the reduction of an image or object to an essential aspect of its form or concept.

accent a specific shape, volume, color, musical note, etc. that has been emphasized. Using an accent, a designer can bring attention to part of a composition and increase rhythmic variation within a pattern.

accent color a color that stands out from its surroundings. Often used to attract attention to a specific part of a design.

achromatic a color (such as black and white) that has no hue.

act a major division in a film or theatrical event. Acts are generally constructed from a group of sequences that increase in intensity.

action-to-action transition in comic books, the juxtaposition of two or more panels showing a sequence of actions.

actual lines lines that are physically present in a design.

actual motion motion that physically occurs in a design.

actual time the duration of an actual temporal event. For example, it takes less than a minute for the bowling ball to roll down the ramps in Jean Tinguely's *Chaos 1*.

additive color color created by combining projected beams of chromatic light. The additive color primaries are red, green, and blue, and the secondaries are cyan, magenta, and yellow.

additive sculpture a physical object constructed from separate parts that have been connected using glues, joints, stitching, welds, and so on.

aesthetics the study of human responses to art and beauty.

afterimage in color theory, a ghostly image that continues to linger after the actual image has been removed.

ambient light the quality of light within an entire space or setting. For example, when we enter an open courtyard on a sunny summer afternoon, we are surrounded by warm ambient sunlight. Everything we see is colorful and bright.

amplified perspective the exaggerated use of linear perspective to achieve a dramatic and engaging presentation of the subject. Amplified perspective is often created using an unusual viewing position, such as a bird's-eye view, accelerated convergence, or some form of distortion.

analogous a color scheme based on hues that are adjacent on a color wheel, such as red, red-orange, and orange.

analogy a similarity or connection between things that are apparently separate and dissimilar. For example, when a teacher describes wet plaster as having the "consistency of cream," he or she is using an analogy.

anesthetic a chemical or action used to induce insensitivity or unconsciousness.

anomaly an obvious break from the norm in a design.

appropriation a postmodern practice in which one artist reproduces an image created by another and claims it as his or her own.

approximate symmetry a form of balance that occurs when roughly similar imagery appears on either side of a central axis.

armature an internal structure created to strengthen and support a three-dimensional object.

aspect-to-aspect transition in comic books, the juxtaposition of two or more panels showing different views of a single setting or event. This transition is often used in Japanese comic books.

assemblage an additive method in which the artist or designer constructs the artwork using objects and images that were originally created for another purpose. Essentially, assemblage can be defined as three-dimensional collage.

asymmetrical balance equilibrium among visual elements that do not mirror each other on either side of an axis.

atmospheric perspective a visual phenomenon in which the atmospheric density progressively increases, hazing over the perceived world as one looks into its depth. Overall definition lessens, details fade, contrasts become muted, and, in a landscape, a blue mist descends.

attached shadow a shadow that directly defines a form.

B

backlight a light source positioned behind a person or object that can either create a silhouette or separate the person or object from the background.

balance the equal distribution of weight or force among visual units.

beat 1. a unit of musical rhythm that creates the pulse of a sound. 2. in acting, the most basic element in a story. A beat is an exchange of behavior, based on action and reaction.

bend one of the five major forces affecting structural strength.

Bezold effect a change in a single color that substantially alters our perception of the entire composition.

boundary the dividing line or edge between objects, images, or experiences.

brainstorming any of a number of problem-solving techniques that are designed to expand ideas and encourage creativity. List making, mapping, associative thinking, and metaphorical thinking are common strategies used.

calligraphic line derived from the Greek words for beautiful and writing, a flowing and expressive line that is as personal as handwriting. Calligraphic lines generally vary in thickness and velocity.

camera angle the angle at which an object or event is viewed. An aerial view can provide the sweeping panorama needed to convey the enormity of a battle, while a low camera angle can provide an expansive view of the sky.

carving the removal of materials from a larger mass, gradually revealing an image or object. Carving is a subtractive process.

cast shadow a dark shape that results from placement of an opaque object in the path of a light source.

categorical (form) in film, a multiple image structure that is based on categories, or subsets of a topic. For example, a film on predators might begin with a discussion of wolves, then move on to lions, and conclude with a discussion of hawks.

causality the interrelation of cause and effect, based on the premise that nothing occurs without cause. Narrative film is based on causality: because the starting pistol was shot, the footrace began.

cause-and-effect critique (or formal analysis) a critique in which the viewer seeks to determine the cause for each visual or emotional effect in a design. For example, the dynamism in a design may be caused by the diagonal lines and asymmetrical balance used.

centricity as identified by Rudolph Arnheim, a compressive compositional force.

characteristic texture the inherent or familiar texture of a material. The gleaming reflective surface of a steel teapot, the transparent and reflective qualities of glass, and the gritty texture of clay are all characteristic textures.

chiaroscuro (from Italian meaning "light-dark") The gradual transition of values to create the illusion of light and shadow on a three-dimensional form.

chroma the purity, intensity, or saturation of a color.

chromatic gray a gray made from a mixture of various hues, rather than a simple blend of black and white.

chronology the order in which events occur.

cliché an overused expression or a predictable visual treatment of an idea.

close-up in film, a type of framing in which the scale of the object shown is relatively large, as in a close-up of an actor's face.

closure the mind's inclination to connect fragmentary information to produce a completed form. Closure is an essential aspect of Gestalt psychology.

codex traditional bound-edged format used for modern books, with separate pages normally bound together and given a cover.

collage an image constructed from visual or verbal fragments initially designed for another purpose.

color harmony use of compatible colors to help unify a composition.

color interaction the way colors within a composition influence one another.

color key a color that dominates an image and heightens its psychological and compositional impact.

color overtone a secondary hue "bias" in a primary color. For example, alizarin crimson is a red with violet overtones, while scarlet is a red with orange overtones.

color theory the art and science of color interaction and effects.

compare/contrast critique a critique in which similarities and differences between two designs are analyzed. Often used in art history classes to demonstrate differences in approach between artists.

comparison recognition of similarity in two or more compositions. Often used in art history to demonstrate connections between images done by different artists or in different periods.

complementary (colors) hues that oppose one another on a color wheel. When paired in a composition, complementary colors create contrast; when mixed, complementary colors produce a wide range of browns.

composite a new material created when two or more materials of differing strengths are fused together. Examples include Fiberglas and foamcore.

composition the combination of multiple parts into a unified or harmonious whole.

compression the forcing or crushing of material into a smaller, denser condition and its visual dynamics and implied psychological effects.

cone of vision in perspective drawing, a hypothetical cone of perception originating at the eye of the artist and expanding outward to include whatever he or she wishes to record in an illusionistic image, such as a perspective drawing. The cone's maximum scoping angle is 45–60 degrees; anything outside the cone of vision is subject to distortion.

containment a unifying force created by the outer edge of a composition or by a boundary within a composition.

content the emotional and/or intellectual meaning or message of an artwork.

continuity degree of connection or flow among compositional parts.

contour line a line that describes the edges of a form and suggests three-dimensional volume.

contradictory texture the unfamiliar use of a texture or the addition of an unusual texture to the surface of an object.

contrast the degree of difference between compositional parts or between one image and another. Contrast is created when two or more forces operate in opposition.

contrasting colors colors that are substantially different in hue, value, intensity, or temperature.

convergent thinking a problem-solving strategy in which a predetermined goal is pursued in a linear progression using a highly focused problem-solving process. Six steps are commonly used: 1. define the problem, 2. do research, 3. determine your objective, 4. devise a strategy, 5. execute the strategy, 6. evaluate the results.

critique any means by which the strengths and weaknesses of designs are analyzed.

cropping the manner in which a section of an image or a fragment of observed reality has been framed. For example, photographers select a fragment of reality every time they look through the viewfinder of the camera. Part of the scene is included, while the remainder is cut away. Photographs are often cropped further in the darkroom, leaving only the most significant information.

cross-contours multiple lines running over the surface of an object horizontally and/or vertically that describe its surface configuration topographically, as in mapping. This process is much like wireframing in three-dimensional computer modeling. Cross-contours can also be used in drawing to suggest three-dimensional form through tonal variation.

crosscutting in film, an abrupt alternation between two or more lines of action.

cross-hatching a technique used in drawing and printmaking to shade an object using two or more networks of parallel lines. Darker values are created as the number of networks increases.

curvilinear shape a shape whose contour is dominated by curves and flowing lines.

cut in film, the immediate change from one shot or frame to another.

definition 1. the degree to which a shape is distinguished from both the ground area and from other shapes within the design. 2. the degree of resolution or focus of an entire image. Sharply defined shapes tend to advance, while blurred shapes tend to recede.

denouement the outcome, solution, or point of clarification in a story.

density the extent to which compositional parts are spread out or crowded together. Visual connections generally occur easily in high-density compositions, while visual connections may be less obvious in low-density compositions.

depth of field the range of focus in a photographic image, from foreground to background. In a photograph with great depth of field, an object that is 15 feet from the camera is in focus, as well as an object that is 10 feet from the camera.

descriptive critique a critique in which the viewer carefully describes what he or she sees when observing a design.

diegetic describes the world created in a film or video.

directed light localized and focused light, such as a spotlight on a singer.

direction actual or implied movement of an element within a design.

disharmony a combination of colors that clash with one another and appear to be jumping out of the picture.

displacement a forming method in which a solid material is physically forced into a new configuration. The stamping process used to mint coins is an example of displacement.

dissolve a transition between two shots during which the first image gradually disappears while the second image gradually appears.

distribution the manner in which colors, shapes, or other visual elements are arranged within the format.

divergent thinking an open-ended problem-solving strategy. Starting with a broad theme, the artist or designer expands ideas in all directions.

dominant describes the principle of composition in which certain elements assume greater importance than others. Also see **emphasis.**

duration 1. the length of time required for the completion of an event; as in the running time of a film, video, or performance. 2. the running time of events depicted in the story (plot duration). 3. the overall span of time the story encompasses (story duration).

dynamic energetic, vigorous, forceful; creating or suggesting change or motion.

dynamic forms forms that imply change.

dynamic space compositional organization that emphasizes movement or the illusion of movement.

earth colors colors made primarily from pigments in soil, including raw sienna, burnt sienna, raw and burnt umber, and yellow ochre.

earthwork commonly, an artwork that has been created through the transformation of a natural site into an aesthetic statement.

eccentricity as identified by Rudolph Arnheim, an expansive compositional force.

economy distillation of a design down to the essentials in order to increase impact.

editing in film, selecting and sequencing the details of an event to create a cohesive whole.

elements (of design) basic building blocks from which designs are made. For example, the essential elements of two-dimensional design are line, shape, texture, color, and value.

elevation in orthographic projection, the front, back, and side views of an object or architectural structure.

emotional in advertising, use of emotion to sell a service, product, or idea. This strategy is often used when a product is neither unique nor demonstrably better than a competing product.

emphasis special attention given to some aspect of a composition to increase its prominence.

engraving a printmaking process in which lines are carved into a metal plate or wooden board, then filled with ink and printed.

environmental work (or environment) an artwork that must be entered physically. Installations (which are usually presented indoors) and earthworks (which are usually presented outdoors) are two major types of environmental works.

ephemera materials that decay rapidly.

exaggerated in advertising, pushing an idea to an extreme to make a point.

exoskeleton an external support structure.

expansion the extending outward of materials to fill more space.

eye level (or horizon line) in linear perspective, the eye level is determined by the physical position of the artist. Sitting on the floor creates a low eye level, while standing at an easel creates a higher eye level. All vanishing points in one- and two-point perspective are positioned on the eye level.

fade a gradual transition used in film and video. 1. In a fade-in, a dark screen gradually brightens as a shot appears. 2. In a fade-out, the shot gradually darkens as the screen goes black.

fidelity the degree of connection between a sound and its source. For example, when we hear the sound of a helicopter and see a helicopter on the screen, the sound matches with the image, creating tight fidelity.

figure the primary or positive shape in a design; a shape that is noticeably separated from the background. The figure is the dominant shape in a figure-ground relationship.

figure/ground reversal an arrangement in which positive and negative shapes alternately command attention.

fill light a diffused light used to lower the contrast between light and dark areas in cinematic and theatrical lighting.

flashbacks in film, alternations in chronology in which events that occur later in a story are shown first.

floodlight a softly defined light with a broad beam.

flying buttress a type of exoskeleton commonly used by medieval architects in designing cathedrals.

focal point primary point of interest in a composition. A focal point is often used to emphasize an area of particular importance or to provide a strong sense of compositional direction.

form 1. the physical manifestation of an idea, as opposed to the content, which refers to the idea itself. 2. the organization or arrangement of visual elements to create a unified design. 3. a three-dimensional composition or unit within a three-dimensional composition. For example, a sphere, a cube, and a pyramid are all three-dimensional forms.

formalism an approach to art and design that emphasizes the beauty of line, shape, texture, etc. as ends in themselves rather than as means to express content. Strictly formalist works have no explicit subject matter.

format the outer edge or boundary of a design.

fractured space discontinuous space that is created when multiple viewpoints are combined within a single image.

frame a single static image in film or video.

freestanding work an artwork that is self-supporting and is designed to be viewed from all sides.

function the purpose of a design or the objective that motivates the designer. For an industrial designer, the primary purpose of a design is often utilitarian. For example, he or she may be required to design a more fuel-efficient automobile. For a sculptor, the primary purpose of a design is aesthetic: he or she seeks to create an artwork that engages the viewer emotionally and intellectually.

fusion the combination of shapes or volumes along a common edge.

geometric forms three-dimensional forms derived from or suggestive of geometry. Examples include cubes, spheres, tetrahedrons, etc.

geometric shapes shapes derived from or suggestive of geometry. Geometric shapes are characterized by crisp, precise edges and mathematically consistent curves.

Gestalt psychology a theory of visual perception that emphasizes the importance of holistic composition. According to this theory, grouping, containment, repetition, proximity, continuity, and closure are essential aspects of visual unity.

gesture drawing a vigorous drawing that captures the action, structure, and overall orientation of an object, rather than describing specific details. Often used as a basis for figure drawing.

gloss 1. in writing, words of explanation or translation inserted into a text. 2. a secondary text within a manuscript that provides comments on the main text.

gradation any gradual transition from one color to another or from one shape or volume to another. In drawing, shading created through the gradation of grays can be used to suggest three-dimensional form.

graphic relationship the juxtaposition of two or more separate images that are compositionally similar. For example, if a basketball is shown in the first panel, an aerial view of the round free-throw zone is shown in the second, and the hoop of the basket itself is shown in the third, a graphic relationship based on circles has been created.

gravity the force that tends to pull all bodies toward the center of the Earth.

grid a visual or physical structure created from intersecting parallel lines.

grisaille a gray underpainting, often used by Renaissance artists, to increase the illusion of space.

group in sequential structure, a collection of images that are related by subject matter, composition, or source. For example the trombone, trumpet, and tuba are all members of the group known as the brass section in an orchestra.

grouping visual organization based on similarity in location, orientation, shape, color, and so on.

handheld a small-scale object that can be held in your hands.

Happening an assemblage of improvised, spontaneous events performed by artist and audience alike, based on a general theme. There is no rehearsal, and any location, from a parking lot to a factory interior, can be used. The Happening is most commonly

glossary

associated with Alan Kaprow and is a precursor to performance art.

hard-sell an advertising approach in which a major point is presented in a clear, direct manner. The narrative is usually linear, and the message is usually explicit.

harmony a pleasing or soothing relationship among colors, shapes, or other design elements.

hatching a technique used in drawing and printmaking to create a range of gray tones using multiple parallel lines.

high definition sharply focused visual information that is easily readable. High definition creates strong contrast between shapes and tends to increase the clarity and immediacy of communication.

hue the name of a color (such as red or yellow) that distinguishes it from others and assigns it a position in the visual spectrum.

human scale a design that is roughly our size.

humorous advertising use of humor to sell a service, product, or idea. By entertaining the viewer, the designer can make the message more memorable.

hybridity the creation of artworks using disparate media to create a unified conceptual statement.

iconography the study of symbolic visual systems.

imbalance the absence of balance.

implied line 1. a line that is suggested by the positions of shapes or objects within a design. 2. a line that is suggested by movement or by a gesture rather than being physically drawn or constructed.

implied motion the suggested change in location of a figure or object.

implied time the suggested location or duration of an event.

installation an artwork or a design that presents an ensemble of images and objects within a three-dimensional environment.

intensity 1. the purity, saturation, or chroma of a color. For example, fire engine red is a high-intensity color, while brick red is a low-intensity color. 2. in time design, the power, concentration, and energy with which an action is performed or the quality of observation of an event.

interdisciplinary art the combination of two or more different disciplines to create a hybrid art form.

in the round a three-dimensional object that is self-supporting and is designed to be viewed from all sides, as in freestanding sculpture.

invented texture a form of visual texture that has been created without reference to perceptual reality.

joint a physical connection between elements or parts in a three-dimensional object. Some joints are fixed,

such as those that are bolted together, while others can be moved, such as a hinge or a ball-and-socket joint.

junction 1. the place at which objects or events meet. 2. a physical intersection between elements or parts in a three-dimensional object.

key light a primary source of illumination.

kinesthetics the science of movement.

kinetic forms forms that actually move.

lap dissolve in film, a dissolve in which two shots are temporarily superimposed.

layered space compositional space that has been deliberately separated into foreground, middle ground, and background.

layering a postmodern practice in which an accumulation of multiple (and often contradictory) visual layers is used to create a single artwork.

line 1. a point in motion. 2. a series of adjacent points. 3. a connection between points. 4. an implied connection between points. Line is one of the basic elements of design.

linear perspective a mathematical system for projecting the apparent dimensions of a three-dimensional object onto a flat surface. Developed by artists during the Renaissance, linear perspective is one strategy for creating the illusion of space.

line weight variation in line thickness.

long shot in film, a type of framing in which the scale of the subject shown is relatively small, as with an image of a human figure within a landscape.

loudness the amplitude of a sound wave; the volume of a sound.

low-definition describes blurred or ambiguous visual information. Low-definition shapes can increase the complexity of the design and encourage multiple interpretations.

maquette a well-developed three-dimensional sketch, comparable to a two-dimensional thumbnail sketch.

mass a solid three-dimensional form.

matrix a three-dimensional grid.

mechanical forms gears, belts, hoses, and other forms suggestive of machinery.

medium the specific tool and material used by an artist or designer, such as brush and oil paint or chisel and stone.

medium shot a type of framing in which the scale of the subject shown is of moderate size, as in a view of an actor from the waist up.

metaphor a figure of speech in which one thing is directly linked to another, dissimilar thing. Through this connection, the original word is given the qualities of the linked word. For example, when we say "She's a diamond in the rough," we attribute to a woman the qualities of an unpolished gem.

glossary

metaphorical thinking the use of metaphors or analogies to create visual or verbal bridges.

meter the basic pattern of sound and silence in music or positive and negative in design.

model in three-dimensional design, a technical experiment or a small-scale version of a larger design.

modeling the process of manipulating a pliable material (such as clay) to create a three-dimensional object.

modernism a collection of artistic styles, most prominent from around 1860 to 1960, that emphasized the importance of form, introduced new materials and production methods, and sought to express universal truths.

moment-to-moment transition in comic books, a transition in which a character or situation is simply being observed over time. This transition is used often in Japanese comic books but rarely in American comic books.

monochromatic a color scheme based on variations in a single hue. For example, a light pastel blue, a medium navy blue, and a dark blue-black may be used in a room interior.

montage time-based structure constructed from multiple and often seemingly unrelated sources; a temporal collage.

monumental scale of objects that are much larger than humans.

movement in design, the use of deliberate visual pathways to help direct the viewer's attention to areas of particular interest.

myth a traditional story collectively composed by many members of a society. The creation of the world, sources of evil, the power of knowledge, and even the nature of reality may be explained through these grand expressions of the imagination.

negative shape (or ground) 1. a clearly defined area around a positive shape or form. 2. a shape created through the absence of an object rather than through the presence of an object.

negative space space surrounding a positive form or shape.

nonobjective artworks artworks that have no reference to perceptual reality.

nonobjective shapes shapes created without reference to specific visual subject matter.

non-sequitur transition the juxtaposition of multiple frames or shots that have no obvious conceptual relationship.

objective criticism the assessment of strengths and weakness in a design based solely on the visual information presented.

one-point perspective a form of linear perspective in which the lines receding into space converge at a single vanishing point of the eye level or horizon line.

opponent theory an explanation for the electric glow that occurs when two complementary colors are placed side by side.

organic forms forms that are derived from nature.

organic shapes shapes that visually suggest nature or natural forces. Also known as **biomorphic shapes.**

organizational lines lines used to create the loose linear "skeleton" on which a composition can be built. Also known as **structural lines.**

orientation the horizontal, vertical, or diagonal position of a composition or design element.

orthographic projection a drawing system widely used by artists and designers to delineate the top, bottom, and four side views of a three-dimensional object. Unlike perspective drawing, which is designed to create the illusion of space, an orthographic projection is constructed using parallel lines that accurately delineate six surfaces of an object.

overlap placement of one shape in front of another to create the illusion of space.

pace the rate of change in a temporal event.

pattern a design created through systematic repetition. Many patterns are based on a module, or a repeated visual unit.

pedestal a vertical support for a sculptural object.

performance art a live presentation, often including the artist and usually combining elements from a variety of art forms, such as film, video, theater, and dance.

permanence the degree of durability, or resistance to decay, in a given material or design.

physical texture actual variation in a surface.

picture plane in linear perspective, the flat surface on which a three-dimensional image is mentally projected.

pitch in music, the relative highness or lowness of a sound. Pitch is determined by wave frequency, as compression and expansion occur within the sound wave.

plane a three-dimensional form that has length and width but minimal thickness.

plinth a horizontal support for a sculptural object.

plot duration the running time of the events depicted in a story.

polyhedra (or polyhedrons) multifaceted volumes.

positive forms areas of physical substance in a three-dimensional design.

positive shape (or figure) the principal or foreground shape in a design and the dominant shape or figure in a figure-ground relationship.

postmodernism a collection of artistic styles that arose in the 1970s as a reaction to modernism. Notable characteristics include conceptual emphasis, social commentary, irreverence, and skepticism about universal truths.

primary colors colors from which virtually all other colors can be mixed. The additive (or light) color primaries are red, green, and blue. The subtractive (or pigment) color primaries are yellow, magenta red, and cyan blue.

primary contours the defining edges of a physical object, such as the extremities of a carved sculpture.

principles of design the means by which visual elements are organized into a unified and expressive arrangement. Unity and variety, balance, scale and proportion, rhythm, illusion of space, and illusion of movement are commonly cited as the principles of two-dimensional design.

process colors in four-color process printing, the subtractive primary colors: yellow, magenta, and cyan, plus black.

proportion the relative size of visual elements within an image.

prototype a well-developed model, as with the fully functional prototype cars developed by automobile companies.

proximity the distance between visual or structural elements or between an object and the audience.

pure form a circle, sphere, triangle, cube, or other form created without reference to specific subject matter.

radial symmetry a form of balance that is created when shapes or volumes are mirrored both vertically and horizontally, with the center of the composition acting as a focal point.

rational a type of advertising in which logic and comparisons of quality are used to sell a service, product, or idea. A rational approach is most effective when the message is compelling in itself or the product is unique.

realistic in advertising, use of a familiar setting or situation to involve the viewer and relate a product, service, or idea to use in everyday life.

recontextualization a postmodern practice in which the meaning of an image or object is changed by the context in which it is placed.

rectilinear shapes shapes composed from straight lines and angular corners.

reflective light that is bounced off a reflective surface back into space.

refracted light that has been bent as it passes through a prism.

relief sculpture in which forms project out from a flat surface. The degree of projection ranges from low to high relief.

repetition the use of the same visual element or effect a number of times in the same composition.

representational artworks commonly, the lifelike depiction of persons or objects.

representational shapes shapes derived from specific subject matter and strongly based on visual observation.

rhetorical a type of sequential organization in which the parts are used to create and support an argument. Often used in documentary films.

rhythm 1. presentation of multiple units in a deliberate pattern. 2. in filmmaking, the perceived rate and regularity of sounds, shots, and movement within the shots. Rhythm is determined by the beat (pulse), accent (stress), and tempo (pace).

rhythmic relationship the juxtaposition of multiple visual elements or images to create a deliberate pulse or beat.

saturation the purity, chroma, or intensity of a color.

scale a size relationship between two separate objects, such as the relationship between the size of the Statue of Liberty and a human visitor to the monument.

scene in film, continuous action in continuous time and continuous space.

scene-to-scene transition in comic books, the juxtaposition of two or more frames showing different scenes or settings.

scope conceptually, the extent of our perception or the range of ideas our minds can grasp. Temporally, scope refers to the range of action within a given moment.

screenplay the written blueprint for a film, commonly constructed from multiple acts.

secondary colors hues mixed from adjacent primaries. In paint, the secondary colors are violet, green, and orange.

secondary contours the inner edges of a physical object, such as the internal design and detailing of a carved sculpture.

sequence 1. in filmmaking, a collection of related shots and scenes that comprise a major section of action or narration. 2. in narrative structure, any collection of images that have been organized by *cause and effect*. In a simple sequence, action number two is caused by action number one. In a complex sequence, there may be a considerable delay between the cause and the effect.

series in sequential structure, a collection of images that are linked simply, like cars in a train.

serious advertising that treats a topic in a somber or solemn manner. Often used for public service announcements, such as drunk driving commercials.

setting the physical and temporal location of a story, the props and costumes used in a story, and the use of sound.

shade a hue that has been mixed with black.

shading in drawing, a continuous series of grays that are used to suggest three-dimensionality and to create the illusion of light; a type of gradation.

shape a flat, enclosed area created when a line connects to enclose an area, an area is surrounded by other shapes, or an area is filled with color or texture.

shear a force that creates a lateral break in a material.

shot in film, a continuous group of frames.

side light a light positioned to the side of a person or an object. Can be used to dramatically increase the sense of dimensionality.

sight line 1. a viewing line that is established by the arrangement of objects within one's field of vision. 2. a straight line of unimpeded vision.

simile a figure of speech in which one thing is linked to another, dissimilar thing using the word *like* or *as*. Through this connection, the original word is given the qualities of the linked word. For example, when we say "He's as strong as an ox," we attribute to a man the strength of an animal.

glossary

simultaneous contrast the optical alteration of a color by a surrounding color.

site-specific an artwork specifically designed for and installed in a particular place.

skeleton (or endoskeleton) a structure that provides internal support.

soft-sell an advertising approach that uses emotion, rather than reason, to sell a service, product, or idea. The narrative is often nonlinear, and ideas or actions may be implied.

solidification a forming method in which a liquid material is poured into a mold or extruded through a pipe, then allowed to harden.

space the area within or around an area of substance. The artist/designer defines and activates space when constructing a three-dimensional object.

spatial context the space in which a sound is generated. A sound that is played outdoors behaves differently than a sound that is played in a small room.

spatial relationship the juxtaposition of two or more images that are spatially different, such as a close-up, a medium shot, and a long shot.

split complementary a complementary color plus the two colors on either side of its complement on the color wheel.

spotlight a light that creates a small, clearly defined beam.

static forms forms that appear to be stable and unmoving.

stereotype a fixed generalization based on a preconception.

stippling a technique for producing an image from multiple dots.

story duration the overall length of a story.

style the recurring characteristics that distinguish one historical period or particular artist's group from another.

subject the person, object, event, or idea on which an artwork is based.

subjective criticism the assessment of strengths and weaknesses in a design based on nonobjective criteria, such as the narrative implications of an idea, the cultural ramifications of an action, or the personal meaning of an image.

subject-to-subject transition in comic books, the juxtaposition of two or more frames showing different subject matter.

subordinate of secondary importance. See **emphasis.**

subtractive color hue created when light is selectively reflected off a colored surface.

subtractive sculpture a forming method in which materials are removed from a larger mass. Carving, drilling, cutting, and turning on a lathe are all subtractive processes.

symbolic color a color that has been assigned a particular meaning by the members of a society. For example, in the United States, the white color of a wedding gown symbolizes purity, while in Borneo white symbolizes death.

symmetrical balance a form of balance that is created when shapes are mirrored on either side of a central axis, as in a composition that is vertically divided down the center.

take in film or video, one version of an event.

temperature the physical and psychological heat suggested by a color's hue.

tempo the pace at which change occurs. A fast tempo is generally used in action films, while a slow tempo is usually used in a dramatic film.

temporal relationship how the shots in a film are related in time.

tension the extension of an object through stretching or bending.

tertiary color a hue that is mixed from a primary color and an adjacent secondary color.

testimonial in advertising, use of a trustworthy character or celebrity to provide endorsement for a product, service, or idea.

texture the visual or tactile quality of a form. Texture can be created visually using multiple marks, physically through surface variation, or through the inherent property of a specific material, such as sand as opposed to smooth porcelain.

three-point perspective a form of linear perspective in which the lines receding into space converge at two vanishing points of the eye level (one to the left of the object being drawn and one to the right of the object being drawn) plus a third vanishing point above or below the eye level. Used when the picture plane must be tilted to encompass an object placed above or below the eye level.

three-quarter work a physical object that is designed to be viewed from the front and sides only.

timbre the unique sound quality of each instrument. For example, a note of the same volume and pitch is quite different when it is generated by a flute rather than a violin.

tint a hue that has been mixed with white.

tone a hue that has been mixed with black and white.

torque the distortion of an object through a twisting movement. Also known as **torsion.**

transition the process of changing from one state or form to another; for example, the surface of a metal sculpture as it shifts from a smooth to a rough surface or the manner in which a computer drawing morphs from one form to another.

translucent a surface that partially permits the passage of light.

transparent a surface that permits the passage of light, such as clear plastic or glass.

triadic describes a color scheme based on three colors that are equidistant on a color wheel.

tromp l'oeil a flat illusion that is so convincing that the viewer believes the image is real. A French term meaning "to fool the eye."

two-point perspective a form of linear perspective in which the lines receding into space converge at two vanishing points of the eye level (or horizon line), one to the left of the object being drawn and one to the right of the object being drawn.

type style the distinctive quality of the letter forms within a given font. For example, Helvetica has a very different look than Palatino type.

unity compositional similarity, oneness, togetherness, or cohesion.

value the relative lightness or darkness of a surface.

value distribution the proportion and arrangement of lights and darks in a composition. Also known as **value pattern.**

value scale a range of grays that are presented in a consistent sequence, creating a gradual transition from white to black.

vanishing point in linear perspective, the point or points on the eye level at which parallel lines appear to converge.

variety the differences that give a design visual and conceptual interest; notably, use of contrast, emphasis, differences in size, and so forth.

viewing time the time an audience devotes to watching or exploring an artwork.

visual book an experimental structure that conveys ideas, actions, and emotions using multiple images in an integrated and interdependent format. Also known as an **artist's book.**

visual movement use of continuity to create deliberate visual pathways. Often used to direct the viewer's attention to areas of particular importance in the composition.

visual texture texture created using multiple marks or through a descriptive simulation of physical texture.

visual weight 1. the inclination of shapes to float or sink compositionally. 2. the relative importance of a visual element within a design.

vitalistic sculpture a sculpture that appears to embody life in an inanimate material, such as fiberglass, stone, or wood.

volume 1. an empty three-dimensional form. 2. in two-dimensional design, a three-dimensional form that has been represented using the illusion of space. 3. in time design, the loudness of a sound.

volume summary a drawing that communicates visual information reductively, using basic volumes such as spheres, cubes, and cylinders to indicate the major components of a figure or object.

volumetric three-dimensional in nature.

weight the visual or physical heaviness of an object.

wipe in film, a transition in which the first shot seems to be pushed off the screen by the second. Wipes were used extensively in *Star Wars*.

Introduction

Page vii: Courtesy of Rusty Smith, University School of Architecture.

xx T: © Bill Viola. Collection: Edition 1: Museo Nacional Centro de Arte Reina Sofia, Madrid. Edition 2, Los Angeles County Museum of Art, Modern and Contemporary Art Council Fund. Photo by Gary McKinnis. Courtesy of artist and James Cohan Gallery.

xx BR: Collection Toni Greenbaum, NY. Photo courtesy of Keith E. LoBue.

xxi T: Designers: Bill Cannan, Tony Ortiz, H. Kurt Heinz. Design Firm: Bill Cannan & Co. Client/Mfr. NASA Public Affairs.

xxi B: Hans-Jurgen Syberberg, Parsifal, 1982.

xxii: The Museum of Modern Art, Film Stills Archive.

xxiii B: Designers: James E. Grove, John Cook, Jim Holtorf, Fernando Pardo, Mike Boltich. Design Firm: Designworks/USA. Client/Mfr: Corona Clipper Co.

xxiv B: Funds from Helen Dill bequest, 1935.1, Denver Art Museum Collection. Photo courtesy of the Denver Art Museum.

xxv: © 2010 Sam Francis Foundation, California/Artists Rights Society (ARS), NY.

xxvi: Collection, University of Illinois at Urbana, Champaign. Photo courtesy of the artist © Alice Aycock, 1994.

xxvii: TM & © 2005 Marvel Characters, Inc. Used with permission.

Chapter 5

Page 110: Courtesy of Georgiana Nehl.

111: Courtesy of Jason Chin.

113 TL: Gift of Gary Laredo. Cooper-Hewitt National Design Museum, Smithsonian Institution/Art Resource, NY.

113 TR: The Museum of Modern Art, New York. Gift of Edgar Kaufman, Jr. Digital Image © The Museum of Modern Art/Licensed by Scala/Art Resource, NY.

114 L: The Museum of Modern Art, New York. Gift of Herman Miller Furniture Company. Digital Image © The Museum of Modern Art/Licensed by Scala/Art Resource, NY. © 2007 Eames Office/www.eamesoffice.com.

114 R: Photo courtesy of Knoll, Inc.

115 C: Courtesy of Ray Rogers.

115 B: Vera Liskova (Czech, 1924–1985), *Porcupine*, c. 1972–1980. Flameworked, h. 10.8 cm. (81.3.11) Gift of Vera Liskova, Collection of The Corning Museum of Glass.

117: © The Trustees of the British Museum/Art Resource, NY.

120 T: The Museum of Modern Art, New York. Mrs. Simon Guggenheim Fund. Digital Image © The Museum of Modern Art/Licensed by Scala/Art Resource, NY.

© 2007 Estate of Yves Tanguy/Artists Rights Society (ARS), NY.

120 B: © 2010 Artists Rights Society (ARS), New York/SIAE, Rome.

124 L: Courtesy of Peter Forbes.

126: Photo by Jeanne Hilary.

Chapter 6

Page 133: M.C. Escher, *Metamorphosis II.* © 2010 The M. C. Escher Company-Holland. All rights reserved. www.mcescher.com.

134 C: Courtesy of Mary Stewart.

134 B: Honolulu Academy of Arts, gift of James Michener, 1991 (21.971). Photo © Honolulu Academy of Arts.

135 T, C: Honolulu Academy of Arts, gift of James Michener, 1991 (21.971). Photo © Honolulu Academy of Arts.

135 BL: © Eddie Chiu, courtesy of the Noguchi Museum.

135 BR: © Deborah Tan, courtesy of the Noguchi Museum.

136 L: Courtesy of Sergio Silva.

136 R: Courtesy of Rusty Smith, University School of Architecture.

138–139: Courtesy of Suzanne Stryk.

Chapter 7

Page 142–143: Gustave Caillebotte, French, 1848–1894, *Paris Street. Rainy Day*, 1877. Oil on canvas, 83 1/2 x 108 3/4 in. (212.2 x 276.2 cm). Charles H. and Mary F. S. Worcester Collection, 1964.336, The Art Institute of Chicago. Photography © The Art Institute of Chicago.

144: Courtesy of Rodger Mack.

145: Stanza della Segnatura, Vatican Palace, Vatican State. Scala/Art Resource, NY.

146: Courtesy of the author.

150–151: Courtesy of Jason Chin.

152 T: The Kansas City Sculpture Park at The Nelson-Atkins Museum of Art, Kansas City, Missouri including *Shuttlecocks* (two of four), 1994 by Claes Oldenburg, American (b. Sweden, 1929) and Coosje van Bruggen, American (b. The Netherlands, 1942). Aluminum, fiberglass-reinforced plastic, paint, 230 9/16 x 191 7/8 inches. (585.63 x 487.36 cm). Purchase: acquired through the generosity of the Sosland Family, F94-1/3-4. Photograph by Louis Meluso.

152 B: Photo by Lynn Whitney.

153 B: Photo by Harry Shunk. Art © Robert Rauschenberg/Licensed by VAGA, New York, NY.

154 R: Moderna Museet, Stockholm. Art © Robert Rauschenberg/Licensed by VAGA, New York, NY.

154 L: Art © Robert Rauschenberg/Licensed by VAGA, New York, NY.

156–157: Courtesy of Kendall Buster.

Chapter 8

Page 158: Collection of the National Palace Museum, Taipei, Taiwan.

159 T: Detail of William Kentridge, *Black Box/Chambre Noire*, 2005, miniature theater with mechanized objects, projections and sound, commissioned by Deutsche Bank with the Guggenheim Foundation for the Deutsche Guggenheim, Berlin. Photo courtesy of Moderna Museet, Stockholm. Courtesy of the artist and Marian Goodman Gallery, NY.

159 B: Courtesy of the author.

160 L: Courtesy of Milton Glaser Studio.

160 R: The Menil Collection, Houston. © 2010 C. Herscovici, London/Artists Rights Society (ARS), New York.

161 TL: Designed by Noon, San Francisco. Courtesy of the ODC, San Francisco.

161 TR: Los Angeles Ballet, Serenade. Balanchine ® is a Trademark of The George Balanchine Trust. Photo: Reed Hutchinson. Graphic Design: Catherine Kanner. Permission granted for LA Ballet.

161 BR: Michael A. Mello, *Dead Wrong: A Death Row Lawyer Speaks Out Against Capital Punishment.* © 1997. Cover design and illustration by Mark Maccaulay. Reprinted by permission of The University of Wisconsin Press.

162: Courtesy of Markus Schaller, Berlin.

163: Ruhr/Paragon, Minneapolis.

164 T: Courtesy of the artist and Chambers Fine Art.

164 B: Courtesy of Kim Martens.

165 T: Courtesy of Richard Saul Wurman, wurrmanrs@aol.com and Pentagram.

165 L: Art © Robert Rauschenberg/Licensed by VAGA, New York, NY.

165 R: Kiki Smith, *Virgin Mary*, 1992. Wax, cheesecloth and wood with steel base, 67 1/2 x 26 x 14 1/2" (171.5 x 66 x 36.8 cm). © Kiki Smith. Photo by Ellen Page Wilson, courtesy of PaceWildenstein, New York.

166 TL: Margaret Bourke-White/TimePix/Getty Images.

166 TR: Alfred Eisenstadt/TimePix/Getty Images.

166 CR: Michael Bierut & Tracey Cameron, Design Firm: Pentagram, NY. Photo: Don F. Wong.

166 B: Courtesy of Sean O'Meallie. Photo by Ric Helstrom.

167: © 1999 Iomega Corporation.

168 T: Courtesy of Jimmy Margulies.

168 B: Museo Nacional Centro de Arte Reina Sofia, Madrid. The Bridgeman Art Library, NY. © 2010 Estate of Pablo Picasso/Artists Rights Society (ARS), NY.

169: Photo provided by the author.

170: © Anthony Kersting/AKG Images.

171: Barbara Kruger, *"Untitled" (We don't need another hero)*, 1987. Photographic silkscreen/vinyl, 109 by 210 inches. © Barbara Kruger. Collection: Fisher Landau Center for Art, Long Island City, New York. Courtesy of Mary Boone Gallery, NY.

172 TL: Mona Hatoum, *Doormat II*, 2000–2001. Steel and rubber, 1 x 28 x 16 in/2.5 x 71 x 40.5 cm. Photo by Orcutt & Van Der Putten. Image courtesy of Alexander and Bonin, New York.

172 TR: Courtesy of Jaune Quick-to See Smith (Salish member of the Confederated Salish and Kootenai Nation, MT).

172 B: Galleria dell'Academia, Venice/Bridgeman Art Library, London / SuperStock.

173: Courtesy of Dan Sutherland.

175: Detail of William Kentridge's *Black Box/Chambre Noire*, 2005. Miniature theater with mechanized objects, projections and sound, commissioned by Deutsche Bank with the Guggenheim Foundation for the Deutsche Guggenheim, Berlin. Photo courtesy of Moderna Museet, Stockholm. Courtesy of the artist and Marian Goodman Gallery, NY.

176–177: Courtesy of Roger Shimomura.

Chapter 9

Page 178: © Eva Hild, Courtesy of Gallery Bienvenu.

179 T: Martin Puryear, *Seer*, 1984. Water-based paint on wood and wire, 78 x 52 1/4 x 45 inches. Solomon R. Guggenheim Museum, Purchased with funds contributed by the Louis and Bessie Adler Foundation, Inc., Seymour M. Klein, President, 1985. 85.3276. © The Guggenheim Foundation, New York.

179 B: Private Collection. Photo: M. Mimlitsch-Gray.

180: Xu Bing, *Book from the Sky*, 1987–1991. Hand printed books, ceiling and wall scrolls printed from wood letterpress type using false Chinese characters, dimensions variable. Installation view at Three Installations by Xu Bing, Elvehjem Museum of Art, University of Wisconsin–Madison, Madison, WI.

181 L: Musée d'Orsay, Paris. Réunion des Musées Nationaux/Art Resource, NY.

181 R: © Larry E. Brackney (The Imagination Factory).

182 T: © David Muench/CORBIS.

182 B: © Bob Evans, Force Fin, www.forcefin.com.

184: Courtesy of the artist and Metro Pictures, NY.

185 TL: Erich Lessing/Art Resource, NY.

185 TR: Erich Lessing/Art Resource, NY.

185 B: © Muntadas 1987, Courtesy of Kent Gallery. © 2010 Artists Rights Society (ARS), New York/VEGAP, Madrid.

208 B: Photo by Satoshi Yamamoto. Courtesy of Stephen Knapp.

209 T: © Krzysztof Wodiczko, Courtesy Galerie Lelong, New York.

209 B: Edition 1: Collection of Marion Stroud Swingle. Edition 2: Collection of the Artist. Photo by Roman Mensing. Courtesy of artist and James Cohan Gallery.

210 BL: Courtesy of Fisher-Price.

210 BR: Courtesy of Toshiyuki Kita/IDK Design Laboratory, LTD, Japan.

211 TL: Do Ho Suh, *Reflection*, 2004. Nylon and stainless steel tube. Courtesy of the Artist and Lehmann Maupin Gallery, New York.

211 TR: © Keith Edmier. Courtesy of Sadie Coles HQ, London.

211 BL: Courtesy of Michael Graves & Associates. Photo by William Taylor.

212 T: © Philippe Caron/Sygma/CORBIS.

212 B: Photo by Robert Stave, 1989. © Adele Linarducci, 1989.

213 TL: George Segal 1924–2000, *Walk, Don't Walk*, 1976. Plaster, cement, metal, painted wood and electric light, Overall: 109 x 72 x 74 3/8 in. (276.9 x 182.9 x 188.9 cm. Whitney Museum of American Art, New York. Purchase, with funds from the Louis and Bessie Adler Foundation, Inc., Seymour M. Klein, President, the Gilman Foundation, Inc., the Howard and Jean Lipman Foundation, Inc. and the National Endowment for the Arts 79.4a–f. © The George and Helen Segal Foundation/Licensed by VAGA, New York, NY.

213 TR: Museo del Templo Mayor, Mexico City. Instituto Nacional de Antropologia e Historia (INAH).

214 TL: Courtesy of Ned Kahn.

214 CL: The Kansas City Sculpture Park at The Nelson-Atkins Museum of Art, Kansas City, Missouri including *Shuttlecocks* (two of four), 1994 by Claes Oldenburg, American (b. Sweden, 1929) and Coosje van Bruggen, American (b. The Netherlands, 1942). Aluminum, fiberglass-reinforced plastic, paint, 230 9/16 x 191 7/8 inches. Purchase: acquired through the generosity of the Sosland Family, F94-1/3-4. Photograph by Louis Meluso.

214 R: © Kim Karpeles/Alamy.

216: Courtesy of Todd Slaughter.

217: Overlooking the Straits of Gibraltar. Commissioned by the port city of Algeciras, Spain. Courtesy of the artist.

Chapter 10

Page 218 L: Courtesy of Humanscale, NY.

218 R: Martin Puryear, *Seer*, 1984. Water-based paint on wood and wire, 78 x 51 x 45 inches. Solomon R. Guggenheim Museum, Purchased with funds contributed by the Louis and Bessie Adler Foundation, Inc., Seymour M. Klein, President, 1985.

85.3276. Photograph by David Heald. © The Guggenheim Foundation, New York.

219: Courtesy Marian Goodman Gallery, NY.

220 T: Courtesy of Hauser & Wirth, New York.

220 BL: Giraudon/Art Resource, NY. © 2010 Estate of Louise Nevelson/Artists Rights Society (ARS), New York.

221 L: © Aaron Macsai.

221 R: Zac Freeman, *Steve*, 2006. Found objects on board, 60 x 48 inches. Photo courtesy of J. Johnson Gallery.

222 T: Photo by Timothy Hursley. Holocaust Memorial Museum, Washington, DC.

222 B: Collection, University of Illinois at Urbana, Champaign. Photo courtesy of the artist © Alice Aycock, 1994.

223 TL: Photo by Don Cole. Courtesy of Fowler Museum of Cultural History, UCLA.

223 TR: Eva Hesse, *Accession II*, 1968. Galvanized steel, vinyl, 30 x 30 x 30 inches. Detroit Institute of Arts, Founders Society Purchase, Friends of Modern Art Fund, and Miscellaneous Gifts Fund, 1979. © The Estate of Eva Hesse. Courtesy Hauser & Wirth, Zurich, London.

223 B: Art @ Judy Pfaff/Licensed by VAGA, New York, NY.

224 T: Courtesy of Mary Boone Gallery, NY.

224 B: Superstock.

225 L: © David Becker/Reuters/CORBIS.

225 R: Courtesy the Library, American Museum of Natural History, New York. AMNH Trans. #2104(2).

226: Courtesy of Theodore Gall.

227 L: Ludovica Canali De Rossi, Milano, Italy.

227 R: Santa Maria degli Angeli, Rome, Italy/Mauro Magliani/Superstock.

227 C: Courtesy the Library, American Museum of Natural History, New York. Trans. #2104(2).

228 T: Kurkje Gallery, Chrong Ku, Seoul, Korea.

228 B: Courtesy of Patricia A. Renick.

229: Designers: James E. Grove, John Cook, Jim Holtorf, Fernando Pardo, Mike Boltich. Design Firm: Designworks/USA. Client/Mfr: Corona Clipper Co.

230 L: Solomon R. Guggenheim Foundation, Peggy Guggenheim Collection, 1976. 76.2553.50 Photo: David Heald. © Solomon R. Guggenheim Museum Foundation, New York. © 2010 Artists Rights Society (ARS), New York/ADAGP, Paris.

230 C: Constantin Brâncusi, French, born Romania, 1876–1957, *Golden Bird*, 1919/20 (base c. 1922), Bronze, stone, and wood, 86 x 11 3/4 x 11 3/4 in. (217.8 x 29.9 x 29.9 cm), Partial gift of The Arts Club of Chicago; restricted gift of various donors; through prior bequest of Arthur Rubloff; through prior restricted gift of William Hartmann; through prior gifts of Mr. and Mrs. Carter H. Harrison, Mr. and Mrs. Arnold H. Maremont through the Kate Maremont Foundation, Woodruff J. Parker, Mrs. Clive Runnells, Mr. and Mrs. Martin A. Ryerson, and various donors, 1990.88, The Art Institute of Chicago. Photography © The Art Institute of Chicago. © 2010 Artists Rights Society (ARS), New York/ADAGP, Paris.

Chapter 11

Chapter 12

photo credits

264 BL: Collection Martha Stewart, Oakland Museum of Art.

264 BR: Private Collection. Photo: M. Mimlitsch-Gray.

265 L: Collection: Rothko Chapel, Houston, dedicated to Reverend Martin Luther King, Jr. © 2010 The Barnett Newman Foundation, New York/Artists Rights Society (ARS), New York.

265 R: Courtesy of P.P.O.W., NY.

266: University of California, Berkeley Art Museum. Photo by Ben Blackwell.

267 TL: Photo by Erik Landsberg. Courtesy of Yong Soon Min.

267 TR: Photo by Henry Arnold. © Maya Lin. Courtesy of PaceWildenstein, New York.

267 B: Private collection. Art © The George and Helen Segal Foundation/Licensed by VAGA, New York, NY.

268 T: Courtesy of Susan Trangmar.

268 B: Olafur Eliasson, *The parliament of reality*, 2006–2009. Concrete, stone, stainless steel, water, trees, other plants. Dimensions variable. Installation at The Center for Curatorial Studios (CCS Bard), New York. The Center for Curatorial Studies and The Luma Foundation. © 2006 Olafur Eliasson.

269 TL: © Barbara Chase-Riboud. On loan to The Philadelphia Museum of Art, Philadelphia, PA.

269 TR: Bequest of Mrs. H.O. Havemeyer, 1929. The H.W. Havemeyer Collection. © The Metropolitan Museum of Art/Art Resource, NY.

269 BL: Scala/Art Resource, NY.

270 T: The Museum of Modern Art, New York. Acquired through the Lillie P. Bliss Bequest. Digital Image © The Museum of Modern Art/Licensed by Scala/Art Resource, NY.

270 B: Steve Raymer/National Geographic Stock.

271 L: Gift of Ginny Williams, 1997.205. Denver Art Museum Collection. Photo © Denver Art Museum. Courtesy Joseph Helman Gallery, NY.

271 R: Courtesy Jay Jopling Gallery/White Cube, London.
© Antony Gormley.

272 T: Courtesy of Pace Wildenstein. Photo: Ellen Page Wilson.
© 2010 John Chamberlain/Artists Rights Society (ARS), New York.

272 B: © Cornelia Parker, courtesy of SITE Santa Fe, 1999.

273 T: Courtesy of The North Face, San Leandro, CA.

273 B: Collection: Caltrans, City of Los Angeles, San Diego Freeway Northbound, Mulholland Drive Exit, Los Angeles.

274 T: Rachel Whiteread, *House,* 1993. Concrete. Commissioned by Artangel. © Rachel Whiteread. Courtesy of the artist, Luhring Augustine, New York and Gagosian Gallery. Photo by Sue Omerod.

274 B: Courtesy of Jack Shainman Gallery, NY. © 2010 Artists Rights Society (ARS), New York/VG Bild-Kunst, Bonn.

275 T: Overlooking the Straits of Gibraltar. Commissioned by the port city of Algeciras, Spain. Courtesy of Todd Slaughter.

275 B: © 2010 Hans Haacke/Artists Rights Society (ARS), New York/VG Bild-Kunst. Bonn.

276 L: © Roald Dahl.

276 R: Lorna Jordan, *Waterworks Gardens: The Grotto*, 1996. Third of five public garden rooms in the King County East Division Reclamation Plant, Renton, WA.

277 L: Courtesy the Library, American Museum of Natural History, New York. AMNH Trans. 1448(4).

277 R: Raymond Duchamp-Villon, French, 1876–1918, *Horse*, 1914. Bronze, 99 x 61 x 91.4 cm. Gift of Margaret Fisher in memory of her parents, Mr. and Mrs. Walter L. Fisher, 1957.165, The Art Institute of Chicago. Photography © The Art Institute of Chicago.

278: The Museum of Modern Art, New York. The Sidney and Harriet Janis Collection. Digital Image © The Museum of Modern Art/Licensed by Scala/Art Resource, NY. © 2010 Artists Rights Society (ARS), New York/ADAGP, Paris/Succession Marcel Duchamp.

279 T: © Peter Arkell/AGE Fotostock.

279 BL: Courtesy of Glen Onwin and Greg Kucera Gallery.

279 BR: Photo by Andrea Pozza, 2008. Courtesy of Adjaye Associates.

280: Nikolai Fine Art, New York.

281: © PhenomenArts, Inc. Christopher Janney, Artistic Director.

282: Courtesy of Rudi Stern.

283: © Christian Marclay. Courtesy of Paula Cooper Gallery, NY.

284: Courtesy of Shelagh Wakely.

285 T: Darroch Donald/Alamy.

285 B: Courtesy of Katherine Wetzel and Elizabeth King.

286 L: Kiki Smith, *Virgin Mary*, 1992. Wax, cheesecloth and wood with steel base, 67 1/2 x 26 x 14 1/2" (171.5 x 66 x 36.8 cm). © Kiki Smith. Photography by Ellen Page Wilson, courtesy of PaceWildenstein, New York.

286 R: © Allen Memorial Art Museum, Oberlin College, OH. Fund for Contemporary Art and gift of the artist and the Fischbach Gallery, 1970.

288 T: Photo by Shelby Duncan, 2006.

288 B: Courtesy of Samuel Yates.

Index

Index

Index

index

Index

index

index